The First World War dealt a profound shock to European society at its outbreak and in the succeeding years of conflict. In this original and stimulating book, Frank Field, a historian of the First World War, looks at the experiences of France and Britain as revealed in the work of some of their most prominent writers responding to the catastrophe. Brooke, Wells, Shaw, Kipling, Lawrence, Owen and Rosenberg are set alongside Jaurès, Barrès, Maurras, Péguy, Psichari and Rolland, as a means of tracing the intellectual and spiritual history of the War (between the two nations and across the political spectrum), affording insights which in turn serve to illuminate the literature itself. The comparative perspective reveals deep differences in French and British experience, and yet a shared ordeal which highlights the terrible ironies with which their common ideals were shattered. Literary images of war as a purification rite were effaced by the bloody realities of the conflict which ensued, and the prophecies of writers who felt increasingly distanced from the essential innocence of the world before 1914 took on a new tone, grimly apocalyptic or bitterly disillusioned. This challenging study, crossing boundaries in an interdisciplinary spirit, enables a fertile conjunction of insights into the impact of the First World War on modern intellectual and literary history.

British and French writers of the First World War

British and French writers
of the
First World War

Comparative studies in
cultural history

FRANK FIELD

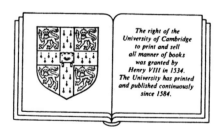

The right of the
University of Cambridge
to print and sell
all manner of books
was granted by
Henry VIII in 1534.
The University has printed
and published continuously
since 1584.

CAMBRIDGE UNIVERSITY PRESS

Cambridge

New York   Port Chester

Melbourne   Sydney

Published by the Press Syndicate of the University of Cambridge
The Pitt Building, Trumpington Street, Cambridge CB2 IRP
40 West 20th Street, New York, NY 10011, USA
10 Stamford Road, Oakleigh, Melbourne 3166, Australia

© Cambridge University Press 1991

First published 1991

British Library cataloguing in publication data
Field, Frank, *1936–*
British and French writers of the Great War: comparative
studies in cultural history.
1. Literature. Influence of World War 1
1. Title
809

Library of Congress cataloguing in publication data
Field, Frank.
British and French writers of the First World War: comparative
studies in cultural history / by Frank Field.
p.   cm.
Includes bibliographical references.
ISBN 0 521 39277 2
1. English literature – 20th century – History and criticism.
2. French literature – 20th century – History and criticism. 3. World
War, 1914–1918 – Great Britain – Historiography. 4. Soldiers'
writings, English – History and criticism. 5. Soldiers' writings,
French – History and criticism. 6. World War, 1914–1918 – Literature
and the war. 7. World War, 1914–1918 – France – Historiography.
8. Literature, Comparative – English and French. 9. Literature,
Comparative – French and English. 1. Title.
PR478.W65F54   1991
820.9'358 – dc20   90-33100   CIP

ISBN 0 521 39277 2

Transferred to digital printing 2004

For Barbara, Libby and Catherine

Contents

Illustrations

Acknowledgements

I am extremely grateful to Josie Dixon and her colleagues at Cambridge University Press for much valuable editorial advice, and to Mrs A.M. Fairclough and Mrs B. Coxon for unstinting secretarial assistance.

I am indebted to the following for permission to take quotations from work in copyright:

Edward Arnold Ltd, *Two Cheers for Democracy* by E.M. Forster

Editions Albin Michel, *Jean-Christophe, Au-dessus de la mêlée, Journal des années de guerre, Le Voyage intérieur*, and quotations from the *Cahiers Romain Rolland*, by Romain Rolland

Chatto and Windus Ltd, *Journey to the End of the Night*, by L.-F. Céline

Editions Flammarion, *Œuvres capitales*, by Charles Maurras

Bernard Grasset, Editeur, *Au signe de Flore*, by Charles Maurras

Hamish Hamilton Ltd, *Testimony*, by D. Shostakovich

The estate of Sonia Orwell, *The Collected Essays, Journalism and Letters of George Orwell*

Laurence Pollinger Ltd and the estate of Mrs Frieda Lawrence Ravagli, *The Letters of D.H. Lawrence* and quotations from works by Lawrence

The Society of Authors, *What I really wrote about the War, Too True to be Good*, and quotations from correspondence by G.B. Shaw

A.P. Watt & Sons, *The Way the World is Going, Tono-Bungay Anticipations, An Englishman Looks at the World, Mr Britling Sees it Through, Boon, War and the Future*, by H.G. Wells

Weidenfeld & Nicholson Ltd, *Memories*, by C.M. Bowra

Introduction

It is hardly surprising that after more than three-quarters of a century the outbreak of the First World War should still haunt the European imagination. Lives, hopes and ideals were all shattered in the course of the conflict. Helplessly we watch the figures moving in the flickering film reels, oblivious of the scale of the catastrophe that is to overwhelm them. If deaths and ironies are permanent and inescapable features of the human condition, both were in plentiful supply in 1914 and the years that followed it.

In *Three French Writers and the Great War* I traced the careers of Barbusse, Drieu la Rochelle and Bernanos, who came out of the experience of battle to encounter the challenge of Communism and Fascism. In the present survey, which deals with civilians as well as combatants, I concentrate far more on the war years and the period that preceded them in order to convey something of the shock experienced by French and British society as a result of the outbreak of the conflict. The most spectacular long-term effects of the war were, of course, to be seen in parts of Europe other than France and Britain – in Russia and Germany, particularly. And yet a study limited to a group of French and English personalities has its own kind of rationale, for France and Britain – despite their pride, their jealousy, and their often infuriating parochialism[1] – lie at the very heart of that Western civilisation whose values and whose self-confidence were to be so deeply undermined in the course of the conflict.

It would be foolish to minimise the profound differences between the French and British experience of the war, and, to underline this, I have dealt with some of the French and British reactions separately in the first two parts of the book. In France the outbreak of a war with Germany had long been expected, and each of the Frenchmen whose careers are examined here looked forward to the possibility of war, either with dread or with anticipation. In Britain, despite the tensions that had been seen in Anglo-German relations before 1914, there was no such general expectation of a major conflict, and those like Kipling, who took a very different attitude and vainly urged the British to follow the example of the continental powers and introduce conscription, were exceptions to the general rule. The British response to the German attack on Belgium was one of moral outrage followed by a declaration of war. To the French, with their memories of battles in the past, the German declaration of war on them one day earlier was one more episode in a long history of antagonism.

Once the war had started the sufferings of France were far greater than those of the British. Not only was the war in the West largely fought on French soil, it was the French army that carried the main burden of the war for the first two years of its duration. The results of this can be seen in the fatality figures. It is significant, for example, that two of the personalities discussed in the book – Péguy and Psichari – were killed in the first few weeks of the conflict. Although, at a later stage in the war, the casualty rate amongst the British junior officers was higher than that of any of the other combatant powers – a situation that was partly the result of the inexperience inevitable in Kitchener's volunteer armies and one that gave a distinctive dimension to the British memory of the battle – the overall cost of the war to the French was staggering. The number of men killed from the British Isles (excluding the Empire) amounted to about 750,000, while French losses amounted to over 1,300,000, of whom the overwhelming majority came from metropolitan France. When it is remembered that in 1914 the population of France was significantly lower than that of Britain it is hardly surprising to discover that in terms of percentage losses of active troops the French fatality rate was higher than that of the Germans and twice that of the British.

Terrible though the British losses were, then, and stoical as France (and especially peasant France) was towards her suffering, statistics like these must be borne in mind when one is considering France's demands for a punitive peace at the end of the war, and the reluctance with which she, even more than Britain, contemplated a renewed conflict with Germany by the late 1930s. As Frenchmen like

Maurras were constantly to proclaim, the First World War may have been an ordeal which the British and the French endured together, but the shares in this ordeal were not equal.

And yet, if the contrasts in the French and British experience of the war cannot be ignored, neither can the many points of resemblance, and perhaps one of the advantages of the comparative approach adopted in this book is that it reveals certain similarities of response that transcend national boundaries. These similarities were the result not so much of cultural affinity – despite the activities of American expatriates like Pound and Eliot during this period, activities that were to be so important for the future, the peak years of Anglo-French literary interchange were in the 1890s and again in the 1920s, and of the writers dealt with here only Kipling and Owen owed a major debt to France – as of situation and circumstance.

In both countries, for example, many writers and artists regarded the outbreak of the war as a rite of purification, as a revolt against the selfishness and greed of the pre-war world. All these hopes were to be doomed. In France Péguy and Psichari dreamt of a revitalised and re-Christianised France that was to be born of the war, but both were killed before the true nature of the conflict became manifest. In England Rupert Brooke celebrated the combatants 'as swimmers into cleanness leaping', but he died of blood-poisoning in 1915 before he had any opportunity to experience the reality of Gallipoli.

In both countries the danger done by the war to established reputations was enormous. On the Right, Nationalists like Barrès and Maurras in France and Kipling in England might see the outbreak of the war as the fulfilment of all the warnings they had given of the German danger, but, not only was the Allied victory of 1918 Pyrrhic in its nature, they themselves were only to survive the war with their glory tarnished and diminished in the eyes of a younger generation that had been repelled by the chauvinism and brainwashing, the *bourrage de crâne*, of civilian propagandists.

On the Left, too, the impact of the war was shattering. In France the Socialist leader Jaurès had striven to avoid a war the horrors of which he had seen more clearly than most of his contemporaries, but was assassinated on the eve of the struggle. In England both Wells and Shaw survived the war, and continued to affirm their belief in the possibility of progress. The arguments they deployed, however, no longer seemed convincing to a generation that had witnessed violence and carnage on an unprecedented scale.

This was a generation that was more likely to listen to the warnings of the prophets of the decline of the West. Spengler is the best known of these, but he was far from alone, and it was the French and English writers discussed in the final part of the book who provided the most poignant variations on this theme. For all of them the First World War was to be a source of bitter disillusionment. Romain Rolland had sensed the decadence of Europe in the years before the outbreak of the war, and in 1914 he appealed to the intellectuals and the youth of the world to rise above the hatreds of the battle, but the call was an unrealistic one and the intensification of a conflict that appalled him led him to the conclusion that Europe was irrevocably doomed. At the start of hostilities D.H. Lawrence regarded the war as the triumph of all those mechanical and industrial forces that were destroying humanity, but he was not then aware of the true dimensions of the nightmare in which he was going to be involved. Isaac Rosenberg and Wilfred Owen reacted to the outbreak of the conflict in apocalyptic terms, but had no inkling in 1914 of the depth of the crisis that Europe was about to endure, or that they themselves would be destroyed by it.

With the exception of the chapter on Jaurès – whose prophetic status is assured, and whose views are of central importance in any discussion of the controversies over peace and war that racked French society in the years before 1914 – this is a survey that concentrates on the careers and achievements of writers as a primary source for the historian. Despite the fact that inter-disciplinary genres of this nature have long been established in the United States – where Paul Fussell's *The Great War and Modern Memory* has made an invaluable contribution to our understanding of the era – this is an approach that until recently has been regarded with a certain amount of suspicion by some English specialists in twentieth-century history. This is partly due, no doubt, to that ingrained English philistinism which regards the activities of imaginative artists as marginal to the serious concerns of life, but it is also due to legitimate objections to the subjectivity of literary evidence.

Provided that the historian is constantly aware of this danger, however, and provided that he handles works of literature with sensitivity, it may be thought that this is a problem that is capable of being surmounted. The potential gains, after all, are considerable. The historian of the First World War is presented with a rich source of material that enables him to embark upon what is now, perhaps, his most urgent task – that of tracing the intellectual and spiritual history, the *Geistesgeschichte*, of the war years and the years that surround them. In return, he may be able to offer to the literary specialist some new insights into the achievement of writers with whose work he is already familiar.

For far too long British universities have preached the virtues of comparative and inter-disciplinary approaches and have then left it largely to the students to make the connections. My hope is that, in however small a way, this book will be of some help in enabling historians and literary historians to communicate with each other.[2] If war is much too serious a thing to be left to military men – as Talleyrand said, and as Briand, Prime Minister of France between 1915 and 1917, reminded Lloyd George during the First World War – it should not be subjected to the demarcation disputes of academics.

PART I

Notre Patrie

Christopher Nevinson (1889–1946), *La Mitrailleuse*

A mesure qu'il s'efforçait à s'approfondir, une résonance lointaine lui revenait, qui roulait de toute une profondeur mysterieuse: 'La guerre est divine.'

(As he tried to examine himself more deeply, a distant resonance came back to him, that reverberated from a great and mysterious depth: 'War is divine.')

Ernest Psichari: *L'Appel des armes* (1913), p. 314

1

Jean Jaurès: the fight against war

Of all the hopes that were shattered by the outbreak of the First World War there can be little doubt that it was the Socialist dream of international fraternity that was the most spectacular casualty. In the years before 1914 Socialists had believed that in the Second International they had a rallying point and an organisation that might prevent a conflict in which the working classes of Europe would be called upon to slaughter one another. Now with the outbreak of the war all this lay in ruins, and all the hopes that had been invested in the International were revealed to be naive and utopian. Nowhere was this more apparent than in France, where Jaurès, the leader of the Socialist party, was assassinated by a Nationalist fanatic on the eve of the conflict.

And yet if the defeat of Jaurès symbolised the defeat of Socialist aspirations in 1914, if it exposed in the most cruel manner possible the hollowness of the Socialist belief in the inevitability of progress, it was a defeat not only for the Left, but for humanity as a whole. For the fact is that, whatever criticisms can be made of him, the leader of the French Socialists had always been far more than an ordinary politician and in the years before 1914 had been one of the few Europeans who had possessed a real sense of the horror that a major conflict would bring. Indeed, one of the many ironies of 1914 is that it was Jaurès, the idealist and the utopian, who saw more clearly than the vast majority of the 'realists' what form the coming war would take.

Perhaps it is no accident that in the midst of all the passions roused by the events of 1914 it should have been the leader of the *French* Socialists who was murdered on the eve of the conflict, for, although the struggle between Socialism and Nationalism was fought in many

9

European countries in the years before the outbreak of the war, it was in France that the battle was waged with particular ferocity. This was due in part to the intensity and ideological fervour that always characterised the conflict between Left and Right in France, a conflict that was further exacerbated by the hatreds aroused by the Dreyfus Affair, in which the Nationalists defended the army while the Socialists further emphasised their anti-militarist stance. But an even more important element in the situation after 1905 was France's growing fear of invasion, her increasing sense of the immediacy of the German threat.

Even the most cursory inspection of the situation of the major powers of Europe in 1914 should serve to demonstrate that it was France above all that felt most vulnerable to the threat of invasion. Austria–Hungary, it is true, was far gone in decline and lived in fear of the Russians, and even of the Serbs, but she was bolstered up by the enthusiastic support given to her by mighty Germany, and it was this very support that was to embolden her to gamble with the threat of war in 1914. France, by contrast, had experienced invasion and defeat by Germany in 1870, and had lived under threat from Germany ever since, a menace that became even more clear after the First Moroccan Crisis and the German pressure that led to the removal of Delcassé as Foreign Minister in 1905.

After that date, in fact, it was impossible for Frenchmen to ignore the danger that hovered on the blue line of the Vosges, and French politics mirrored this anxiety. There was, admittedly, a slackening of tension after 1906, but in 1911 there was a rebellion in Morocco against the Sultan, which led the French to strengthen their grip on the country. The Germans sent a gunboat, the Panther, to Agadir, ostensibly to protect German interests. After the resulting Second Moroccan Crisis France had to surrender 220,000 square kilometres of land in the Congo in return for Germany's recognition of the French protectorate over Morocco, and there were renewed anxieties over France's military position. In 1913 the fiercely patriotic Poincaré was elected President of the Republic, and in the same year the French Chamber, after ferocious and prolonged debate, approved the measure extending the period of compulsory military service from two years to three. While the Balkan Wars of 1912 and 1913 passed by without the great powers of Europe becoming involved, the great issues of nationalism and internationalism had in no way been resolved in France by 1914. In April of that year the Left, an alliance of Radicals and Socialists, won a near-absolute majority (if an extremely unstable one) in the elections, and throughout the period up to the outbreak of the war Poincaré was involved in maintaining the renegade Socialist Viviani in office as a device to frustrate the Left's endeavours to reverse the decisions over military service that had been taken the previous year.

In the summer of 1914, therefore, French politics were in a process of flux, and the hatreds between Left and Right had in no way been appeased. Few could have realised then that in the space of a few weeks France would be involved in the most terrible war in its history, and that the battle between Nationalists and Socialists would lead to the assassination of Jaurès on the eve of the outbreak of the war.

For Jaurès himself 1914 was to be the climactic year of a career in which he seemed destined to attract extremes of both adulation and hatred. It was a career that began inauspiciously, however. He was born in fairly humble circumstances into a decayed bourgeois family in 1859 at Castres, about fifty miles to the East of Toulouse, where his father was an unsuccessful businessman. The boy's ability was recognised at an early age, however, and after two years at the Collège of Sainte-Barbe in Paris he secured admission to the Ecole Normale, where Emile Durkheim and Henri Bergson were among his contemporaries.

At a time when the study of philosophy at the Ecole Normale was dominated by the clash between positivism and neo-Kantianism it is typical of Jaurès that he should have attempted to reconcile the two. The world, he was convinced, is a living organism in which there is a constant inter-penetration of matter and spirit: idealism and materialism are not necessarily opposed, for truth lies in a synthesis of the two. The eclectic nature of Jaurès's philosophy is obvious, and this was an element that persisted after his conversion to Socialism, for he was deeply indebted to the theories of 'Integral Socialism' formulated by Benoît Malon in the 1890s, a body of thought which attempted to reconcile Marxism with the French Utopian Socialist tradition, a tradition which was strongly idealistic and humanitarian in its emphasis. Despite his protestations to the contrary, therefore, Jaurès was never an orthodox marxist.

On both the Left and the Right in French politics, in fact, Jaurès was often seen as an academic who was out of place in the world of politics, a professor who was ignorant of many of the basic realities of existence. Alexandre Ribot, Prime Minister of France at the time of the Panama Affair and again in the early months of 1917, once exclaimed, partly in admiration, partly in exasperation, that Jaurès was 'a child, a great child'.[1] But for Jaurès himself his involvement in politics was a natural expression of his philosophical beliefs, which demanded that theory should involve action. In October 1885, largely through the influence of his cousin, Admiral Jaurès, he was elected to the French Chamber as an independent Republican. Defeated in the elections of 1889, he returned in January 1893 as an independent Socialist.

In later years he was constantly attacked by his opponents on the Left as a bourgeois progressive who had joined the Socialist movement for opportunistic reasons. Jaurès repudiated the charge of careerism, maintaining that his Socialism was the logical outcome of his earlier Republicanism, and pointing out, quite correctly, that if he had wanted ministerial office the last grouping he would have joined would have been the Socialists. He was always to be sensitive to the accusations that he knew little about the working classes, however, and there is no doubt that he tended to take a somewhat sentimental view of the masses. Briand, who was Jaurès's principal lieutenant in the years at the beginning of the century, and who, like so many of his young followers, was eventually to desert him for the chance of office, once observed maliciously:

He really has a timid temperament which dares not affront the common people . . . Try to persuade him of the rightness of a thesis, a tactic or a programme: after a thousand discussions and innumerable controversies he'll come round to your point of view. He'll find wisdom itself in it. But let a workman in dungarees come up and sustain the opposite point of view and he'll abandon you in a minute.[2]

In the 1890s, however, Jaurès's main problem was to find his bearings in the midst of the extraordinary fragmentation that characterised the Socialist movement in France. For a period in the middle of the decade it seemed that the moment for unity amongst the many competing groups might have arrived: support for Socialism was increasing; there was growing co-operation between the different factions; and Jaurès himself looked forward to the day when all the various elements in the Socialist movement – Guesdists, Broussists, Blanquists, Allemanists, Independents – would achieve synthesis and harmony. But it was a long and complicated process, and the movement towards unity was seriously delayed by the quarrels provoked by the Dreyfus Affair.

To Jules Guesde, the leader of the Marxist Parti Ouvrier Français, and to many others, the Affair was a dispute that had broken out between elements of the bourgeoisie, a dispute that had little relevance to the problems that preoccupied Socialists. To Jaurès and his supporters Dreyfus was a symbol of the sufferings of humanity as a whole, a cause that raised profound issues concerning individual liberty, issues which Socialists could not ignore. Above all, the Republic must be supported and defended against its enemies, even if this meant Socialist participation in bourgeois ministries. When Alexandre Millerand, with the support of Jaurès, accepted office in the Waldeck-Rousseau government of 1899, therefore, the prospects for the warring Socialist factions coming together were seriously diminished. That unity was eventually achieved in 1905 after a lapse of several years was due partly to German support for Guesde at the meeting of the Socialist International at Amsterdam in 1904 when Jaurès's tactic of participation was rejected and 'Millerandism' was condemned, and partly to Jaurès's decision to accept this decision.

He did not abandon his position without a struggle, however. Whilst the German Social Democrats claimed that the Third Republic was a bourgeois republic and that the record of the French bourgeoisie in its treatment of the working class in the past had been marked by bloodshed and repression, Jaurès counter-attacked by pointing out that the Republic, now strengthened by the victory of the Dreyfusards, offered the workers the opportunity for real political advance, and contrasted the situation in France with that in Germany where the most powerful Socialist movement in Europe possessed no such opportunities:

En ce moment, ce qui pèse sur l'Europe et sur le monde, sur la garantie de la paix, sur la garantie des libertés publiques, sur le progrès du socialisme et du prolétariat, ce qui pèse sur tout le progrès politique et sociale de l'Europe et du monde . . . ce ne sont pas les expériences aventureuses des socialistes français . . . pour sauver la liberté, le progrès, la paix du monde, ce qui pèse

sur tous, c'est l'impuissance politique de la démocratie socialiste
allemande . . . le prolétariat allemand . . . n'a pas historiquement une
tradition révolutionnaire. Ce n'est pas lui qui a conquis sur les barricades le
suffrage universel. Il l'a reçu d'en haut . . . Eh bien, parce que vous n'avez
pas cette tradition révolutionnaire, vous la regardez avec une sorte de
déplaisir chez les peuples qui y recourent . . .[3]

(At this moment what weighs most heavily on Europe and on the world, on
the guarantee of peace, on the guarantee of freedom, on the progress of
Socialism and the proletariat, what weighs on every kind of social and
political progress in Europe and the world . . . is not the bold attempt of
French Socialists . . . to safeguard liberty, progress, the peace of the world,
what weighs on all of us is the political impotence of German Social
Democracy . . . Historically the German proletariat . . . has no revolutionary tradition. It was not that party that gained universal suffrage through
action at the barricades. It was given to it from on high . . . And so, because
you do not possess this revolutionary tradition, you regard with a certain
displeasure those people who do have this experience . . .)

It is worth bearing this speech in mind when considering the
constant attacks made by Nationalists on the 'pro-German' sympathies of Jaurès in later years.

And yet, although the speech was an oratorical triumph – it was
received in stunned silence by the German delegation and wildly
applauded in other parts of the hall – Jaurès for the moment had to
resign himself to the fact that on the matter of Socialist unification on
Guesdist terms he was bound to be defeated. Another issue had to be
found in which he could utilise his talents to relate Socialism to the
wider needs of humanity. As he left the Congress he revealed that
another campaign was in the making:

Trois millions d'électeurs sociaux-démocrates sont à peu sans action sur la
politique impériale. Je vais étudier les questions militaires.[4]

(Three million Social Democrat electors have practically no influence on
imperial policy. I am going to study military questions.)

In any examination of Jaurès's views on foreign and military policy it
soon becomes clear that in the course of his career these views
underwent a considerable evolution. During his period as an
independent Republican in the 1880s and early 1890s, for example,

he had welcomed the prospect of an alliance between France and
Russia as a factor making for increased stability in Europe. In 1891 he
had denied that there was any resemblance between the Russian
monarchy and the monarchies of the Triple Alliance, maintaining
that

la Russie est encore dans cette période historique où la monarchie, sauf
quelques erreurs réparables, confond avec la nation elle-même . . . elle est
l'âme même du peuple.[5]

(Russia is still in that period of historical development when the monarchy,
apart from some errors that can be corrected, is identified with the
nation . . . it is the soul of the nation itself.)

But after his conversion to Socialism he became bitterly hostile to
Tsarism as a repressive force within Russia and increasingly critical
of the alliance itself. At the time of Nicholas II's visit to Paris in 1896,
he argued that the alliance was being used by right-wing Republicans like Méline and Hanotaux to consolidate the forces of
conservatism and reaction in the internal affairs of France, and
warned that the French Right wanted to lead the country into a
revived Holy Alliance that in foreign policy would be directed
against England and in internal affairs would be used to combat the
growing power of Socialism.

   Indeed, as the 1890s progressed he became increasingly radical in
matters of foreign policy and more and more critical not only of the
alliance system but of the whole international order that was
beginning to develop in the classic age of imperialism. In a speech to
the French Chamber in 1895 he maintained that it was the advent of
capitalism with its competitive and anarchic spirit that had increased
the dangers of a major European war:

Toujours votre société violente et chaotique, même quand elle veut la paix,
même quand elle est à l'état d'apparemment repos, porte en elle la guerre,
comme la nuée dormante porte l'orage.[6]

(All the time your violent and chaotic society, even when it wants peace,
even when it is in a state of apparent repose, carries war within it, as the
rain-cloud carries the storm.)

And by the time of the Fashoda Crisis and the Spanish American War
it was the danger of a world conflict that now haunted him:

Elle sera terrible et vaste. Pour la première fois, il y aura une guerre universelle, mettant aux prises tous les continents. L'expansion capitaliste a élargi le champ de bataille; c'est toute la planète que se disputent maintenant les capitaux; c'est toute la planète qui sera rougie du sang des hommes.[7]

(It will be vast and terrible. For the first time there will be a universal war, setting all the continents against one another. Capitalist expansion has enlarged the field of battle, the different capitalisms fight over the whole planet, and now it is the whole planet that will be stained red by men's blood.)

In the early 1890s he had considered disarmament to be a 'dangerous chimera'.[8] Now he regarded it as 'inevitable' since the development of modern science made war suicidal. Nevertheless, he repudiated the idea that, since conflict was endemic in the nature of the capitalist and imperialist system, then war was something that could not be avoided, and he was also hostile to the notion that war should be welcomed by the Left as the engine for revolution. His studies in the history of the French Revolution (research that resulted in a pioneering *Histoire socialiste de la révolution française*) convinced him that it was the declaration of war in 1792 that had caused the Revolution to degenerate into the Jacobin dictatorship, the Terror, and ultimately into the military dictatorship of Napoleon, and he was adamant that the Left should not make the same mistake again:

D'une guerre européenne peut jaillir la révolution et les classes dirigeantes feront bien d'y songer; mais il peut sortir aussi, pour une longue période, des crises de contre-révolution, de réaction furieuse, de nationalisme exaspéré, de dictature étouffante, de militarisme monstrueux, une longue chaîne de violences rétrogrades et de haines basses, de représailles et de servitude. Et nous, nous ne voulons pas jouer à ce jeu d'hasard barbare . . .[9]

(A European war can lead to the outbreak of revolution, and the ruling classes would do well to think about it; but it could also lead for a long period to counter-revolutionary crises, violent reaction, inflamed national-ism, stultifying dictatorship, fearful militarism, a long process of retrograde violence and hatred, reprisals and servitude. And we for our part do not wish to engage in this barbaric game of chance.)

But if war was to be avoided, then the Left should take the lead in fighting the idea, and it was not until after the Amsterdam Congress of 1904 that Jaurès threw himself wholeheartedly into the campaign for peace. Various explanations can be offered for the delay, explanations that all have an element of truth in them. Cynics could maintain that during the period that Jaurès had supported the government of Waldeck-Rousseau's successor, Emile Combes, he had found it convenient to trust the latter not to engage France in an adventurous foreign policy while they both concentrated on internal affairs, like the attack on the Church. Cynics would further maintain that, after Jaurès was impelled by the Amsterdam Congress to withdraw support from Combes, he had suddenly become interested again in foreign policy on opportunist grounds, in order to regain his ascendancy in the soon-to-be-united French Socialist party and to identify the party with the kind of vague humanitarian cause that suited his particular rhetorical gifts.

As usual, cynics would be partly right and partly wrong. It would be a complete misreading of the political career of Jaurès ever to minimise the sheer pragmatism that governed his conduct. On the other hand, it would be an even graver injustice not to recognise that by 1904–5 he was impelled by moral imperatives and by a blinding sense of the horror of any coming war.

Why did Jaurès's fear of war intensify in 1904 and 1905? There is no doubt that it was the outbreak of the Russo-Japanese war in February 1904 and the onset of the First Moroccan Crisis in the following year that were the main factors that were responsible for his change of attitude. As far as events in the Far East were concerned he was worried by the international implications of a war in which France's ally Russia clashed with England's ally Japan, a war that might easily exacerbate Franco-British rivalry, and, although that particular danger was averted and Jaurès was able to welcome the conclusion of the Entente Cordiale between France and Britain in April 1904 as a development that strengthened the power of the democratic idea in Europe, there was a further element in the confrontation between Russia and Japan that deeply disturbed him – the development of trench warfare in Manchuria in the course of the conflict.

As will be seen later, this was a development which convinced him that it was imperative to rethink military strategy. He was also profoundly affected by the suffering of the soldiers in the trenches. In a newspaper article written in October 1904 he attempted to explain to the French public something of the realities of modern warfare:

Dans le Grand Palais des Champs Elysées, tout au fond de l'exposition ouverte au profit des blessés russes, se dresse la blanche tente de la Croix Rouge. Des mannequins figurent le médecin, les infirmiers, le blessé qu'on rapporte sur un brancard. Comme tout cela est propre, décent, presque tendre! C'est la guerre vue à travers des vitraux roses et bleus. Le blessé lui-même est d'une tenue irréprochable: son pied, fracassé par un éclat d'obus, est enveloppé de linges blancs, mais ni sur ses vêtements ni sur son bonnet de fourrure il n'y a une tache de boue, un grain de poussière, une goutte de sang. C'est la guerre brossée, correcte, coquette, presque pimpante; sur le visage même du blessé, qu'aucune souffrance ne contracte, se joue une nuance de mélancolie. Qui pourrait se représenter, par ces enchantillons innocents et discrets, l'horrible pestilence qui se dégage des charniers du champ de bataille et des hospitaux encombrés, tout le large flot mêlé de sang, de pourriture et de boue qui coule par toutes les places de la guerre?[10]

(Right at the back of the exhibition in the Grand Palais of the Champs Elysées in aid of the wounded Russians is the white tent of the Red Cross. Dummies represent the doctor, the orderlies, and the wounded man who has been brought in on a stretcher. How clean, decent and almost touching it all is! It is war seen through rose-coloured spectacles. The wounded man himself is immaculately attired; his foot, which has been shattered by a shell, is covered in white bandages, but neither on his clothes nor on his fur hat is there a bit of mud, a speck of dust, or a drop of blood. This is war cleaned and tidied up, elegant, almost smart; on the face of the wounded man himself there is a suggestion of melancholy but no grimace of pain. Who would imagine from these charming and innocent representations the terrible disease that stalks the field of battle and the crowded hospitals, the whole mixture of blood, putrefaction and mud that is to be found in every theatre of war?)

All these concerns were eventually to bear fruit in his ideas for a reorganisation of French military policy that was to appear in his treatise L'Armée nouvelle that was published in 1911.

Already in the course of 1904, then, Jaurès's decision to concentrate on military affairs in the aftermath of his defeat at the Amsterdam Congress had been more than justified by events. The First Moroccan Crisis in the next year only confirmed him in his view that action was now urgent.

Under the terms of the Anglo-French Entente the French had

recognised Britain's position in Egypt, while Britain gave France a free hand in Morocco. Angered by France's attempts to consolidate her position in Morocco the German government reacted swiftly, at a time when France's ally, Russia, was weakened by her war with Japan. In March 1905 the Kaiser visited Tangier and dramatically assured the Moroccan leaders that Germany regarded the future of their country as an international question. When Delcassé ruled out German proposals for an international conference the German government demanded his resignation. The Germans were further emboldened in their demands by the defeat of the Russian fleet by that of Japan at Tsushima in May 1905, a defeat that sent shock-waves through Asia and Europe, encouraging both the development of the Asian revolt against European imperialism and the onset of the 1905 revolution in Russia.

In the course of the ensuing Franco-German crisis Jaurès did not conceal his dislike of the methods that Germany had used in this attempt to test the strength of the new Anglo-French Entente, but it was the extent to which the affair revealed how Delcassé had kept his colleagues in the dark about his intentions during the entire period of the Combes administration that now concerned him. While Combes, with Jaurès's assistance, had been happily engaged in reducing the power of the Church and blocking the promotion of Catholics and royalists in the army and the civil service after the Dreyfus Affair, Delcassé had been strengthening the Franco-Russian Alliance and encouraging the forward extension of French influence in Morocco. In defence of the French Foreign Minister it could be maintained that his policies were a necessary response to Germany's increasing preoccupation with *Weltpolitik*, but all this had now to be paid for, and, under intense German pressure, the new Prime Minister, Rouvier, had no option but to get rid of Delcassé, a severe and public humiliation of France, although Germany gained little at the subsequent international conference on the Moroccan question held at Algeçiras in 1906, when Britain and Spain supported the French position.

From now on, Jaurès (whose faith in the potentially civilising mission of French imperialism had lingered for some years after his conversion to Socialism) was to be a determined opponent of any further provocation of Germany by renewed activity in Morocco. At the same time, the adventurism that had come to characterise Russian foreign policy and had led to the Russo-Japanese war, together with the savage repression by the Tsar of the democratic forces in Russia after the failure of the 1905 Revolution, convinced him that France's alliance with Russia should at the very least be subjected to constant scrutiny. Ultimately, however, the only guarantee for a lasting European peace would lie in concerted action by the Socialist movement.

It would require a far more exhaustive treatment than is possible here to go into details of the long campaign that Jaurès conducted after 1905 within the French Socialist party and the Second International to convert his fellow-socialists to the view that the danger of war was imminent and that the only policy to avert such a danger was to invoke the threat of a general strike of workers in all the combatant nations if the powers involved would not agree to arbitration. What would be more useful, perhaps, would be to single out one particular, and prophetic, aspect of his campaign – his attempt to transform French defence policy. This is intended to offset at least part of the mockery and ridicule to which he has been subjected on the grounds that his overall policy was utopian and impractical.

That his overall policy *was* impractical barely needs emphasising, and the opposition that Jaurès experienced came from both Left and Right within the Socialist spectrum. While Lenin and Rosa Luxemburg preached revolution instead of a general strike to combat capitalist war, the majority of German Socialists and, even more, the majority of German trade union leaders, were opposed to Jaurès's ideas on quite different grounds. They were sceptical about the practicality of a general strike at a time of international crisis and war, and feared the backlash that a general strike in these circumstances would provoke against their powerful and prosperous organisations. They also thought that Jaurès's fears of war were exaggerated – a view that seems extremely short-sighted in retrospect, when one considers the extent to which the *Weltpolitik* of the Imperial government in Germany from the late 1890s onwards was itself a response to its deteriorating position within German domestic politics, but a view that seemed to be confirmed by the ability of the international system to preserve the peace between the Great Powers until 1914, by which time it was beginning to appear even to Jaurès himself that he had cried wolf too often.

In any case it was believed by many inside and outside Germany that, with the increasing number of votes that the Social Democrats received in the Reichstag elections, the German Socialists, by far the most powerful Socialist grouping in Europe, would take power without undue difficulty some time in the near future. Seen in this perspective Jaurès's agitation for a general strike to prevent war seemed both alarmist and demagogic. Typical of the German reaction to Jaurès was a remark that had been made as early as 1904 by Karl Kautsky, the most prominent ideologist of the German party, in a letter to Viktor Adler, the leader of the Austrian Socialists:

Jaurès breaks people of the habit of thinking clearly. He is a rhetorical genius, but that is why he thinks he can do anything with words. He carries this national French vice to extremes . . . For the rest his talents are those of a parliamentary string-puller.[11]

Although the German Social Democrats went along with the famous compromise resolution of the Stuttgart Congress of the Second International in 1907 – which managed to embrace all the different viewpoints on the policy to be followed by Socialists in time of war – and although, amidst the general euphoria at the end of the Congress, Jaurès himself was deluded into thinking for a time that this resolution represented a significant step forward, the fact remains that on this most basic of issues the European Socialist movement, despite all Jaurès's efforts, was permanently split.

The same was true of the unified French party. There, despite the support that Jaurès received from leading personalities like Edouard Vaillant of the Blanquist section and many of the rank and file, there were many who followed the policies of the rabid anti-militarist Gustave Hervé, who had once exclaimed that the tricolour should be planted on a dung-hill, and took the line that not a general strike but a general insurrection was necessary in case there was a threat of war. It was symptomatic of the intransigent position of the German Socialists and the increasing war-fever in France in the years before 1914 that Hervé abandoned this view in 1913 after frustrating encounters between the French and German trade unionists. In any case it was a view that had no chance of success in a France where

trade union strength was relatively weak, where the wave of
syndicalist strikes had spent itself by 1909, and where the latent
Jacobinism of the French Left would never accept a policy of
sabotage if Germany declared war on Republican France.

Still, Hervé's influence within the movement was considerable,
and Hervé was not the only opponent that Jaurès had to face. There
was above all his main rival within the party, Jules Guesde, the
supreme ideological pontiff of French Marxism, the 'Torquemada in
spectacles', as he was once described. Guesde held that war was
inevitable under capitalism, that a general strike or insurrection was
futile, and that, instead of trying to devise means of avoiding war,
Socialists should stick to the sacred formula of 'la lutte des classes'.

Guesde's theoretical Marxism did not stand up to the test of events
in 1914, and soon after the outbreak of the First World War the man
who had opposed participation in bourgeois governments at the time
of the Dreyfus Affair found himself a member of a coalition
administration pledged to defend France against Germany, while
Hervé became a fire-eating patriot. But long before 1914 Jaurès had
realised that the schematic simplicities of Guesde and Hervé were
utterly inadequate to the problems that faced them. He agonized over
the immoral nature of France's alliance with the enemy of all
European liberty, Tsarist Russia, and he was passionately concerned
to avoid war between the three most advanced societies of Europe –
France, Britain and Germany – that might result from an Austro-
Russian conflict in the Balkans.

How could this problem be resolved? In the short term he hoped to
achieve a remodelling of the French armed forces so that a
professional army devoted to the offensive could be transformed into
a citizen army concerned above all with defence. In the long term he
probably hoped to see a progressive transformation of the existing
alliance system into a Paris–London–Berlin–Rome combination that
would leave decadent Austria–Hungary and autocratic Russia to sort
out their own problems in the Balkans or have solutions to these
problems imposed on them by a Grand Alliance of the West.

His views on the changes that were necessary to the alliance
system are of necessity open to some speculation, but the idea that he
wanted eventually to abandon the Russian alliance in favour of a
more Western-based system seems to fit in with the whole logic of

Jaurès's evolution after 1905. The most interesting formulation of the idea that he was in favour of such a 'renversement des alliances' is, of course, to be found in the biography of Lucien Herr by Charles Andler that was published in 1932.[12] Andler was for many years Professor of German at the Sorbonne, a Socialist who quarrelled with Jaurès in the years before 1914 over the way in which he and his ally Lucien Herr – who from his post as librarian of the Ecole Normale exercised an enormous influence on successive generations of the intellectual youth of France – attempted to minimise the importance of Pan-German influence on certain elements in the Social Democratic Party within Germany in order to portray that party as a party devoted to peace. It might be thought from this that Andler is a somewhat suspect source, but there is no reason to impugn the essential veracity of his account of the views of Jaurès and Herr in this biography. Talk of the necessity for an alliance for peace between England, France and Germany was common currency amongst leaders of Western European progressive thought in the years before 1914. Vaillant and the British Labour leader Keir Hardie supported the idea. So did Bernard Shaw, as will be seen later. And, as far as Jaurès is concerned, Andler's speculations secure implicit, if not explicit, confirmation in many of Jaurès's speeches before 1914 and in the proposals that he later made for a transformation of French defence policy.

The fact is that, whilst bitterly critical of the Franco-Russian alliance, Jaurès could never openly and unequivocally call for its abrogation for fear of alienating French public opinion. Instead, whilst denying that he wanted to destroy the alliance, he called for it to be progressively 'enlarged'. This position may have satisfied Jaurès, but it hardly satisfied many of his contemporaries, and when, in furtherance of this policy, he welcomed the conclusion of the Entente between England and Russia in 1907 and depicted the now 'enlarged' Triple Alliance as a stabilising force in European politics, as a further stage in the movement towards a European League for Peace, it is hardly surprising that he should have been severely criticised by radicals within the European Socialist movement like Rosa Luxemburg.[13]

It is easy to understand her exasperation. In contemplating Jaurès's career it is continually tempting to conclude that his intellectual facility and rhetorical skills were only means for avoiding unpleasant truths, that his gifts as a conciliator and a compromiser were only devices that enabled him to escape from the problems, quarrels and contradictions that afflicted the rest of humanity. Clemenceau once exclaimed that one could always tell if an article was written by Jaurès because all the verbs would be in the future tense. And one of Guesde's friends, Lucien Roland, produced a devastating parody of Jaurès's oratorical style:

Idéal! citoyen! lumière! humanité!
L'orage, les éclairs, la flamme, le simoun!*
Franchise! Nègre blanc! Immense loyauté!
Raplapla! Badaboum! Ratapla! Zim boum boum!
Le néant, le progrès! Nuages éthérés!
Plutarque! Karl Marx! Michelet! Chantaboum!
Électeurs décorés! Badaboum! Rataplan! Zim boum boum![14]

(Ideal! citizen! light! humanity!
The storm! The flashes of lightning, the flame, the simoon!*
Frankness! White negro! Immense loyalty!
Rapapla! Badaboum! Ratapla! Zim boum boum!
Emptiness! progress! Ethereal clouds!
Plutarch, Karl Marx, Michelet! Chantaboum!
Honourable electors! Badaboum! Rataplan! Zim boum boum!)

* A hot stifling wind from North Africa.

In defence of Jaurès, however, it could be said that it was precisely his gift for conciliation and harmony that was the essence of his genius, and that it was this that enabled him to offer fresh and creative solutions to problems in situations where others could only see conflict and confrontation. At their worst Jaurès's ideas seem to be the product of wishful thinking. At their best they seem to point the way forward to a new way of looking at issues that had seemed to be incapable of resolution. Both aspects of his thinking can be seen in his approach to French military policy.

    Jaurès's ideas on a citizen army, formulated in *L'Armée nouvelle*, had long roots within the French and European revolutionary tradition that disliked professional standing armies as instruments of class oppression. And as ideas they have certain obvious advantages and disadvantages. Like many of Jaurès's projects, the idea of a citizen army can be dismissed as utopian – a possibility for professionally neutral countries like Switzerland, but hopelessly impractical for a great power like France. When similar proposals were debated within the German Social Democratic party Max Schippel pointed out in a famous observation that one could not put a cannon in the bed of every former gunner and give every old sea-dog a little warship to be put in his farmyard trough or wash-tub.[15] Later on, during the First World War, General Galliéni quoted an instance of a detachment of territorial troops fleeing in terror from the onrush of the initial German offensive in 1914, adding that in his ideas on the citizen army Jaurès had not foreseen a situation like that.[16]

But while these are obviously important objections, it is equally important to remember that, amidst all his chimerical notions, Jaurès, the rhetorician and optimist, the eternal Mr Micawber of French politics, had one great insight. Together with a group of junior French army officers who also disagreed with the current revival of Napoleonic offensive tactics by Foch and Colonel de Grandmaison, he had studied the emergence of trench warfare in Manchuria at the time of the Russo-Japanese war and had come to the conclusion that the next European war would be a terrible, murderous and long drawn-out affair in which the state of military technology dictated that the ultimate advantage would lie with troops trained to perform a primarily defensive role. As he warned the Chamber of Deputies when outlining the main proposals of L'Armée nouvelle in December 1911:

Et qu'on n'imagine pas une guerre courte, se résolvant en quelques coups de foudre et quelques jaillissements d'éclairs; ce sera, dans les régions opposées, des collisions formidables et lentes, comme là-bas celles qui se produisirent en Mandchourie entre Russes et Japonais; ce seront des masses humaines qui fermenteront dans la maladie, dans la détresse, dans la douleur, sous les ravages des obus multipliés.[17]

(Do not imagine a short war, resolving itself in a few flashes of lightning and a few showers of sparks. In the regions concerned it will consist of slow tremendous collisions like those that occurred down there in Manchuria between the Russians and the Japanese. It will consist of masses of human beings, fermenting in sickness, distress and misery, subjected to the ravages of a multiplicity of shells.)

Although Jaurès could not possibly foresee the full horror of the
First World War his predictions concerning the likely character of a
future conflict – predictions that included a forecast that the main
thrust of the German attack would be through Belgium and proposals
that France should build fortresses from Sedan to Dunkirk to match
those that existed on the eastern frontier – are not unimpressive,
even if they wholly failed to influence the French Chamber, which
ignored his warnings. No doubt his views on the coming war and the
necessity for a defensive strategy to deal with it fitted in extremely
neatly with his political and ideological preoccupations, one of
which was his desire to help the German Socialists to undermine
German militarism by demonstrating that France had no aggressive
intentions in Europe – a laudable aim, but one which gave an
unregenerate Germany the possibility of a free hand in eastern
Europe. Another criticism that can be made of him, of course, is that
he himself refused to believe his own most pessimistic insights about
the coming war and, instead, radiated optimism in the crisis of 1914.

But these objections should not be allowed to obscure the
prophetic nature of his vision or the fact that, for much of the time
during the closing years of his life, he was far from hopeful that a
conflict could be avoided. In 1911 and 1912, for example, he was no
stranger to the temptation of despair. At the time of the Second
Moroccan Crisis in July 1911 he lamented that there was not an atom
of good faith between nations anywhere. And when the Balkan wars
started in 1912 he wrote in *L'Humanité* on 20 October:

Des insensés nous mènent à l'abîme. Par le Maroc sera suscitée la
Tripolitaine. Par la Tripolitaine sera suscitée la guerre des Balkans. Par la
guerre des Balkans sera suscitée la guerre générale.

(Madmen are leading us to the abyss. Morocco will stir up Tripoli, Tripoli
will stir up war in the Balkans. And the war in the Balkans will stir up a
general war.)

A few weeks later he made what was perhaps the most famous speech
of his career at the emergency Congress called by the Second
International at Basel, a speech in which his sense of foreboding
overshadowed his ultimate affirmation of hope:

Je pense à la devise que Schiller inscrivit en tête de son magnifique poème
'Le Chant de la cloche': Vivos voco: j'appelle les vivants pour qu'ils se

défendent contre le monstre qui paraît à l'horizon. Mortuos plango: je pleure sur les morts innombrables couchés là-bas vers l'Orient et dont la puanteur arrive jusqu'à nous comme un remords. Fulgora frango: je briserai les foudres de la guerre qui menacent dans les nuées.[18]

(I think of that motto that Schiller inscribed at the beginning of his magnificent poem 'The Song of the Bell': Vivos voco: I appeal to the living to defend themselves against the monster which appears on the horizon. Mortuos plango: I weep for the innumerable dead laid down there towards the East whose stench reaches us in reproach. Fulgora frango: I will break the thunderbolts of war that menace us from the skies.)

As matters turned out, however, his anxieties seem to have been exaggerated. Admittedly in the course of 1913 France was plunged into the bitter debate that surrounded the proposal to extend the period of military service. And at the beginning of the year, when Fallières left the Elysée Palace after the election of Poincaré as President of the Republic, the former was heard to murmur that he was making way for war.[19] But in the event Europe managed to negotiate not only one but two Balkan wars without a major conflagration, and it was this that led Jaurès to take a basically sanguine view of events in 1914, a view that he maintained until the day before his assassination on 31 July.

Until that time he was still hopeful that a major European war could be averted, that both governments and capitalists now realised the economic futility of war (he was greatly taken by the arguments of Norman Angell in *The Great Illusion*), and that with every year that passed the Social Democrats were moving closer towards taking over power in Germany. Even after the crisis of 1914 started he still refused to despair. The forthcoming Congress of the Internatonal in Vienna might have to be postponed because of Austria's declaration of war on Serbia, but he believed there was a chance that the other powers would not become involved. Even if war broke out between Austria and Serbia, he hoped that it would be of limited duration and that, later on in the year, he would be able to press the German Social Democrats and their new leader, Hugo Haase, to agree to the strategy of a general strike to prevent a general European war. In return, he hoped that he would be able to announce to the International that the long-standing division between the French Socialist party and the

French trade unions (always a source of weakness in the French Left) had been overcome, and that the French labour movement was on the verge of fighting against war as a united force.

'Ce sera comme pour Agadir. Il y aura des hauts et des bas. Mais les choses ne peuvent pas ne pas s'arranger'.[20] (It will be like Agadir. There will be ups and downs. But things are bound to sort themselves out.) Jaurès addressed these remarks to the Belgian Socialist leader Vandervelde on 30 July, just before he returned to Paris from the emergency meeting of the Bureau of the Second International held at Brussels to discuss the war between Austria and Serbia, a meeting at which Viktor Adler had confessed that he could do nothing to prevent the tide of hatred that was rising in Austria against the Russians and the Serbs. And there is no doubt that Jaurès's attitude at this point in the crisis has done little to enhance his reputation, for we know that by this time the First World War was virtually inevitable. We know now the full extent to which the German government had encouraged Austria in her determination to have a showdown with the Serbs. We know now that the hesitations of Wilhelm II and the German Chancellor as the crisis developed were to be overborne by the Russian decision to implement full (instead of partial) mobilisation, a decision which caused the German army to press for an immediate declaration of war in order that their one military plan, the Schlieffen plan (which envisaged a holding operation in the east until France had been knocked out in the west), could be put into effect.

Still, it is difficult not to be moved by another of Jaurès's conversations, one that took place after his return to Paris, when he heard the news of the Russian mobilisation and of Germany's declaration that she was putting herself on a war footing. As the full horror of the situation began to dawn on him, he saw Captain Gérard, one of the officers on whose expertise he had relied in the formulation of his proposals on military policy in *L'Armée nouvelle*. His parting words to Gérard demonstrate once again his insight into the real nature of the coming war, an insight that has only rarely received its proper recognition in the standard histories:

Ah! Pourvu que nos jeunes officiers ne soient trop braves! Pourvu qu'ils aient bien compris cette terrible guerre et qu'ils n'aillent pas se jeter sur les mitrailleuses![21]

(Ah! If only our young officers are not too daring! If only they understand this terrible war and do not throw themselves on the machine guns!)

This moves and impresses us now, but it was the kind of statement that could only move the majority of Frenchmen to anger when they were faced with the German threat in 1914. Already since the time of the Dreyfus Affair Jaurès had been the subject of merciless attacks by Maurras and the Nationalist Right. These attacks now reached a climax in the bitter disputes that had surrounded the three years military service law of 1913 and the election of a Chamber with a potential left-wing majority that might reverse the law in 1914. On 18 July 1914, for example, the newspaper of Maurras and his Action Française proclaimed that 'Chacun le sait. M. Jaurès c'est l'Allemagne' ('Everybody knows it. Monsieur Jaurès is Germany'). And even if Barrès admired Jaurès personally while believing his ideas to be mistaken, there were plenty of other enemies around anxious to see Jaurès's influence extinguished. Indeed, in the period after the First Moroccan Crisis when the internationalist stance of the Socialists became increasingly pronounced, his old opponents on the Right were now joined by an even more fearsome breed – former allies of Jaurès in the Dreyfusard cause who now regarded him as a traitor to the patriotism of the Jacobin tradition.

Foremost and most murderous of these new enemies was the editor of the *Cahiers de la quinzaine*, the poet, dramatist and polemicist Charles Péguy. At the height of the battle over the three years military law Péguy attacked Jaurès and Herr (and the Parti Intellectuel at the Sorbonne that supported them) in the most violent terms, proclaiming that they constituted

le point d'infection politique, le point de contamination, le point d'origine de virulence qui a corrompu, qui a empoisonné le dreyfusisme, le socialisme, l'esprit révolutionnaire même.[22]

(the source of political infection, the point of contamination, the source of the virulence that has corrupted and poisoned the Dreyfusard cause, Socialism, and the revolutionary spirit itself.)

In the same essay by Péguy page after page of invective against Jaurès as an agent of Imperial Germany culminates in a vision of the Socialist leader being guillotined on the outbreak of the war.

Many of the attacks that were made on Jaurès were, of course, not only barbaric but also in many ways unjust. Far from taking the line of revolutionary defeatism in time of war advocated by Lenin, Jaurès ardently believed in the defence of Republican France. Far from being in any way an agent of Germany, he was always regarded with deep suspicion by the German Social Democrats. On the Left Rosa Luxemburg respected him for his humanity and for the largeness of his vision, but was fiercely critical of his constant advocacy of reformist remedies to problems that required revolutionary solutions:

The melodies that Jaurès still sings remind me of the good old arias of Verdi: once in sunny Italy they were on the lips of every happy, dark-eyed urchin like the promise of a people's spring, and now we hear them still, but ground out with horrible monotony on barrel-organs. Tempi passati. And the organ-grinder stares into space with an air of detached boredom as he grinds; the same song, but the spirit has gone.[23]

And on the Centre and Right of the German party, too, Jaurès was never forgiven for his electrifying indictment of the impotence of German Social Democracy at the Amsterdam Congress in 1904.

Indeed, far from wanting to submit France to the domination of Germany, as Maurras and Péguy alleged, Jaurès's ultimate aim, as some German Socialists realised, was to liberate the International from the stultifying grip of the German party, and, with the aid of men like Keir Hardie – who had supported Jaurès and Vaillant in their attempts to persuade the Germans to agree to the policy of a General Strike to prevent war – to reassert France's historic role as the leader of the forces of Progress in Europe. As Barrès instinctively realised, Jaurès, too, was a descendant of Michelet and Hugo, a man who believed that France could never commit an irrevocable sin against humanity, a man who was passionately convinced that the cause of France was that of civilisation as a whole.

By the high summer of 1914, however, all this was now irrelevant. A terrible war, far more terrible than even Jaurès could have anticipated, swept both him and Péguy away. Already on 31 July, the day of Jaurès's assassination, the German ultimatum had been sent to Russia, and within the course of the next few days, the majority of European Socialists rushed to support their governments.

In Germany, following the Russian mobilisation, the vast bulk of the Social Democrats felt justified in giving their support to the struggle against Tsarism. In France, after Germany's declaration of war against Russia on 1 August and on France two days later, French Socialists rallied to the Union Sacrée, in which the political parties sank their differences to support the country against the invader. In England the bulk of the Labour movement, where many of the trade union leaders had always been sceptical of the talk of a general strike in time of war, ignored Hardie's advice and supported the British ultimatum to Germany on 4 August. In December 1913 Hardie had chaired a great peace rally at the Albert Hall in London, where the speakers had included Jaurès, Vandervelde, the German Social Democrat Molkebuhr, and Anatole France. Now the great dream of Socialist internationalism had been exposed as an illusion.

Keir Hardie died broken-hearted in 1915. What would Jaurès's attitude have been had he survived to see the outbreak of the war? There can be little doubt that, although his last intention before he was shot by Raoul Villain – at the Café du Croissant just after 9.40 in the evening of 31 July – was to go on after dinner to the offices of L'Humanité to write a new 'J'accuse', blaming the Russian mobilisation for the escalation of the crisis into a major European war, once Germany had declared war on France he would have supported France against the aggressor. At the same time it is equally certain that he would have maintained that both sides must bear some responsibility for the conflict, that both sides must work for an end to the war, and that he would have been one of the leaders of a peace campaign following the downfall of Tsarism in 1917.

Whether activities like these would ultimately have enhanced his reputation, however, is a question that is more difficult to answer. While Jaurès was a man of the utmost personal integrity he was a bad judge of men, and the devious Radical politician and former Prime Minister Caillaux, who had been an ally of Jaurès at the time of the elections in 1914, was one of those contemplating a compromise peace in 1917, even to the extent of letting it be known that if Germany, now under the political domination of its army, granted a generous peace to France in the west, she would be allowed to make annexations in the east. Jaurès himself is hardly likely to have been prepared to sanction anything like this, but, seen against the background of his campaigns for peace before 1914, it is easy to understand why Clemenceau is reported to have said that had Jaurès survived until 1917 it would have been necessary to shoot him.

Although Jaurès's Nationalist admirer, Maurice Barrès (whose son Philippe served in the same regiment as Jaurès's son, Louis, who was killed in 1918), continued to defend his reputation throughout the war,[24] and although his memory was cherished by millions of Socialists — as well as by intellectuals as diverse as Proust,[25] Bernard Shaw and Anatole France — perhaps it was fortunate for Jaurès's continuing renown that he should have died when he did. Now that the battle had begun, the men of war and the men of violence were in control. Shortly after the outbreak of the conflict it was with contempt that Lenin dismissed the argument of one of his followers who maintained that by following the Bolshevik line on the war he was in danger of encouraging Germany to destroy democracy in France:

Let them destroy it. France is nothing but a backward republic of usurers and rentiers fattening on their gold . . . for us revolutionary Marxists it makes no difference who wins . . .[26]

A new era had begun, an era of ruthlessness, duplicity and force, an era in which Jaurès had no place. But on one matter he had not been mistaken. As Captain (now Commandant) Gérard explained to a brother soldier as the heavy shells exploded around him in the middle of one of the battles of the war:

Il me semble avoir déja vu tout cela . . . Jaurès avait prophetisé cet enfer, cet anéantissement total.[27]

(It seems to me that I have seen all that before . . . Jaurès prophesied this Hell, this total annihilation).

— 2 —

Maurice Barrès, Charles Maurras, Charles Péguy: the defence of France

It is no accident that Nationalism should have become a significant force within French politics in the years before the outbreak of the First World War, for France, the greatest power in Europe at the time of the Napoleonic Wars, had seen her position deteriorate seriously in the course of the nineteenth century, a decline that was accentuated by her defeat in the Franco-Prussian War, by the unification of Germany, and by the onset of a process of German industrialisation and population increase that left France far behind. If Kipling in England was concerned by the growing might of Germany, and her increasing inclination to embark on *Weltpolitik*, for France the implications of the dynamism of Wilhelminian Germany were even more serious: in terms of military and industrial potential she was in danger of slipping out of the ranks of the great powers, while, domestically, she found herself governed by a Republican system that was subject to a series of scandals and crises that culminated in the crisis over the Dreyfus Affair.

Seen against this background it is not suprising that in the course of the Affair the anti-militarism of the Left should have been challenged by ideologists like Barrès and Maurras, who emerged as the standard bearers of a new form of right-wing Nationalism. Admittedly the anti-Dreyfusards were defeated by their opponents at the end of the Affair, but their analysis of French weakness and decadence could not indefinitely be ignored, and, after France's humiliation at the hands of Germany at the time of the First Moroccan Crisis, the Nationalist ideologists of the Right were now joined by Republican publicists like Péguy in calling for French rearmament and a policy of firmness towards Berlin.

With the outbreak of the First World War it seemed that all their warnings had been justified. For four years France was faced

33

with the most terrible struggle in her history, and for four years many Frenchmen turned to the members of the Nationalist revival for encouragement and inspiration. Péguy was killed at the beginning of the battle of the Marne. Too old or too unfit for military service, Barrès and Maurras devoted themselves to the fight to sustain French morale and to prepare the way for eventual victory.

When that victory came in 1918, therefore, the prestige of the Nationalists was very high. France was once again the greatest military power on the continent of Europe, and, amidst the euphoria, the French elected the first Chamber with a right-wing majority for over forty years. Nevertheless, as the magnitude of the suffering caused by the war became fully apparent in the years that followed the end of the conflict, as it became clear that the problem of French decline had not been solved but had only been exacerbated by the war, the message of the Nationalists was subjected to a prolonged process of scrutiny and re-examination. So rigorous was this re-examination that few reputations survived unscathed.

Perhaps it was inevitable that it should have been the prestige of Barrès that suffered most severely during the period of reassessment that took place in the years after the First World War, for, already in the years before the outbreak of the conflict, there were signs that his position was no longer secure. Indeed, well before 1914 his reputation as the doyen of the Nationalist ideologists was coming under a mounting challenge from those who were turning to the far more rigorous and intellectually demanding system of Maurras, while his role as a literary lion, as the 'prince de la jeunesse', as the arch-exponent of individualistic self-examination, was being increasingly criticised by Gide and others who regarded him as a lightweight and a dilettante.

His conduct during the war itself did little to remedy the situation. Admittedly he threw himself wholeheartedly into the struggle and was tireless in his efforts to rally the nation, but his position was so closely identified with that of the official Establishment that in the general revulsion against the horrors of war in the 1920s he was increasingly seen as the archetypal war-propagandist, a man who had inflamed the civilians with hatred of Germany, who had constantly attempted to identify himself with the sufferings of the soldiers but had revealed in the process how utterly out of touch he was with the day-to-day experience of the men at the front.

The bill of indictment that was made out against Barrès in the years after the First World War was a formidable one, and it would be foolish to attempt to explain it away. Seen in retrospect Barrès was a typical member of a generation of European *littérateurs* who came to maturity in the 1890s – Thomas Mann, Hugo von Hofmannsthal, Gabriele d'Annunzio and W.B. Yeats are other obvious examples – who as aesthetes preached revolt and rebellion against bourgeois society but who were yet hopeful for a reconciliation between themselves and traditional institutions. At various times in their careers all of them showed a fascination with the idea of violence – d'Annunzio, of course, more than the rest of them – but none of them had very much notion of the realities of violence in modern mass society. As a result of this, and despite their formidable literary gifts, the verdict of posterity on many of their political activities has tended to be harsh.

And yet, despite the narcissism that characterised so much of their behaviour, the fascination exercised by this generation still remains. Perhaps this is due to the fact that this was the first generation of artists to experience in full measure a sense of isolation and vulnerability in the modern world. Already in the middle of the nineteenth century, it is true, writers like Baudelaire and Flaubert had been preoccupied with similar themes, but it was the generation that grew up after them that experienced the full impact of the development of mass democracy and industrialisation. The claims of society were now so overwhelming that they could no longer be ignored or repudiated. Some kind of compromise, some sort of modus vivendi had to be achieved, and, although the kind of compromises that were made by Barrès and his contemporaries are no longer found to be convincing, their attempts at political involvement retain an abiding interest.

Barrès, in particular, is a personality whose faults and deficiencies are so glaring to modern eyes that it is easy to underestimate him and to dismiss him out of hand. The influence that he exerted on his own generation and on the generation that succeeded him cannot be ignored, however. Many of his admirers may have become exasperated by his 'solutions' to the problems of France, but the significance of his initial diagnosis of the dilemmas of the individual in a mass society should not be minimised.

He was born at Charmes-sur-Moselle in Lorraine in 1862. The fact that the province of Lorraine was to be mutilated in the peace settlement at the end of the Franco-Prussian War (a war that Barrès remembered vividly from his childhood – one of his early memories was that of a company of Prussian Uhlans occupying the small town) was to be of lasting significance for his future development. As a youth, however, he was far more interested in literature than in politics, and, after desultory law studies in Nancy and Paris, he had managed by the middle of the 1880s to establish himself as a seemingly permanent fixture on the Parisian literary scene.

As was often to be the case in the course of Barrès's life his sense of timing in the launch of his career was perfect: France was beginning to recover from the trauma of defeat by the Germans; intellectual and artistic speculation was beginning to revive after the sterile years of the 1870s; and there was an increasing desire to overcome the opposition between aestheticism and naturalism that had dominated the literary scene for so long. Zola was at the height of his influence, and the death of Victor Hugo in 1885 meant that the last great representative of the Romantic era had now disappeared, but there were signs of a growing opposition to the dominant role of positivism and materialism in French intellectual life. It was in this situation that Barrès appeared with his *Culte du moi*.

In *Sous l'œil des barbares* published in 1888, and, above all, in *Un Homme libre* which appeared in the following year, Barrès frankly acknowledged the utter alienation that must be felt by any intelligent person in a society given over to gross philistinism, materialism and opportunism. He also maintained that a necessary stage in the therapy that must be developed to meet this situation involved a withdrawal into the self in order to divine the essence of the 'moi', and that this innermost essence must be protected from the enemy without by means of the mask or the façade. But this did not mean a permanent withdrawal from society. Indeed, to take this route would lead one into the same impasse of aestheticism that had trapped 'les poètes maudits', and in *Un Homme libre* he specifically warned against the dangers of perpetual self-contemplation. On the contrary, the 'moi', once established, should seek enrichment and enlargement not only in literature and art, but also in action, *élan* and adventure. It was in accordance with this programme, therefore, that Barrès was able to demonstrate both his contempt for the mediocrity of the parliamentary system in France and his desire for political as well as literary glory by participating in the Boulangist movement, a course of action that finally resulted in his election as Boulangist deputy for Nancy in 1889.

At this stage in his career he still thought of himself as a man of the Left. He was influenced for a considerable period in the 1890s by the vogue for a sentimental and vaguely 'anarchisant' form of Socialism, as can be seen in his novels of the time, such as *Le Jardin de Bérénice* of 1891 and *L'Ennemi des lois* of 1893. And although in an article he contributed to *Le Figaro* on 4 July 1892 he gave currency to the idea (and to the name) of 'Nationalism' as a principle of order that was to be preferred to the dangers of cosmopolitanism, it was only with the publication of *Les Déracinés* in 1897 that he fully indicated the extent to which he was now moving to the Right. Under the influence of such men as Taine, with his emphasis on the determining influence of the 'milieu', and Jules Soury, with his emphasis on the importance of 'race', Barrès was now searching for a new accommodation between the 'moi' and the rest of society. This was to take the form of a new kind of national self-consciousness, a new form of 'National Socialism', based on fidelity to the eternal verities of 'la terre et les morts'.

Les Déracinés, as the title implies, argues the case for rootedness, for attachment to one's city, to one's province, to one's *patrie*. Like so many of Barrès's works it is open to the criticism that it is over-ambitious and yields far less than its promise (and its title) might suggest. Certainly, apart from a few striking phrases, its ideological content is thin. Nevertheless, in spite of all this, it still provides a vivid picture of the options open to intelligent Frenchmen in the 1890s, and, by utilising the device of a novel that examined the careers of a disparate group of provincials from Lorraine, Barrès's message – that society is not a mechanical artefact but an organism, and that future French regeneration must be sought in a synthesis of Bonapartist energy and an attachment to provincial virtues – entered the literary and political vocabulary of France.

Once again, his sense of the opportune moment was exact. As a result of a number of factors – the growing rapprochement between the Republican and anti-Republican bourgeoisie during the time of the Ralliement in the 1890s, the increasing use of the army to police industrial disputes, the accelerating influence of Marxist doctrines concerning the primacy of internationalism and the class struggle within French Socialism – new divisions between Left and Right were opening up within French society. For a time Barrès was hopeful that these divisions could be healed: in 1896 he offered himself (unsuccessfully) as a Socialist candidate to the electors of Boulogne-Billancourt under the patronage of Jaurès; and in 1898 he reminded the electors of Nancy that Nationalism inevitably contained Socialist measures as part of its programme. But the onset of the Dreyfus Affair made such attempts to transcend the quarrels within French politics impossible, and, faced with the choice of supporting or attacking the Dreyfusard cause, Barrès (to the extreme disappointment of many of his young Socialist admirers like Léon Blum) chose the latter course. From now on he was to be irrevocably associated with the Right, and *Les Déracinés* was brought into service as one of the key texts of the anti-Dreyfusard cause.

It would be tedious to go into the details of the many controversies in which Barrès became engaged during the Dreyfus Affair and the many campaigns that he fought to defend the cause of Right-wing Nationalism in the years before 1914. Suffice it to say that during the Affair itself his main contention was that the security of France must be the first priority and that any attempt to undermine the morale of the army and of the intelligence service must be resisted. To the extent that the Dreyfusards were anti-militarists and internationalists, to the extent that they derived so much of their support from minority groups such as Protestants, Freemasons and Jews, therefore, Barrès regarded them not only as political opponents but as enemies of France itself. He took the same line in the aftermath of the Affair. When the triumphant Dreyfusards went on to consolidate their triumphs by attacking the Church and by discriminating against the promotion of Catholic and Royalist officers within the army, Barrès deployed all his polemical talent against them, accusing them of dividing the French people and of reducing France's ability to meet the German threat.

The menace of Germany was also the theme of the series of novels that he entitled (with his customary flair) *Les Bastions de l'est*, which began to appear in 1905. With his uncanny ability to anticipate events he had started writing the first novel of the series, *Au service de l'Allemagne*, only a few weeks before the First Moroccan Crisis. Its publication soon after the crisis, and its theme – the fidelity of the Alsatians to France, symbolised by the figure of Ehrmann, who sees it as his duty to remain behind after the German annexation and to wait for 'the day of anger' that is eventually to come – helped to maintain Barrès's position at the forefront of the Nationalist movement in the years before 1914.

And yet, despite the increasing threat from Germany, despite the growth of the Nationalist movement in France after 1905 (and particularly after the Second Moroccan Crisis in 1911), and despite his own increasing prominence as a leading public personality, a position that was enhanced by his election to the Academy, the decade before the outbreak of the First World War was not a period in which Barrès made any significant or permanent advance.

As he himself would freely admit, this was largely due to the fact that, like so many writers who discover with surprise that they are now middle-aged, he had said what he had to say long ago and was now repeating themes that he had first treated many years in the past. But it was also the result of a situation in which significant elements of his Nationalist message were being increasingly accepted and in which his original quarrel with established society was dwindling. The younger generation showed that they were aware of this development. When students were questioned by 'Agathon' (a pseudonym for Henri Massis and Alfred de Tarde) in his enquiry into the opinions of French university youth in the years before 1914, their replies revealed that young men had the sense that Barrès was resting on his laurels.[1] They were also increasingly conscious of the contradiction between his demands for action and his own growing detachment from action. Faced with Barrès's increasing identification with the *bien-pensants*, his disciples were beginning to look for other masters and other certainties.

The fact is that Barrès's taste for politics, and particularly for partisan politics, was fast diminishing in the years after 1905. To the degree to which the passions aroused by the Dreyfus Affair tended to subside and the attacks on the Church and the army that took place in the aftermath of the Affair were brought to a halt, to the degree to which French society as a whole was gradually alerted to the German threat, Barrès's dissatisfaction with the French political system lost much of its ferocity. Like his mentor, Stendhal, his temperament was basically Bonapartist. He believed that France needed a powerful leader, and he had supported the Boulangist cause in the 1880s and early 1890s. His contempt of existing political institutions at the time of the Dreyfus Affair had been extreme, and he had sympathy with Paul Déroulède, the leader of the Ligue des Patriotes who had attempted to incite the army to a military *coup d'état* at the height of the Affair. But any attempt to see the confused amalgam of Nationalism, Socialism, anti-semitism and authoritarian leadership peddled by Barrès at the turn of the century as a serious and sustained exercise in what was later to be called Fascism must be treated with considerable caution.[2] Despite his cult of energy and his worship of Napoleon there was in his 'ideology' little of the truly amoral activism, the perverted and barbarised Nietzscheanism, that was so characteristic of full-blooded Fascism. Some disciples of Barrès like Drieu la Rochelle may ultimately have embraced Fascism, but it was a highly intellectualised version of the ideology that bore little relationship to the brutal realities of Hitler's Europe. And certainly, as far as Barrès himself is concerned, even his most vehement critics would concede that he possessed neither the energy nor the fanaticism necessary for the leadership of a Fascist-style movement. His intelligence was far too keen, his sympathies were far too wide, his susceptibility to boredom was far too acute, for him ever to be able to accept the limitations that would be imposed on him by a rigid ideology or the single-minded pursuit of power.

He asserted his independence of thought in a number of ways in the years before 1914. During this period, it is true, he was still deeply involved in politics through his journalism. He was a regular attender at the debates within the French chamber to which he was re-elected as deputy for a Paris constituency in 1906. And in 1914, on the death of Déroulède, he took over the leadership of the Ligue des Patriotes. But behind this façade of activity he was increasingly disenchanted with politics as an end in itself. It was no accident that it was during these years that he was most attracted by Catholicism, an attraction that was increased by the long campaign that he waged to defend the Church during the protracted struggle that took place between the French government and the Papacy following the separation of Church and State in 1905. In 1910 he noted in his notebooks:

Je sens depuis des mois que je glisse du nationalisme au Catholicisme. C'est que le nationalisme manque d'infini.[3]

(Over the months I have felt myself slipping away from Nationalism to Catholicism. That is because Nationalism lacks the sense of the infinite.)

In the event his temperament was far too sceptical for him ever to be able to make a return to the Church, but the dilemmas of a soul divided in its sympathies between pantheism and Catholicism form the major theme of one of his most ambitious novels, *La Colline inspirée*, which was published in 1913.

If his freedom from dogma was exhibited in the religious sphere, it was also a factor at work in his approach towards the politics of the Nationalist movement. Although he and Maurras were allies on so many issues of the day, his correspondence with Maurras and the entries in his notebooks demonstrate his impatience with the narrowness and rigidity of Maurrassian ideology. He was repelled by the fact that while Maurras ardently defended the Church he took no account of the things that are unknown,[4] that he always dealt with religion under its political aspect and not from the point of view of the interior life. In terms of the solutions that were necessary to France's political problems, too, there were profound differences between the two men. As befitted a personality so greatly influenced by the Bonapartist tradition, Barrès could not accept Maurras's proposals for a restoration of the monarchy as the most reasonable and practical remedy for France's ills. A return of the monarchy would be divisive, whereas the greatness of Napoleon had been that he had accepted so many of the achievements of the Revolution whilst reasserting the principle of order. By his blanket condemnation of the Revolution, Napoleon, Romanticism, and what the leaders of the Action Française called 'the stupid nineteenth century', Maurras was denying to the Nationalist movement the political and spiritual legacy of a whole epoch of French history, an epoch in which France had reached the summit of her political power and influence.

Barrès found it difficult to excuse such myopia. He complained to
Maurras of the 'durs petits esprits' (harsh, little minds) that he was
creating in his disciples.[5] He compared the fanaticism of the Action
Française with that of the royalist émigrés in Mainz and Koblenz
during the 1790s, an emigration that had wished to destroy the
Revolution with the aid of the outsider. He predicted that royalism
could only triumph in France in the wake of a major defeat. And in a
strangely prophetic entry in his notebook in 1904 he commented:

Ce seront les conservateurs qui accepteront, appelleront l'étranger. Oui,
ceux qui sont aujourd'hui les patriotes, les hommes fiers, las de vivre une
France amoindrie et une vie humiliée, appelleront . . . une intervention de
l'étranger qui leur donne enfin la joie de participer à une grande vie
collective – et nous verrons au contraire la résistance à l'étranger personifiée
par la demagogie pacifiste.[6]

(It will be the conservatives who will call for and accept the foreigner. Yes,
those who are the patriots today, the men of pride, tired of living a life of
humiliation in a diminished France will call for . . . the foreigner to
intervene to give them the joy of participating in a larger collectivity – and
on the other hand we will see resistance to the foreigner organised by pacifist
demagogy).

Whereas Maurras, after the defeat of France in 1940, maintained his
hatred of the Germans but welcomed the advent to power of Pétain as
a 'divine surprise', there can be little doubt that Barrès, had he
survived, would have followed the example of his son Philippe in
supporting de Gaulle.

Symptomatic of Maurras's limitations as a political philosopher,
Barrès believed, was his failure to recognise the greatness of Jaurès.
Many of Jaurès's ideas might be naive, and Barrès did not hesitate to
subject them to a vigorous attack during the Dreyfus Affair and
during the long campaign for peace that Jaurès waged in the years
before 1914. But Barrès could never forget the generosity with which
Jaurès had treated him in the course of his own 'Socialist' phase in the
1890s, and, however much he might disagree with his ideas, he never
failed to be impressed by the vast erudition and the humanitarian
passion of the Socialist leader. In his view Jaurès was a true
'professeur d'énergie', and his idealism and rhetorical powers were
true manifestations of the French genius. It is typical of Barrès that, in

the privacy of his notebooks, he admitted that Jaurès had the accent of a prophet in his campaign against war, and compared his voice to that of the 'muezzin on the minaret'.[7] And in 1914, when the news of Jaurès's assassination was greeted with barely concealed delight by the bulk of the Nationalist Right, he made a point of calling on Madame Jaurès to express his condolences.[8]

Unlike Maurras, then, Barrès always hoped for reconciliation amongst Frenchmen, and with the outbreak of the war and the declaration of the Union Sacrée these hopes now seemed to be on the point of fulfilment: the former anti-militarist Gustave Hervé now praised the memory of Déroulède; the writer Rémy de Gourmont, who had once said that in order to regain Alsace-Lorraine he would not offer the little finger of his right hand, which he needed for writing, nor that of his left hand, which he needed for flicking the ash off his cigarette, now told the soldiers that they would look back on the outbreak of the war as the happiest time of their lives; Anatole France, that great luminary of the Left, offered himself for military service at the age of sixty-nine; while, the day after the declaration of war, Joseph Reinach, one of Barrès's principal opponents in both the Panama Scandal and the Dreyfus Affair, a founder of the Ligue des Droits de l'Homme, now applied for membership of the Ligue des Patriotes.

Barrès was delighted. Already in the years immediately before the outbreak of the war he had been able to make his peace with a Republican establishment that was headed by a patriot and a fellow 'man of Lorraine' like Poincaré. Now he had the opportunity to appeal to all the diverse spiritual families of France – Nationalists and Socialists, Republicans and anti-Republicans, Catholics, Protestants, Freemasons, Jews – to forget the quarrels of the past and to defend France against the German attack that he had long predicted.

For the next few years he was indefatigable in his efforts to sustain French morale and the morale of the French army. He made numerous visits to the front in France. He fought a successful campaign in the chamber and in the press for the French soldiers to be issued with steel helmets. He was behind the proposal to institute the Croix de Guerre. He interested himself in the soldiers' cooking facilities, medical care and leave arrangements. He was solicitous about their pay and their families, and proposed that every war widow should be given her dead husband's right to vote.

Meanwhile he visited the British troops in France and praised their 'calmness' and 'serenity'.[9] And, at the end of July 1916, in an exchange for Kipling's tours of the front in France, he came to Britain for a month. During his stay he breakfasted with Lloyd George, 'the Celt', and dined with Asquith, 'the powerful Norman'. He toured Portsmouth dockyard, and was charmed by the typically English setting of an officers' mess, the building clad with ivy and with miniature cannons sitting amidst beds of geraniums. He also went to Oxford (where he noted that All Souls would have provided the perfect setting for Renan), Woolwich Arsenal and Sheffield, and paid a call on the fleet in the Firth of Forth. Everywhere he found intense admiration for the epic defence of Verdun, and Paul Cambon, the French ambassador, told him that although the British had come into the war for the sake of Belgium they were now absolutely committed to the cause of France. At first Barrès was somewhat disconcerted by the well-lit and cheerful atmosphere of London compared with the subdued character of Paris, where people would even remonstrate against such innocent pastimes as schoolchildren practising on the piano. But, as the appalling casualty lists came in from the Somme, a battle in which Asquith's eldest son Raymond was to be killed in September 1916, he was reassured to discover that, now that the British were totally engaged in the struggle, they would never let go. Germany would find that she had no more terrible enemy.

Back in France he gritted his teeth and resumed his anxious watch on the situation at Verdun. Clearly, for a time, he had been excited by the war. In October 1914 he had described one engagement as a 'delicious Van der Meulen'.[10] In January of the following year he took pleasure in imagining a situation in which Germany would be eventually defeated and starving after the Russians had killed hundreds of thousands of blonde blue-eyed German soldiers.[11] Statements such as these were to form part of the terrible dossier that was prepared against him by the Dadaists and others in the years that followed the First World War, but as the conflict dragged on Barrès's mood became far more sombre. He could not remain indifferent to the fearful martyrdom that France endured during these years, and inevitably he had the melancholy task of composing tributes to the fallen – those to Péguy,[12] to Ernest Psichari[13] and to Kipling's son, John,[14] immediately spring to mind.

He always attempted to take a positive and affirmative view, however. He did this over Verdun in 1916. And he did the same in the critical year of 1917, when a frenetic gaiety reasserted itself in fashionable Paris, when Cocteau, Satie and Picasso entertained the cultural avant-garde with the ballet *Parade*, while inflation, strikes and a political deadlock over the future prosecution of the war dominated the public scene. In his notebooks Barrès did not attempt to disguise the doubts that he felt about the disastrous Nivelle offensive in 1917, nor did he try to conceal his anguish over the mutinies in the French army that followed that offensive, but he was always convinced that France would be triumphant in the end, and he was indefatigable in his pursuit of the defeatists of 'Le Bonnet Rouge', of Malvy, the Minister of the Interior who protected them, and of Malvy's patron, the former Prime Minister Joseph Caillaux. There were flashes of the old polemical and partisan Barrès – the Barrès of the novel *Leurs Figures* and the attack that he had launched against the parliamentary corruption revealed by the Panama Scandal of the 1890s – in the onslaught that he now directed against the defeatists in 1917:

De toutes les crevasses que les convulsions de ce monde souterrain font s'ouvrir, on entend sortir le même nom. Au fond de tous ces puits, on distingue le même personnage, Caillaux, toujours![15]

(From all the crevasses that the convulsions of this underworld are causing to appear one hears the same name mentioned. At the bottom of all these sinks of iniquity one can distinguish the same person. It is always Caillaux!)

When Clemenceau was triumphant at the end of 1917, and Malvy and Caillaux had lost their power to influence events, therefore, Barrès was exultant. Once again the French people could present a united front against the aggressors:

L'Allemand comprend mal la psychologie de la France et de nos soldats. Il entend chez nous des discussions, des critiques; il en infère qu'il y a démoralisation. En effet, s'il se produisent chez elle la moitié des scandales qui se produisent chez nous, ce serait l'effondrement de la conscience populaire dans le doute.[16]

(The Germans badly misunderstand the psychology of France and of our soldiers. When they see us immersed in discussions and criticisms they conclude that we are demoralised. But if they had half of the scandals that we have, public opinion would collapse into despair.)

These words were written just before Ludendorff's great spring offensive of 1918, Germany's final attempt to win the war in the west. They could serve as a summary of all Barrès's efforts to sustain the spirit of the French nation in the course of the First World War.

Some idea of the expenditure of energy and spirit in which he was involved during these years can be gauged from the extent of his war journalism for *L'Echo de Paris*, journalism which was eventually collected and published in fourteen volumes under the title of *Chronique de la Grande Guerre*. Little though these works may be read today, they still have great value as indispensable works of reference for anyone attempting to understand the atmosphere of France between 1914 and 1919. And as a portrait of Barrès himself, attempting, however inadequately, to come to terms with the horror of the war, they are full of revealing touches. On meeting a man whose son had just been killed Barrès embraced him:

J'ai tenté de lui expliquer ce que je sentais si bien: que tout le monde le plaignait et, qu'aux yeux de tous, son fils et lui étaient couverts d'honneur. Mais il a dit: 'L'honneur, je m'en fous.'[17]

(I tried to explain to him what I felt so deeply: that everybody was sorry for him, and that everybody thought that he and his son were covered with honour. But he said: 'I don't give a damn for honour.')

On another occasion he talked for some time with a soldier whose arm had been amputated:

Quand je me suis éloigné, j'ai fait a ce blessé pour la vie un geste qui lui disait d'avoir confiance. Je lui ai dit 'Au revoir mon camarade.' Est-ce donc un geste vain, un mensonge?[18]

(As I was moving away from this man who was now wounded for life I did something that was intended to encourage him to have confidence. I said to him 'Au revoir mon camarade.' Was this a futile gesture, a form of insincerity?)

At other times Barrès interrupted his tone-poems on the scenes of desolation at the front to reflect on the wider significance of what he has seen. He returned from a visit to the outer trenches where on the previous day he had witnessed the burial of three decomposed bodies. Dusk was falling:

De temps à autre, nous croisons des gens à nous, en train de faire la cuisine dans des dépressions du plateau. Ils rient, s'interpellent. Puis nous rentrons dans le silence et dans la nuit qui s'épaissit. Cette fin de notre visite aux avant postes ressemble à un retour de chasseurs, mais il s'y mêle une anxiété extraordinaire du cœur. Jamais je n'ai ressenti une aussi vive émotion de fraternité que dans cette journée; jamais, un plus profond sentiment du mystère où baignent nos existences.[19]

(From time to time we come across some of our men cooking their meal in the hollows of the plateau. They laugh and talk together. Then we go out again into the silence and the gathering night. The end of our visit to the front trenches is like that of hunters, returning from the chase, but mingling with this is an extraordinary heartfelt sense of concern. I have never felt such a deep sense of brotherhood as I did on this day; never such a deep sense of the mystery that surrounds our lives.)

Publicly Barrès professed himself to be immensely proud of his war journalism, and claimed that it should be regarded as his most important work. Privately he was full of doubts. With that disarming candour that is so frequently to be found in his notebooks he confessed to a sense of dissatisfaction:

Les hommes politiques n'ont pas su penser cette guerre. Elle a débordé tous les cerveaux, celui de Briand, celui de Lloyd George. Ils ne l'ont pas dirigée. Quel événement qui remet tout en question. Quel chaos! Que va-t-on voir demain? Eh bien! la faillite des intellectuels n'a pas été moindre. Anatole France, c'est le silence. Bourget se tait après quelques mois de réflexion. Ils n'ont pas cherché à dégager les directives. Un seul, Romain Rolland, osa. Il pécha par l'orgueil, les autres par l'humilité. Étrange péché, si j'interroge mon cas, je vois bien que je l'ai commis. Je n'aspirais qu'à servir. Continuellement j'ai fait une besogne inférieure. C'était bien de soutenir le moral chaque jour, mais ne me suis-je pas noyé dans cet excès de travail?[20]

(The politicians have not been able to think through the implications of this war. It has surpassed the understanding of any of them, even of Briand and Lloyd George. They have not been able to give it direction. What an event it has been, one that has put everything into question. What chaos! What is going to happen tomorrow? Indeed, the failure of the intellectuals has been no less striking. Anatole France is silent. After a few months of reflexion

Bourget, too, has relapsed into silence. They have not looked for the guiding principles. One man only, Romain Rolland, has dared to attempt the task. He has been guilty of the sin of pride, the others have offended by their humility. If I look at my own case I am well aware that I am guilty of the same offence. My only desire was to serve. Continually, I have not been at my best. It was a good idea to sustain morale every day, but have I not drowned myself in this excessive load of work?)

But others were prepared to offer much harsher verdicts. While Barrès accused Romain Rolland of spiritual pride because of his condemnation of the war from a position above the battle in Switzerland, the latter had already commented in his own *Journal* on Barrès's war activities:

Dans la même page, Barrès module sur la mort et les meurtres ses plus mélodieux chants de flûte. Il est le rossignol du carnage. En temps de paix, il trainaît son ennui et sa nostalgie de cimetière. Sur les tombes fraîches, il s'épanouit; son art est en plein fleur. Si belle que soit la fleur, je vois la tige qui sort du ventre des charniers.[21]

(On the same page Barrès modulates on death and murders with the most melodious strains of his flute. He is the nightingale of the carnage. In peacetime he languished with boredom and nostalgia for the cemetery. Now he comes into bloom on the freshly-dug graves; his art is in full flower. However beautiful the flower, I see the stalk that grows out of the entrails of the charnel-houses).

To many of the soldiers who survived the war, too, Barrès was now a discredited figure. One of his disciples, Henri Massis, once recalled Barrès's words to the generation departing for the war:

En revenant vous serez monté si haut, avec des actes si forts, que vous surpasserez tous nos rêves, comme l'aigle survole le rossignol. Les maîtres ont fini leur enseignement en vous; de vos mains heureuses vous saisirez le fruit du miracle, le fruit formé à notre insu dans les années que nous croyions stériles.[22]

(When you come back you will have ascended so high, with actions so heroic, that you will have surpassed our dreams, in the way that the eagle flies higher than the nightingale. The masters have finished their teaching and you will seize the fruit of the miracle in your joyful hands, the fruit that was being created without our knowing it in the years that we believed to be barren).

But if Massis, who was wounded in the war and received the Croix de Guerre, continued to regard Barrès with veneration and respect, this did not prevent him from transferring his allegiance to Maurras and the Action Française, while to many others the master now appeared as the incarnation of the spirit of the 'Derrière', a man who, cut off from the daily death, mutilation and comradeship of the 'Avant', had sentimentalised and trivialised the experience of the war generation. The fact that, once released from the constraints of the war, Barrès returned to the literature of exquisite sensation in his oriental fantasy *Un Jardin sur l'Oronte* only seemed to strengthen the view that his was an essentially superficial and self-regarding talent.

For once his sense of timing had deserted him. Having survived so many changes of fashion in the past he was now to be one of the most spectacular victims of the post-war era. On 13 May 1922, the Dadaists opened the first session of their famous mock trial. With a wooden dummy substituting for Barrès himself, André Breton as president of the tribunal, and Louis Aragon and Philippe Soupault as 'defence' counsel, the proceedings turned into a massive indictment of the man who had started off his career with the liberating message of *Un Homme libre* and had then turned into the Academician, the war propagandist, and the pillar of the Establishment. Called as a witness, Tristan Tzara declared that Barrès was the biggest scoundrel that had emerged in Europe since Napoleon. A figure symbolising the Unknown Soldier denounced Barrès in German. At the end of the affair the accused was found guilty of 'crime contre la sûreté de l'esprit'[23] ('crime against the safety of the mind').

Seen against this background it was perhaps fortunate that Barrès had only another eighteen months to live, for, as the years went by and the frivolity of 'les années folles' of the 1920s intensified, both his reputation and the values that he believed in were subjected even more to the merciless forces of time and chance. Bitterly disappointed as so many Frenchmen were by the failure of the Versailles peace-makers to give the left bank of the Rhine to France as security against Germany, Barrès enthusiastically devoted himself to the task of encouraging the Rhinelanders to separate themselves from Prussia and to form themselves into an independent republic, a state that, he hoped, would be able to mediate – politically, economically and culturally – between France and Germany. In fact, the French purpose in encouraging Rhenish separation was to secure a French satellite state that would further weaken Germany, and Barrès was guilty of self-deception when he maintained that this is what a majority of the people of the Rhineland really wanted. He was also deluding himself when he defended Poincaré's action in sending French troops into the Ruhr in January 1923 to enforce the continued payment of war reparations on the grounds that it would teach the Germans to obey the provisions of the Peace treaty.

On the contrary, the British, embarrassed by French demands and more concerned with their Empire and the outside world than with Europe, regarded the French action as provocative, the Americans had already refused to ratify the hypocrisies of a peace settlement where the principle of self-determination was everywhere interpreted to Germany's disadvantage and had retreated into isolation, while German nationalism was only further inflamed. It is possible to sympathise with the French desire for security, but long-term peace in Europe could only have been guaranteed if Germany had been treated equitably after her defeat in the First World War. The only situation in which France might have been persuaded to accept such a settlement would have been one in which she felt she had the total and unequivocal commitment of the British and Americans to defend her against a resurgent Germany. Since such a guarantee did not exist the French felt they had no option but to treat Germany with severity. As time was to show, a Germany that had been neither totally crushed (as Maurras and Kipling wanted) nor conciliated and won over to the cause of peace (as Wells, Shaw, Rolland and Owen wanted) would continue to pose a major threat to European stability.

Barrès did not live long enough to see that his hopes for the post-war world were not going to be fulfilled, however. He died suddenly in December 1923, at the early age of sixty-one. He had worn himself out by his labours during the war, and was both physically and emotionally a spent force. As he once confessed in the middle of the conflict, he himself was bored and tired with 'Maurice Barrès', the public personality,[24] and his life was probably shortened even further by a family tragedy that occurred in 1922, when his niece was murdered by her husband.

Now that he was gone the attacks on him were redoubled. Gide was now emboldened to launch a frontal assault on his reputation, attacking him for the restraints that he placed on individual freedom by his call for rootedness, while, shortly after Barrès's death, one of his former admirers, Henri de Montherlant, published a notorious essay in which Barrès was savaged as an eternal voyeur – 'voyeur of war, voyeur of religion, voyeur of love'.[25] Apart from Mauriac, Massis and Philippe Barrès, there were relatively few amongst the men who had returned from the war who were now prepared to defend him. To the last generation of young men who had been influenced by him – Aragon, Drieu la Rochelle and Malraux amongst them – the essential truth of Montherlant's attack was too evident to be denied. In the course of the next twenty years the necessity for some kind of total commitment, whether to Communism or to Fascism, seemed to be far more important to many of his former followers than the cultivation of a private sensibility.

Whether his admirers were any wiser than Barrès in their choice of the cause to which they gave their allegiance is a matter that is open to some argument, however. And whether they were more honest with themselves than Barrès is yet another issue on which there can be considerable disagreement. His contradictions were many and glaring: by instinct a radical and a sceptic, he gave comfort to the forces of conformity; by temperament an Athenian, he sang the praises of Sparta; a prophet of French regeneration, he was at his most effective in writing on the melancholy of decline in Toledo, Seville, Venice and Versailles.

But any criticism that can be made of him is usually only a rephrasing of criticism that he had long ago made of himself. He was intensely aware of the mutability of all things, including his own reputation. As he once confessed:

La vie n'a pas de sens. Je crois même que chaque jour elle devient plus absurde. Se soumettre à toutes les illusions et les connaître nettement comme illusions, voilà notre rôle.[26]

(Life is absurd. I do believe it gets more absurd each day. Our role is to submit ourselves to all the illusions and to recognise them clearly as illusions.)

'Vous parlez de mon orgueil', he wrote in his notebooks; 'je n'en ai pas, mais si petite que se sois, je me sens le point le plus sensible de l'univers'[27] ('People talk of my arrogance. I have none. But however

insignificant I may be, I feel myself to be the most sensitive point in
the universe').

Comments like these help to explain his enduring appeal. They
also indicate how inevitable was the disfavour into which he fell in
the years that followed the outbreak of the First World War.

At first sight it might have seemed in the early 1920s that Maurras had
weathered the trials of the First World War with far greater success
than Barrès. Certainly his basic position was far stronger. Whereas
Barrès had never been a 'thinker' in the real meaning of the word but
an isolated *littérateur* relying on his charm and skill to attract his
public, Maurras had employed his considerable abilities as a
theoretician to construct a whole system of doctrine in the years
before 1914, a system that (whatever its defects) proved strong and
resilient enough to maintain itself in the post-war world as a
formidable and influential force. Behind Barrès there was no one.
Behind Maurras there was the newspaper and the membership of the
Action Française. Few could have predicted in the years immediately
after the war that the power of Maurras would prove to be as
vulnerable as that of Barrès to the long-term consequences of the
conflict, or that over the next twenty years the Action Française
would enter into a period of decline at the end of which there was to
be an even more spectacular fall.

Six years younger than Barrès, Charles Maurras was born at
Martigues in Provence in 1868. Maurras's Provençal background is
important, for, while Barrès's attachment to his native Lorraine (like
Kipling's regard for his adoptive Sussex) always had a certain
element of the artificial about it − few personalities were more
naturally Parisian − Maurras remained a provincial through and
through. Passionately attached to Provençal culture and the poetry
of Mistral, he tended, like so many inhabitants of the Midi, to regard
those Frenchmen who live north of Lyons to be spiritually German,
incapable of fully appreciating the priceless contribution of the
Latin, Mediterranean and classical heritage to the greatness of French
civilisation. Despite the sophisticated nature of his intelligence he
remained to the end of his days an aggressive outsider on the French
intellectual scene, suspicious of the north, of centralisation, of Paris.

His distrust of the world was, of course, greatly increased by the
fact that from the age of fourteen he was afflicted with serious

deafness, for this affected his future evolution profoundly. He had dreamed of following a career in the navy, but this was now impossible. For the same reasons he felt that both university studies and marriage were denied to him. For a number of years during his adolescence he suffered emotional and spiritual turmoil because of his affliction. From this period, too, dates his loss of religious faith, his tendency towards misanthropy, his capacity to isolate himself from human contacts, and his ability to concentrate with an extraordinary single-mindedness on the pursuit of abstract truth. As he wrote in his 'Ballade de la Nature du Désir:'

> Ecoute-moi, jour après jour
> Se fait la nuit qui toujours dure,
> Le temps de la jeunesse est court
> Et dans la pulpe à peine mûre
> L'ombre de l'âge te torture:
> Mieux vaut te dire, ami mortel,
> Qu'en vain s'approche la froidure,
> Le désir est spirituel.[28]

> (Listen, day after day
> Approaches the night that lasts always,
> The time of youth is short
> And in the pulp that is scarcely ripe
> The shadow of age tortures you:
> It would be better to tell you, mortal friend,
> That the advance of the coldness is in vain,
> Desire is spiritual.)

Arriving in Paris with his mother to pursue a career as a journalist in December 1885 he was bewildered and angered by the cosmopolitan atmosphere of the city. He was also repelled by the signs of intellectual and spiritual decadence that he saw all around him, and in later years, whatever the differences that were to separate them, he was unstinting in the praise that he accorded Barrès for acting as the guide and mentor to his generation. The latter's analysis of the plight of the alienated intellectual in the novels of the 'Culte du Moi', his hatred of the corruption and incoherence of the French political system, his call for a reintegration of the individual into the society of the nation – all these were to have a profound effect on Maurras. But whereas Barrès moved easily in the world of the literary salons and the French Chamber, Maurras's sense of alienation from society was far more profound. All the greater was his determination to discover some point of stability, some principle of order, to give meaning and purpose to human existence. Gradually during the late 1880s and early 1890s – a period that culminated in one of the decisive experiences of his life, his journey to Greece in 1896, when he was sent by the *Gazette de France* to cover the first Olympic Games – he was able to construct that synthesis of Nationalism, positivism, royalism and classicism that was to have so potent an influence on the French political and intellectual scene in the course of the next fifty years.

In the long term it may be that his work will turn out to be of more permanent significance for the world of the arts than for that of politics, that the clarity and concision of his poetry, the ardour of his defence of the principle of the finite against the anarchy and imprecision of Romanticism, the verve of some of his non-political essays such as *Les Amants de Venise* (a devastating attack on the insatiable George Sand, the masochistic Alfred de Musset, and the illusions of romantic love), will be remembered when most of his *œuvres de circonstance* are forgotten. But in his time it was Maurras the political polemicist who was to the fore, and it was the political implications of his 'system' that were to give him his fame and notoriety.

The salient points of his ideology can quickly be summarised. Basically Maurras attributed most of the anarchy and disorder of the modern world to an unbridled desire for individual liberty, a desire first made manifest at the time of the Reformation – that revolt of northern Europe against the civilisation of the south – and then stimulated by two further developments that ultimately derived from the Reformation – the French Revolution and Romanticism. In the world of the arts these movements had been responsible for a wild and disordered subjectivism. Politically they had led to liberalism and democracy, to the chaotic and fragmented system of the Third Republic in France, to a régime that was incapable of guaranteeing stability at home or French power and prestige abroad.

The only solution to this situation was to work for a restoration of the principle of order. In the arts this meant a reassertion of the classical virtues of Greece and Rome. In French politics it meant a restoration of the monarchy, a restoration that was necessary, not for sentimental reasons, but because it was the most rational, the most 'scientific' solution to France's problems. These problems were all the more acute since, as Maurras had come to realise during his excursion to Greece, everywhere in the world French power was in visible decline, challenged by monarchical systems like those of Britain, Germany and Russia, systems that were intent on protecting and furthering their own national self-interest. Only by restoring the monarchy could France compete with these powers. Only by asserting her own nationalism could France liberate herself from the alien forces – Protestants, Freemasons and Jews – that had acquired so much influence in the Third Republic. The republican system represented merely 'le pays légal'. The eternal France, 'le pays réel', was that of the monarchy. Only by overthrowing the former could France face the challenge of all the other nationalisms that had developed in the world in the course of the nineteenth century.

Even from this brief résumé it is not difficult to see why these ideas began to make headway in France in the early years of this century. Maurras and the Right may have been defeated in the course of the Dreyfus Affair, but they could point to the enormous damage that had been done by that affair to the state of France. Army morale had been undermined by reductions in the military budget (so that between 1906 and 1910 Germany spent nearly twice as much on defence as did France), by the falling-off of officer recruitment, and by the crippling of the military intelligence service. What hope could there be for France in a situation like this? Admittedly the necessity for France to have strong defences was realised by many Republicans after the Moroccan Crises. But was there any guarantee that the existing political system could adequately ensure that France was strong and secure? The fact was that, during his tenure of office as prime minister between 1906 and 1909, Clemenceau, the Republican patriot, had neglected the French armed forces, and, despite the emergence of Poincaré and the passing of the three years military service law in 1913, this tougher policy could still be repudiated by a future Chamber, a danger that was underlined when the Radical and Socialist coalition appeared to be triumphant in the elections of April 1914. The great peril, according to Maurras, was that the endemic instability of France might tempt Germany into a war against her, and that France would be faced with the prospect of 500,000 young Frenchmen 'couchés, froids et sanglants sur leur terre mal defendée'[29] ('lying bloody and cold on their ill-protected soil').

The only way in which this could be avoided was by means of the 'integral' nationalism of the Action Française, a nationalism that insisted on going to the root of French weakness by demanding that the 'established disorder' of the Republican system should be overthrown. Time and again Maurras returned to the terror that he had experienced when he first realised the extent of France's weakness on his visit to Greece in 1896:

Sorti de mon pays, je le vis enfin tel qu'il est. Que je fus effrayé de la voir si petit! Comme il apparaissait isolé et flottant dans le vaste monde, différent de l'idée que je m'en faisais! Jusque là j'étais vaguement fier de certains actes de relèvement, tel que l'alliance russe: dans Athènes le cœur me saigna pour le genre et le nombre des difficultés que cette espèce de protectorat tsariste nous imposait par tout l'Orient, pour les menaces, les dangers, qui en résultaient. Ailleurs je me heurtais au monstrueux développement scientifique, économique, financier, politique, militaire, de l'Allemagne.[30]

(After I left my country I saw it at last for what it is. How terrified I was to see how small it was! Isolated and floating, as it seemed, in the vast wide world, how different it was from my conception of it! Up to that moment I had taken a vague amount of pride in a number of signs of recovery like the Russian alliance. But in Athens my heart bled as a result of the number and nature of the difficulties, dangers and threats, that this Tsarist protectorate imposed on us throughout the East. At the same time I came across the gigantic development, scientific, economic, financial, political and military, of Germany.)

The only remedy that France could turn to in this situation was to ask for the return of the King. Under a monarchy, Maurras argued, France would no longer be the cat's paw of her allies. By utilising French resources properly at home, and by mobilising France's many natural supporters in 'the immense Canada'[31] and in Central and Southern America, the monarchy would be able to liberate the nation from the yoke of the Russians and the English by organising a vast Latin bloc in the world, a bloc under French leadership, a bloc that would be capable of negotiating on a bilateral basis with Germany in order to secure concessions from her over Alsace–Lorraine and other issues.

This would be an infinitely better state of affairs than the present arrangement under the Republic, in which the interests of France were constantly subordinated to those of London and St Petersburg. Only under the monarchy could France behave again as a great power. To anyone who disputed this proposition Maurras could point to the publication of *Faites un roi, sinon faites la paix*, a book by the Socialist Marcel Sembat, which appeared in 1913. Sembat's aim in writing this was to calm the hysteria of the debates over the extension of military service that took place in France that year, and to argue that the only true Republican response to the international situation must be one that favoured peace and disarmament. It was still an implicit admission – an admission that Jaurès found intensely embarrassing – that the Republic, as it was constituted, was unfitted to compete with the aggressive foreign policy of Imperial Germany.

In the event, the despised Third Republic – with the indispensable aid of those very Allies whom Maurras regarded with such suspicion – proved capable of waging and surviving the First World War. But the cost was enormous – over 1,300,000 dead, against the 500,000 that Maurras had envisaged before 1914 – and it can be argued that in the long term his diagnosis of the weakness and ineptitude of the parliamentary Republican system in France was correct, that the Third Republic never recovered from the effects of the 1914–18 war, that its collapse in 1940 was inevitable, and that the unsuitability of the system was further demonstrated by the inability of the Fourth Republic to deal with the problems of the Algerian War, a war that led to its disintegration in 1958. On the other hand, it by no means follows that a restored monarchy was the answer to France's problems. Quite apart from the decline of genuine royalist sentiment in France in the twentieth century, quite apart from the periodic (and ludicrous) squabbles that broke out between Maurras and successive pretenders to the French throne, the truth is that the weakness of France in the years after 1870 was due far more to her economic and social backwardness than to the iniquities of the Republican system. On economic affairs Maurras was almost entirely ignorant, with only one recipe for success: a system of prohibitive tariffs against the foreigner. On matters of social policy, too, he tended to make assertions without offering any evidence to suggest that he had subjected the problems to any kind of empirical investigation – his claim that a restoration of the monarchy would lead to a reduction in alcoholism and arrest the decline in the French birth-rate is a case in point.

Some of these might seem to be trivial objections in themselves, but everywhere throughout his work Maurras attached a magical significance to the presence or the absence of a king. This was true not only of his examination of French affairs but also of his descriptions of those more fortunate countries where monarchs were still in possession of their thrones. English readers of his work, in particular, will be intrigued to discover that, according to Maurras, Edward VII played a preponderant role in the formulation of British foreign policy, and that in the years of the Edwardian era the British possessed a 'perfect political organisation' which left to a widely experienced King 'full authority' in the affairs of state, an organisation that gave England the means of never having to hurry or to improvise.[32] On some occasions Russia is depicted by Maurras as having the good fortune to be ruled by the strong and unscrupulous system of Tsarism. At other times, when Maurras was demonstrating his opposition to the Russian alliance and the Socialist peril, the Russian monarchy is revealed to be ravaged by Jewish and anarchist leprosy and to be pursuing a foreign policy too ambitious for its means. In the various accounts that he gave of Wilhelm II over the years, Maurras was divided between his royalism and his Germanophobia. He finally seems to have decided that, while Germany was the seed-bed of the Reformation and Romanticism, its impulses towards anarchy and destruction were restrained by the Kaiser until he was overwhelmed by them in 1914.

On closer examination, therefore, many of Maurras's arguments in favour of a restoration of the monarchy, however ingenious as exercises in Cartesian logic, seem not only implausible but also capricious and specious. His regret for the days of Louis XIV, when France had truly been 'La Grande Nation', is understandable. But whether there was a real opportunity for the France of the years before 1914 to regain the leading role that she had once played in the affairs of Europe is another matter. Indeed, behind all Maurras's triumphalist talk of the future of France under the monarchy it is possible to detect not only an extreme nostalgia for the past but also a deep pessimism over the present, a pessimism which led him to advocate policies which amounted to little more than a sophisticated version of isolationism.

The line of argument that led Maurras towards isolationism is not difficult to follow. If France's allies are so consistently Machiavellian in their intentions towards her – Russia using her to support her intrigues in the Balkans, Britain manipulating her in the fight against German economic power and imperial ambitions – then the implication is that France would be better off without allies. If French colonial expansion is a diversion of strength from the European theatre, as Maurras consistently maintained, then it would be better if France had no Empire. And if the Third Republic is so completely incapable of managing France's affairs, as Maurras suggested, then it might be better for France to refuse to be entangled in the European struggle for power until she had sorted out her own internal problems. It was not until the 1930s and 1940s that the isolationist, and ultimately defeatist, implications of Maurras's phrase 'la France seule' were to become fully apparent, but already in his writings before 1914 there is more than a hint of that desire to escape from the complexities of the modern world, that hope that France might be able to opt out of a Europe dominated by barbarians and unreliable allies, that dream that France might be able to shelter behind massive defences whilst concentrating her energies on the task of domestic counter-revolution, that was to dominate Maurras's thinking in the closing decades of his life.

Having said all this, however, it is only fair to point out that 1914 was not 1939, that France in 1914 was prepared to contemplate the possibility of war with far greater equanimity than she was to do a quarter of a century later, and that the France of the Belle Epoque had not yet experienced the terrible blood-letting of 1914–18 that was to contribute so powerfully to Maurras's deepening pessimism in the 1930s. Above all, there is the obvious but important fact that, unlike the situation in 1939, it was Germany that took the initiative in provoking hostilities in western Europe in 1914.

In this situation the duty of Frenchmen in 1914 was clear: to resist the aggressor and to support the Union Sacrée. Maurras had not wanted the First World War. He was always to argue that the conflict would not have broken out had the nation adopted his policies in the years before 1914. And, in the crisis of July 1914 itself, the Action Française was far from provocative, with Jacques Bainville arguing in the movement's newspaper that the Quai d'Orsay should press the Serbs to accept the Austrian ultimatum in order that France should not have to make the terrible choice between going to war for a pan-Slavist ideal in which she did not believe or abandoning the Russian alliance altogether.[33] But events were to move too quickly for the hesitations of the Action Française to be of any account. In his article Bainville himself had added the proviso that if a war was to be the inevitable result of the crisis then it was imperative that France should be united, and, as matters turned out, it was Germany that ensured this unity by its declaration of war on 3 August.

From this moment onwards the leaders of the Action Française set their hesitations aside and put themselves at the forefront of the Union Sacrée. While Léon Daudet was indefatigable in his many campaigns – part scurrilous, part ridiculous, part valuable – to root out potential traitors, and while Bainville sketched out the foreign policy opportunities that were open to France, Maurras, the sheet anchor of the movement, proclaimed that defeatists like Caillaux must be destroyed, that Germany, like Carthage, must be destroyed, and that the future of the entire West depended on France's ability to defend civilisation against the barbarian hordes who were attacking it from without.

Such was the patriotic atmosphere of the time that even Gide gave his support to the Action Française for a time in 1916, and without any doubt the years of the First World War saw Maurras at the height of his influence. Faced with the simple issue of resistance to Germany or capitulation Maurras displayed his polemical skills to their maximum advantage, and, as the battle became increasingly desperate, his immense reserves of stoicism came into their own. At the time of the German spring offensive in 1918, for example, when Russia had been knocked out of the war and Ludendorff was attempting one final blow against the French and British before American troops arrived in sufficient strength to turn the balance on the Western Front, it was Maurras alone amongst the leaders of the Action Française who met the crisis with determination and calm.[34] In his essay L'Avenir de l'intelligence, published in 1902, he had declared that in politics despair is an absolute folly. And in 1918, at a time when even Daudet and Bainville were driven to the point of despair by the ferocity of the German bombardment of Paris and the speed and magnitude of the enemy advance – an advance that might have knocked France out of the war had Germany not been obliged to keep a million men on the Eastern Front to hold on to the gains made at Brest-Litovsk – it was Maurras alone who insisted that the only aim worth considering was that of victory. Like Barrès at the same moment, he proclaimed that the one thing to be avoided was doubt, for it was doubt, and not the Germans, that could defeat the French:

N'en a-t-on pas cédé, et plus vite que cela, après Charleroi? N'en a-t-on pas perdu de même à l'Yser? N'en a-t-on pas perdu identiquement à Verdun? Cependant Verdun n'a pas lâché, on a tenu l'Yser, et l'on a réagi après Charleroi, plus vite et mieux qu'on n'eût jamais osé l'espérer. Il n'y a donc rien de plus vrai que ces mots d'ordre répétés chaque jour de Français à Français: – C'est un nouveau Verdun. On tiendra. Ils ne passeront pas.[35]

(Did we not retreat more rapidly than that after Charleroi? Did we not lose ground in the same way at the Yser? Did we not lose ground in an identical way at Verdun? Nevertheless Verdun was not abandoned, we held on at the Yser, and we recovered after Charleroi, more quickly and in better shape than anyone could have dared to hope. So there is nothing truer than the words that Frenchmen repeat to each other every day: – It's another Verdun. We will hold on. They shall not pass.)

With the end of the First World War and France's victory in that war, therefore, it might seem that the triumph of Maurras was complete. Germany had been defeated. The threat to France seemed to have been removed. And, as has already been seen, in the elections of 1919 the French people had elected the first Chamber with a right-wing majority since 1876. Meanwhile Maurras's fame as an ideologist was spreading rapidly outside France. This influence was primarily confined to the countries of Latin civilisation like Italy and Spain, but even in England a somewhat watered-down version of his ideas was on offer. T.S. Eliot had come in contact with Maurras's ideas in Paris before 1914, and when he affirmed in the preface to *For Lancelot Andrewes* in 1928 that his position could now be defined as 'classical in literature, royalist in politics, and Anglo-Catholic in religion', the imprint of Maurras was unmistakable. Even if many of Eliot's

disciples in England could not accept the master's religious or
political attitudes, therefore, and even if some of them, in their
insular way, must occasionally have wondered how much real
knowledge of the European scene there was behind Eliot's very
American taste for polymathic allusiveness, their sympathy for
Eliot's anti-Romanticism inevitably meant that they were ultimately
influenced by Maurras, towards whom Eliot himself was consistently
respectful in the pages of *The Criterion* in the inter-war years.

And yet, already by the time that Eliot was making his major
declaration of loyalty in 1928, Maurras's influence was on the wane.
The first major blow to his prestige came in 1926, when the Action
Française, which had exercised an enormous intellectual influence on
French Catholicism in the years before 1914 – on one occasion Pius X
had described Maurras as 'an incomparable defender of the faith' –
was formally condemned by the Vatican. Rome had already come to
the conclusion by 1914 that, despite Maurras's vociferous support
for the Church in its quarrels with the Third Republic, it could no
longer tolerate a situation in which many Catholics were looking for
leadership to a man who was an avowed agnostic, a disciple of
Machiavelli, who insisted on the slogan of 'politique d'abord', the
primacy of political over spiritual activity, a man who regarded the
Church primarily as a manifestation of classical civilisation and a
buttress of the social order. Certainly the Vatican could hardly ignore
for long the provocative nature of many of Maurras's assertions, such
as his statement that the Bible was a collection of 'turbulent oriental
writings',[36] or his claim that the greatness of the Church lay in the
degree to which it had curbed the revolutionary, anarchic and
Jewish nature of Christianity. A formal condemnation was out of the
question during the First World War, when such a move would have
seemed to compromise the neutrality of the Holy See, but the end of
the war and the election of the energetic Pius XI in 1922 meant that it
could now be put into operation.

There can be little doubt that the Action Française was seriously
damaged by this condemnation. Thousands of members and sympathisers (including men like Jacques Maritain) came to the conclusion that they must obey Rome and withdraw their support. Maurras
himself made matters worse by his declaration of "non possumus',
announcing the inability of the movement to meet Rome's demands,

and then by attempting to argue matters out with the Vatican in public. And while patient negotiations (and prolonged prayer) on the part of intermediaries, together with the election of Pius XII, led to a rapprochement and the lifting of the ban in 1939, by that time the damage had been done. A generation of French Catholics had grown up away from the domination of the movement, and a body of left-wing Catholic opinion had emerged that would ensure that the Church would never be subjected to the same degree of Maurrassian influence that had been apparent in the years before 1926.

But if the defection of many Catholics was a serious blow to Maurras, the decline in the power of the Action Française was further accentuated in the course of the 1920s and 1930s by the number of young men who were now leaving it for Fascism. This was a development that Maurras deplored, seeing Fascism as he did as an end-product of those traditions of Romanticism and plebiscitary democracy that he detested. On the other hand the young could claim that by his corrosive attacks on liberalism and democracy Maurras had shown the way towards Fascism, and certainly they could argue that some radical shift in policy was necessary if the challenge of the Left was to be contained. For the truth of the situation was that, despite Maurras's perpetual talk of the imminent appearance of a figure in the army who, like General Monk in England in 1660, would sweep away an enfeebled political system and invite the King to return, despite all the theorising about the possibility of a *coup de force*, the lack of real revolutionary élan within the Action Française had been obvious for some time. For years Maurras had prided himself on the strength and organisation of his movement, but the reality was that behind the newspaper there was nothing.[37] For years he had spoken of the necessity of rallying the workers to the monarchy, but had sabotaged all real attempts – such as the Cercle Proudhon in the years before 1914 – to turn the policy into reality. More and more it became clear that, despite the increase in popularity that Maurras had experienced during the war, the passions of the conflict had only served to disguise the fundamental weaknesses of the Action Française, and had only postponed the moment when these weaknesses would be fully exposed.

Now in the post-war years, as the movement began to lose its cutting edge, as it became increasingly sympathetic to right-wing

Republicans like Poincaré, as it began to talk less and less of revolution and more and more of uniting the bourgeoisie against the threat of Communism, the radicals within the Action Française began to desert it. Some went over to the Communists. More became Fascists. It is a revealing comment on the loss of dynamism within the movement that at the height of the Stavisky riots in 1934, when it seemed that the Republican régime was crumbling before the anti-parliamentary leagues, Maurras sat in the offices of the newspaper working on a poem in Provençal. Increasingly the movement seemed out of date and out of touch, with any initiative for rejuvenation stifled by a group of old men who jealously clung on to their power. Maurras's election to the Academy in 1938 only served to demonstrate the extent to which the *enfant terrible* of the years before 1914 was becoming part of the right-wing Establishment.

But if by the late 1930s the decline of the Action Française could no longer be concealed, neither could the renewed threat that France faced from Germany. Like Kipling, but unlike Barrès, Maurras had never deluded himself that something might be salvaged from the wreckage of the Versailles settlement, believing that the only safety for France lay not in weakening but in annihilating Germany, preferably by reducing her to the state of fragmentation that existed at the time of the Treaty of Westphalia in 1648. If that had not been accomplished at Versailles it was because France had been betrayed by the Americans and the British for their own selfish reasons. For the same reasons the Anglo-Saxons had refused to police even the feeble settlement they had created. In this situation France must resign herself to the fact that war was, sooner or later, inevitable.

Throughout the 1920s, then, Maurras insisted on the harshest and most rigorous interpretation of the treaty, and was fanatically opposed to statesmen like Briand who attempted to secure German co-operation as well as Anglo-American approval by a more moderate approach. With Hitler's advent to power in the 1930s, Maurras, again like Kipling, gave his support to the Stresa Front, the London–Paris–Rome combination that was designed to restrain Hitler and prevent any German takeover of Austria. When the unity of that front was broken by Britain's signing of the Anglo-German Naval treaty in her own interests without consulting her Stresa allies, and then by Britain's refusal to recognise Mussolini's ambitions in

Abyssinia, the Action Française still hoped for a Western bloc between France, Mussolini and Franco that would restrain German expansion. But the polarisation of French politics between Left and Right in the era of the Popular Front made such a combination impossible, and although Maurras never totally abandoned his hopes that Italy might be detached from Hitler – despite his dislike of French Fascism he accepted Italian subsidies for his newspaper and could tolerate Mussolini as a fellow-Latin and a man who had preserved the monarchy – the territorial demands that Mussolini would have made on France as his price for any such change of policy (Corsica, Tunisia and Nice) would have proved exorbitant.

Where, then, did France's best interests lie? Increasingly by the late 1930s Maurras was driven back to the cry of 'la France seule!' Since Hitler's ambitions in Central and Eastern Europe could no longer be resisted, France should not waste her energies on a war with Germany over Czechoslovakia in 1938. Nor should she be dragged by the British and the Jews into a war with Hitler over Poland a year later – despite the fact that Maurras supported France's guarantees to Warsaw in the spring of 1939. The long-term hope must be that Hitler would eventually turn against the Soviet Union and that the Nazis and the Bolsheviks would destroy each other. Meanwhile the French must rearm at all speed and rely on the fortifications of the Maginot Line for their security. The problem that Maurras and those who thought like him did not face, of course, was the situation that would be created if Hitler secured a rapid victory over Russia and then turned his forces against the West, but the attitude of the Action Française was widely shared in a France that was determined not to go through another holocaust like that of 1914–18.

Events did not turn out in the way that Maurras hoped, however. The conclusion of the Nazi–Soviet pact postponed a German attack on the Soviet Union, while, after some hesitation at the last moment, the French government joined with Britain in declaring war on Germany over Poland in September 1939. Nine months later the Western Allies collapsed before the German onslaught, and France was plunged into one of the most tragic periods in her history. The arguments for and against the policies pursued by the Vichy régime are too numerous and too well-known to be rehearsed in detail, but even if it is conceded that the Armistice was necessary and that some kind of French administration was needed to deal with the Germans if France was to escape the fate of Poland and rule by Nazi Gauleiters, there is little doubt that Maurras was deceiving himself when he claimed that Vichy would be able to retain a meaningful degree of independence. He might express his delight at the downfall of the Republic and the advent of Vichy's 'National Revolution', a revolution which included the persecution of Republican politicians, Freemasons, and above all, the Jews. He might claim that Vichy represented the only hope for French recovery, and that both the Resistance and the Collaboration were instruments of the foreigner. But the logic of events made the progressive capitulation of Pétain to the Germans inevitable, and it was with the same inevitability that Maurras himself was drawn into the terrible cycle of violence that was created in France as Vichy and the Germans attempted to quell the rising tide of the Resistance. Born in an atmosphere of civil war, the Action Française was to perish in one that was far more terrible.

At his trial in Lyons after the Liberation Maurras claimed that in the support that he had given to Vichy he had been faithful to the ideal of 'la France suele'. He also attempted to demonstrate the consistency of the Germanophobia that he had expressed throughout his career, pointing out that he had urged Vichy to withdraw support from Darnand's para-military Milice in the middle of November 1943 when it became clear that its counter-subversive activites were becoming inextricably enmeshed with those of the Waffen SS.[38] The fact remains that, once he had decided to continue to publish the Action Française newspaper in Lyons after the German invasion of the formerly unoccupied zone at the end of 1942, he was then subjected to a censorship that insisted that all attacks on the Collaboration should be deleted. Meanwhile he was allowed to publish his denunciations of the Resistance. From now on the public appeals he continued to make for the death penalty against named Resistance members meant that the distinction that he attempted to draw between the 'legitimate' nature of Vichy's repressive activities and the 'illegitimate' nature of those of the Germans became more and more academic. 'C'est la revanche de Dreyfus!' ('It is the revenge of Dreyfus!'), he exclaimed at the end of his trial after he had been found guilty of giving intelligence to the enemy and been sentenced to life imprisonment. While it is possible to understand his anger, the cry itself betrays his inability to respond to any new developments that had taken place in the world in the last forty years. It demonstrates once again the monotonous and unchanging nature of his preoccupations, the degree to which he remained trapped in the hatreds of the past.

He lived on in prison until 1952, arguing, justifying, expostulating, complaining. He predicted the downfall of the Fourth Republic. He did not live to see the triumph of the hated de Gaulle. The latter had many ideas in common with Maurras on the necessity of restoring order at home and French prestige abroad, but de Gaulle was a man of action rather than an ideologue, and, despite its limitations and archaisms, his vision of France was always far wider than that of the leader of the Action Française.

In part this was due to de Gaulle's family background, a family in which his father, while a devout Catholic, is reported to have been convinced of Dreyfus's innocence. Another factor, no doubt, was that in his youth he had been influenced by other leaders of the Nationalist revival like Barrès and Péguy. But perhaps the most decisive experience in de Gaulle's early career was that of the First World War. To many of those who fought in it and survived it a part of their youth remained with them to the end. To many of those who were already middle-aged in 1914 the cataclysmic changes wrought by the conflict were something to which they could not adapt. As Bernanos constantly pointed out, to a personality as rigid and unyielding as Maurras, the war meant petrifaction, a fate that was to have consequences as cruel and as remorseless in their operation as those of antique tragedy.

It has often been said of de Gaulle that he loved France but not the French, and yet this is even more true of Maurras, whose attitude towards his country has rightly been compared to that of an aesthete, who regarded France as being so precious that he lived in constant terror that she might break. Barrès once recalled that in September 1914, when Paris was partly evacuated and the government had moved to Bordeaux, he and Maurras had walked round the deserted streets of the capital in the early morning and that the latter had confessed that in the face of monuments that testified to human ingenuity he had always been haunted by a fear of their fragility.[39]

At the end, however, it is possible that there was some alleviation of his tensions, some breach in the defence mechanisms that had operated throughout his career. In April 1952 he was transferred to a clinic, where he was still under surveillance. Shortly before his death in November of that year the aged sceptic received the sacraments, and shortly before he died he is reported to have said that for the first time he could hear someone coming.[40] Like so many dying words – like Goethe's appeal for more light – this can mean very little or a great deal. It all depends on the point of view of the observer.

If the career of Maurras closed in tragedy, that of Péguy ended on a note of triumph. His death at the beginning of the Battle of the Marne on 5 September 1914 ensured him entry into the pantheon of French war-heroes. His disappearance at the start of the conflict also meant that he did not see the terrible cost that France was to pay in the years between 1914 and 1918. There is yet a further factor that has helped to preserve his reputation. As the danger of another war came nearer and nearer in the course of the 1930s attention was increasingly focussed on the libertarian inspiration behind Péguy's message, his conviction that it was the freedom of Europe as a whole that was at stake in the quarrel between France and Germany in the years before 1914. Whereas the reputations of Barrès and Maurras have tended to go into eclipse in the last fifty years, therefore, that of Pèguy is still alive, retaining even now a capacity to stimulate and to provoke.

In fact, to few people in the history of twentieth-century France is it more difficult to give a fair assessment than it is to Péguy. He is viewed by many on the Right as a turbulent and anarchic spirit. On the Left he is regarded as a turn-coat because of his abandonment of Socialism and his emergence as a prophet of Nationalism and Catholicism. To a small group of passionate admirers in his own time and since, however, his career was marked by a fundamental consistency.

To this last group Péguy's work was characterised by a lifelong opposition to the materialism and opportunism of the bourgeoisie, whether expressed in his attacks on the anti-Socialist and anti-Dreyfus forces at the turn of the century, or in his tirades against Jaurès and the alliance of Socialists and Radicals that made up an important part of the Establishment of the Third Republic in the years after the Dreyfus Affair. Péguy's espousal of a patriotic line after the First Moroccan Crisis in 1905, it is pointed out, represented no radical departure from his Jacobin and libertarian past. His growing identification with his own, intensely idiosyncratic, version of medieval Catholicism in the years before 1914, a Catholicism deeply impregnated with a virulent anti-clericalism and a passionate hostility towards the rich, was also, it is argued, implicit right from the start of his career. Péguy's ability to combine an ardent Republicanism and an ardent Catholicism – a rare combination in France before 1914, and made even rarer by the papal condemnation of Marc Sangnier and the Sillon movement that he had created – was, it is maintained, no sign of self-contradiction but a result of his fidelity to the experiences of his childhood, when his mother had sent him to the Republic primary school on weekdays, and to the *curé* to be taught diametrically opposite ideas on Sundays.

'Avant que nous ayons douze ans tout est joué' ('Before we are twelve years old everything is decided'). Péguy wrote these words at the age of forty, and the key to an understanding of his career can only be found in his childhood. He was born at Orléans, the city of Joan of Arc, in 1873. His father, a cabinet-maker, died soon after he was born. His mother, Cécile, was a remarkable woman. Possessed by a demonic energy, she had learned the trade of mending cane chairs, and by working up to sixteen hours a day throughout her life she was able over the years to buy a number of cottages which she let to tenants whose conduct and behaviour were closely supervised and controlled by her. When she died at the age of eighty-six in 1933 a chair seat was found beside her on which she had been working to the end.

Years after Péguy's death one of his friends called on his mother and was struck by the physical similarities between the two:

Il lui ressemblait extraordinairement. Il avait sa bouche volontaire, ses lèvres energiques, son front puissant, ses yeux clairs, physionomie dont le dessein un peu rude trahissait la race robuste, solidement enracinée dans le sol. Il avait surtout son sourire. Jamais je n'a vu un visage subir une pareille transformation. Soudain il en était non pas seulement illuminée mais comme réchauffée. Une flamme intérieure jaillisait et communiquait son éclat à tous les traits.[41]

(He was extraordinarily like her. He had her firm mouth, her mobile lips, her powerful forehead, her bright eyes, a somewhat rough physiognomy that was the product of robust ancestors, deeply rooted in the soil. Above all he had her smile. I have never seen a face that underwent so striking a transformation. It was not only that it was suddenly illuminated, it seemed to be rekindled. The fire within him flared up and was reflected in all his features.)

An only child, Péguy did not merely resemble his mother in a physical sense. If his was to be a life that echoed to the sound of splintering friendships he never lost a healthy respect for his mother, who was quite capable of giving him a box round the ears even after he was a husband and father. From her he inherited his fierce independence, his authoritarianism, his sense of craftsmanship, and his industry. 'J'ai toujours tout pris au sérieux', he once confessed. 'Cela m'a mené loin'[42] ('I have always taken everything seriously. That has taken me far'). But it was not his mother but his maternal grandmother, who lived with them, who had the most direct influence on him during his early childhood. It was she who prepared his meals, taught him to walk, and scolded him. Above all it was she, an illiterate, who told him stories – stories of the Devil and of fantastic occurrences, stories of her poverty-stricken childhood, stories of the time when she had taken his mother (who was illegitimate) away from the harshness of life in the hills of the Bourbonnais down the Allier and Loire rivers to Orléans, where they had settled. Through her Péguy was to acquire that sense of the importance of the oral and epic tradition within French civilisation that was so profoundly to influence his work. Men like Barrès and Maurras could never be anything but bourgeois; Péguy never felt that he could be anything other than a peasant. He never set foot outside France, nor ever showed any desire to do so. He was conscious of the fact that he was the first of his 'race' to have the advantages of education. The physical act of writing was always for him a kind of ceremony.

A hard-working and intelligent child, Péguy absorbed all that his teachers at the new Republican primary school had to tell him of the glories of the revolutionary and Republic tradition. With the local curé he learned by heart long passages from the Scriptures and from the lives of the Saints, a fact that was to be of considerable importance later in his life after he recovered the religious faith that he had lost during his adolescence and embarked on a remarkable

career as a religious poet. Between 1892 and 1893 he completed a
year's military service, and, in the autumn of 1894, he secured a place
at the Ecole Normale in Paris, a striking tribute to the opportunities
that existed for the able child within the French educational system
compared with that of England. In the course of the next few years he
became so deeply involved in Socialism and the Dreyfusard cause –
his military training came in useful when he and other students were
involved in street battles with anti-Dreyfusards – that he abandoned
his university studies, much to the annoyance of his mother who
wanted him to have a good safe conventional career. It was during
these years, too, that he came into close contact with the Jewish
anarchist Bernard Lazare, one of the earliest Dreyfusards, a man of
shining idealism and integrity, whose whole career, including his
ultimate conversion to Zionism and early death, were to have a
profound influence on him. In January 1900 Péguy published the
first of his *Cahiers de la quinzaine*, the magazine that was intended to
act as the intellectual forum and spiritual conscience of the Socialist
movement. 'La révolution sociale sera morale, ou elle ne sera pas'
('The social revolution will be a moral one, or it will not take place at
all'), he proclaimed in the issue of 25 April 1901.

In the years after 1900, however, Péguy increasingly turned away
from Socialism. This was partly due to his disgust at the way in which
the idealism of the Dreyfusards was manipulated by men like Jaurès
(whom he had once idealised) into support for the anti-clerical
policies of Emile Combes, a development that prompted his famous
statement that 'tout commence en mystique et finit en politique'
('everything begins in mysticism and ends in politics'). But his
disillusionment went deeper than that. His Socialism had always
been marked by a strong individualistic and moral emphasis – his
enemies talked of his 'anarchism'[43] – and he always found it
impossible to accept the discipline and compromises that were
inevitable in mass politics. Already in his first drama on the subject
of Joan of Arc, the so-called 'Socialist' *Joan of Arc* of 1897, his
concern had been to show his heroine's contempt for commonly
accepted wisdom, her insistence on obeying her 'voices'. In many
ways Péguy's Joan is reminiscent of Simone Weil.

As Péguy's career developed, the incompatability between his
own vision of the world and that of the Socialists became increasingly apparent. Like his friend, Georges Sorel, the self-appointed

ideologist of anarcho-syndicalism (with whom he inevitably quarrelled because of the latter's anti-semitism) he despised the parliamentary process. He was offended not only by the deviousness of
Socialists like Jaurès, but also by their optimism, the naiveté of their
belief in positivism, materialism, 'science' and 'progress'. Of humble
origins himself, he was acutely aware that many of the Socialist
leaders were bourgeois, men who were fascinated by the political
game in the Chamber of Deputies but had little conception of the
tragic nature of life as it was led in the lower depths of society.
Strongly influenced by Pascal and Bergson, he was hostile to many of
the intellectual and artistic trends that found favour amongst
progressives. Zola might be praised by the Left for the pioneering
qualities of his Naturalism, but he was in truth only a 'tourist' of
misery.[44] A man like Durkheim knew all that there was to know
about suicide but was totally ignorant concerning the mystery of his
own death. Modern historians and sociologists might take pride in
their 'scientific' and objective methods, but all they had done was to
dethrone God from the centre of the universe and set themselves up
in his place.

The outbreak of the Russo-Japanese war in February 1904 further
convinced him of the shallow nature of much contemporary
optimism, and his scepticism that the world was entering into a new
era of peace and harmony was confirmed by the First Moroccan Crisis
in the next year, a crisis which reactivated his instinctive patriotism,
as he demonstrated in his famous Notre Patrie:

en l'espace d'un matin tout le monde . . . sut que la France était sous le coup
d'une invasion allemande imminente . . . Tout le monde . . . tout le monde
en même temps connut que la menace d'une invasion allemande est
présente, qu'elle était là, que l'imminence était réelle.[45]

(In the space of a morning . . . everyone knew that France was under the
threat of an imminent German invasion . . . Everyone . . . all the people
simultaneously, became aware that the menace of a German invasion was
present, that the menace was there, that its imminence was real.)

If the human condition was characterised by precariousness and
misery, where then did salvation lie? More and more it seemed to him
that the only solution lay in a return to the Catholicism of his youth.
To those who objected to the increasingly Nationalist and Catholic

emphasis in his work after 1905 his reply was that this was not a volte-face but the result of a prolonged meditation on the real meaning of the beliefs that he had always held. What he had experienced was not a 'conversion' but a long period of 'approfondissement'.

Péguy's basic consistency cannot, in fact, be denied, for, after his return to Catholicism, he proved to be an extremely difficult ally for the Catholics to handle. In deference to the wishes of his wife and the plight of his unbaptised children he refused to attend mass, and was furious with his friend Jacques Maritain when the latter attempted to put pressure on his wife's family to conform. Relations with Maritain were finally broken off completely when Péguy insisted on publishing in the *Cahiers de la quinzaine* Julien Benda's violently anti-clerical novel *L'Ordination*.

Here, indeed, in Péguy, the clericalist and ultramontane tendencies that were at work in French Catholicism in the years before 1914 had met their match. On the one hand, in his second drama on Joan of Arc, *Le Mystère de la charité de Jeanne d'Arc* which he wrote in 1909, and in his poetry – in pieces like 'Le Mystère des Saints innocents', 'Le Porche du mystère de la deuxième vertu', and in the various 'Tapisseries' – Péguy undoubtedly produced some of the most intensely felt and moving literature that was to appear from the Catholic revival that took place in France in the years before the outbreak of the First World War. On the other hand, in his passionate commitment to social justice, in his concern to avoid minimising the difficulties inherent in Christian belief, in his reverence for the tradition of Stoicism, in his conviction that Christ by his incarnation and by his sense of abandonment on the Cross represented the fulfilment of and the ultimate answer to the teachings of Stoicism – in all these things Péguy showed himself to be a pioneer in the modern 'lay' approach to Christianity. The essence of his message, that God has need of Man in order to fulfil his mission, is conveyed in 'Le Porche du mystère de la deuxième vertu':

> Comme la victime se rend aux mains du bourreau,
> Ainsi Jésus s'est livré en nos mains.
> Comme la victime se livre au bourreau,
> Ainsi Jésus s'est livré à nous.
> Et comme le prisonnier se livre au gardien de prison,
> Ainsi Dieu s'est livré à nous.

Comme le dernier des misérables a pu souffleter Jésus,
   Et il fallait qu'il en fût ainsi,
Ainsi le dernier des pécheurs, un malheureux infirme,
Le plus infime des pécheurs peut faire avorter, peut faire aboutir
   Une espérance de Dieu;
Le plus infime des pécheurs peut découronner, peut couronner
   Une espérance de Dieu.

Et c'est de nous que Dieu attend
   Le couronnement ou le découronnement d'une espérance de lui.

Effrayant amour, effrayante charité,
Effrayante espérance, responsabilité vraiment effrayante,
Le Créateur a besoin de sa créature, s'est mis à avoir
   besoin de sa créature.
Il ne peut rien faire sans elle.[46]

(As the victim delivers himself into the hands of the executioner,
   So Jesus has delivered himself into our hands.
As the victim delivers himself to the executioner,
   So Jesus has delivered himself to us.
And as the prisoner delivers himself to the prison warder,
   So God has delivered himself to us.
As the worst of wretches was able to smite Jesus,
   And it had to happen like this
So the worst sinner, a wretched cripple,
   The lowest sinner is able to thwart, to render in vain an
   expectation of God.
The lowest sinner is able to frustrate or fulfil the hope of God.

And it is for us that God is waiting
   for the fulfilment or the frustration of his hope.

Terrifying love, terrifying charity,
Terrifying love, a responsibility that is truly terrifying,
The Creator needs his creature, has put himself in a position
   to need his creature.
He cannot do anything without it).

Faithful to this message, Péguy was adamant in the attack that he launched against that alienation of the Church from the poor, that growing alliance of the Church with the bourgeoisie, that had taken place in the course of the nineteenth century. And he was remorseless in his criticisms of the clerical caste that had arrogated to itself so many of the responsibilities and privileges that should rightfully belong to mankind as a whole. Christ had not died to serve the interests of a group of priests. He had placed himself at the axis of *all* human misery. But the aim of the clergy had always been to obstruct and oppose the operation of grace, to work against it with a kind of remorseless and terrifying insensitivity:

Ils se conduisent comme des terrassiers dans un jardin; et encore ils mettent dans un jardin des entreprises de démolition. Et surtout quand Dieu, par le ministère de la grâce, travaille les âmes, ils ne manquent pas, ils ne manquent jamais de croire, ces bons curés, que Dieu ne pense qu'à eux, qu'il ne travaille que pour eux, qu'il travaille, qu'il pense uniquement à eux, pour eux, souvent même à et pour leur avantage temporel, quelque fois même à et pour leur domination temporelle . . . On ne peut, il ne faut que suffoquer, et dire: C'est effrayant. Et ce qu'il y a de plus effrayant, c'est qu'ils ne font que cel depuis le commencement du monde.[47]

(The conduct themselves like navvies in a garden; furthermore, they undertake enterprises of demolition in the garden. Above all, when God, by the ministry of grace, operates on souls, they do not fail, they never fail to believe, these good priests, that God thinks only of them, that he works only for them, that he only works for, that he only thinks about, them, for them, often about and for their temporal advantage, sometimes even, often even, about and for their temporal domination . . . There is nothing that one can do except to swallow hard and to say: it is terrifying. And the most terrifying part of it is that this is all that they have been doing since the beginning of the world.)

By taking this attitude, the clergy had disqualified themselves from judging the modern world. But still they went on, compounding their sins by the attack that the Catholic Church was now mounting against a man like Bergson. By his attack on the exorbitant claims made on behalf of the scientific method, by his insistence on the importance of time, memory and the human imagination, the latter had pioneered the revolt against the materialism and positivism of the nineteenth century that was now widespread in France in the years before the outbreak of the first World War, and the implications of his philosophy showed the way in which this revolt could be harnessed to the service of religious faith. But, after making use of Bergson, the Church (under the influence of men like Maurras and Maritain, who detested the fluidity of Bergson's thought and the subversive nature of his criticism of dogma) now regarded his influence with increasing hostility, a hostility that was eventually to result in a decision to place his works on the Index.

This was not exactly a surprising development, for the pontificate of Pius X witnessed a series of hysterical denunciations of Modernists and all kinds of other potential heretics, but to Péguy the situation was a scandal. 'Les Catholiques sont vraiment insupportables dans leur sécurité mystique', he told Joseph Lotte, his lieutenant at the office of the *Cahiers*. 'Le propre de la mystique, au contraire, est une inquiétude invincible. S'ils croient que les saints étaient des messieurs tranquilles, ils se trompent!'[48] (The Catholics in their mystical security are quite intolerable. On the contrary, the essence of mysticism is an invincible anxiety. If they think that the saints were placid gentlemen they are mistaken!') The trouble with contemporary Catholicism, he maintained, was that it had compromised far too much with the centralising and trivialising tendencies of the modern world. All facile and superficial interpretations of Christianity must be rejected − the views of Maurras and his sympathisers, as well as those of Marc Sangnier. In his defence of Bergson Péguy was quite capable of accusing the Pope himself of heresy.[49] Against the background of suspicion and terror that characterised Pius X's many campaigns against centres of dissidence in the years before 1914 it is more than likely that Péguy would have been condemned in turn, had the war not broken out when it did.

Péguy's relations with the Catholics were far from easy, then. But to the Nationalists, too, he was far from being a comfortable bedmate. Faithful to the Dreyfusard sympathies of his youth he continued to regard himself as a man of the Left, and again and again affirmed his detestation of the anti-semitism of the Right, a factor that was certainly present in the growing persecution of Bergson:

Je suis de plus en plus contre l'antisémitisme . . . Si on veut recommencer l'affaire Dreyfus, nous la recommencerons . . . Je marche avec les Juifs parce qu'avec les Juifs je peux être Catholique comme je veux l'être; avec les Catholiques je ne le pourrais pas.[50]

(More and more I am against anti-semitism. If they want to restart the Dreyfus Affair we will restart it . . . I stand with the Jews because it is with the Jews that I can be a Catholic in the way that I like; with the Catholics I could not do it.)

He was scathing, also, in his comments on the leaders of the Nationalist cause. Despite the considerable help that he received from Barrès in his constant (and largely fruitless) attempts to secure literary recognition and financial security he regarded Barrès himself as a worldly dilettante, a slave of fashion. At the time of the Dreyfus Affair he had described him as a 'mouldy Tartuffe',[51] and over the years his initial judgement did not alter: 'il a tout, l'Académie, l'État, la Gloire, et il tremble devant n'importe quel morveux de journaliste'[52] ('he has everything, the Academy, the State, Glory, and he trembles before every snotty-nosed journalist'). Maurras he felt to be even more detestable, an ideologue who was more devoted to his precious 'doctrine' than the best security of France, a man who, for all his monarchism, was far more a descendant of the divisive Catholic League of the sixteenth century that had plunged France into civil war than a follower of the great reconciler, Henri Quatre. Men like Briand and Poincaré, who were obviously men of ability, men who in the epoch of the monarchy would have been regarded as excellent servants of France, were attacked by the Action Française as mere lackeys of a corrupt system. But this was all that one could expect from theoreticians. The men of the Action Française were not traditionalists at all. Essentially 'modern' in their cynicism and frivolity, they were incapable of restoring the monarchy,

mais ils s'emploient tant qu'ils peuvent à démolir le respect, qui était le fondement même de l'ancien régime. On peut dire littéralement que ces partisans de l'ancien régime n'ont qu'une idée, qui est de ruiner tout ce que nous avons gardé de beau et de sain de l'ancien régime . . .[53]

(but they busy themselves as much as they can in demolishing the sense of respect that was the fundamental basis of the Ancien Régime. One can literally say that these partisans of the Ancien Régime have only one idea, that of ruining everything fine and sane that we had kept from the Ancien Régime . . .)

In divining the negative and demoralising implications of Maurras's 'Nationalism' for France, Péguy was, of course, being

remarkably prophetic. Prophetic, too, were the terrible attacks that
he launched against his old hero and ally Jaurès in the years after
1905. In a series of polemics, each one more inflammatory than the
last, Péguy castigated Jaurès's ultimate optimism, his belief that Man
was fundamentally too rational a creature to embark willingly on a
major war, and ridiculed all the rhetorical and political skills that
enabled him to secure meaningless compromise resolutions at
congresses of the French Socialist party and the Second International, resolutions that gave the misleading impression that
European socialists really had an effective policy to deal with the
problem of war.

Péguy could see with a merciless clarity all the inherent paradoxes
and weaknesses of Jaurès's position. He did not live to see the
growing divisions and hesitations of the Socialist party that
developed in the course of the First World War, divisions which led
in 1917 to the party withdrawing its support from the Union Sacrée,
but they could not have surprised him. Nor would he have been
surprised by the events that took place within the Left in the years
after 1918, when the hatred of war that was so understandably a part
of the Socialist tradition, allied with memories of the murderous
offensives of 1914–18 and the well-founded Socialist hostility to the
hypocrisy of the Treaty of Versailles, were to have dire consequences
over the next twenty years, when Jaurès's successor, Léon Blum, was
to fight in vain against the pacifist section of the party that supported
both the Munich agreements that abandoned Czechoslovakia to
Hitler in 1938 and the advent to power of Pétain in 1940.

Indeed, in many ways Péguy's nightmare vision of European
freedom being extinguished by Germany while Socialists remained
divided and irresolute fits the situation of the 1930s even better than
it does that of 1914, and it is on this insight into the coming era of the
dictators that much of Péguy's present-day reputation is based.
When commentators now class Péguy with Bernanos and Orwell as
one of the great prophets and opponents of modern tyranny it is
because they can now see the significance of Péguy's apocalyptic
vision, dating from the time of the First Moroccan Crisis of 1905, of
the inevitability of future conflict, the vulnerability of Western
civilisation, and the restricted geographical boundaries of liberty in
the modern world:

Les peuples de culture et de liberté, les nations libérales ou libertaires, enfin les peuples de quelque culture et de quelque liberté, – de si peu de culture et de si peu de liberté, je le sais, autant que personne, mais tout de même d'un petit peu de culture et d'un petit peu de liberté, – France, Angleterre, Italie (du Nord), quelques fragments de l'Amérique, des fragments de la Belgique, de la Suisse – occupent sur la carte du monde une étroite bande, quelques parcelles, misérable et précaire, étroite en largeur, étroite en profondeur aussi, une mince pellicule, fragile . . . Les parcelles de culture et de liberté que l'humanité, que certaines humanités ont péniblement acquises, et conquises, sont incessamment menacées par d'énormes vagues de barbarie, barbaries montant de presque partout, de presque tous les autres peuples; et dans ces peuples mêmes, dans ces peuples élus, au moins de quelque *self* élection.[54]

(The free and cultured peoples, the liberal and libertarian nations, that is, the people who have some culture, some liberty – how little culture, how little liberty I know as well as anyone, but who just the same have at least a little culture, a little freedom – France, England, Italy (the North), some parts of America, some fragments of Belgium and of Switzerland – on the map of the world they occupy a narrow band, a few patches miserable and precarious, narrow in width and restricted in depth also, a thin fragile skin . . . This free humanity, more or less free, this small part, the only part, which has some degree of liberty, this little fragment which floats, but which, unstable as it is, could founder, is the world's only hope . . . these parcels of culture and of freedom, which some parts of humanity have painfully acquired and conquered, are incessantly threatened by enormous waves of barbarism, barbarism arising almost everywhere, arising in almost all the other peoples; and in these peoples too, in these chosen people, at least chosen by some kind of self-election).

This vision obviously applies to the Europe of Hitler and Stalin even more than it does to the situation before 1914. In 1939 and 1940, too, Péguy's affirmation that, despite the hesitations and contradictions of the likes of Jaurès over the question of war, France was the principal bastion of libertarian values in Europe and that in order to protect the liberty of Europe these values must be incarnated, defended and if necessary died for, obviously struck a responsive chord in those who were opposed to any continued appeasement of Hitler. Seen in this perspective the diligence and enthusiasm that Péguy displayed in fulfilling his duties as a reserve officer in the French army can be seen as a preparation for the fight against modern

totalitarianism, and his death at the beginning of the battle of the
Marne can be taken as an early example of that kind of 'engagement'
that became almost mandatory for any serious European writer in the
course of the 1930s and 1940s.

Like the apologia that can be made for Jaurès in terms of his
prophetic understanding of the nature of the war that was to come in
1914, a similar apologia can thus be constructed for Péguy in terms of
his insight into the conflict that was to take place in Europe between
1939 and 1945. But while this is a legitimate exercise, it is only fair to
point out that Péguy's prophetic intuitions, like those of Jaurès, were
accompanied by serious deficiencies. For Péguy, it was Germany
which stood for 'barbarism' in 1914: he ignored or excused the
nationalism that was evident elsewhere in Europe, and he was not
interested in the complicated nature of the alliance system and the
state of military planning that led to the war, a situation that meant
that no power was without some degree of responsibility for its
outbreak. Equally alarming was Péguy's ignorance of the likely
nature of the coming war, a struggle in which, he hoped, the moral
superiority of the French cause and the *élan* of the French army
would be sufficient to ensure a relatively speedy elimination of the
German threat.[55]

That this was a somewhat optimistic view, given the state of
military technology and the disparity in military and economic
strength between France and Germany in 1914, hardly needs
emphasising. Despite the many prophetic qualities of his work there
is, in fact, a damningly antiquated quality about all Péguy's
panegyrics to his beloved France, all those passages in which his
veneration for the France of Joan of Arc, Michelet and Hugo,
achieves passionate expression:

La grâce ne peut se concevoir que là où la liberté existe, et c'est parce que la
France est le seul pays de la terre où l'on sait vraiment ce que c'est que d'être
libre, que le peuple français, impie, mal élevé, indocile, a sur lui des grâces
que manifestement n'ont pas tant d'autres peuples pieux, sages, appliqués,
bons élèves . . .[56]

(Grace can only operate where liberty exists, and it is because France is the
only country in the world where one really knows what it is to be free, that
the French people, lacking in piety, badly brought up, without docility, is

the recipient of graces that so many other peoples, pious, wise, zealous, good pupils, manifestly lack . . .)

To a certain extent, of course, he was aware that he was a survivor from an earlier epoch, and this helps to explain a great deal of the fury that animated his polemics against the modern world in general and the French Left in particular. But his capacity for self-insight was always limited, and, far more than he ever realised, he was the poet of an archaic peasant-dominated France that was already being seriously eroded before 1914, a France that was destined to disappear in the course of the twentieth century.

His inability to see that, whatever the outcome of the coming war, the France that he represented was ultimately doomed is a major weakness in his work. But by far the greatest obstacle to any canonisation of Péguy is his increasing obsession with themes of frustration, violence and death in the closing years of his life. This is an aspect of his personality that his admirers have tended to minimise, but it is one that cannot be ignored. Continually in Péguy's writing before 1914 there is the cry that he belongs to a failed generation, a generation that had been forced to watch the mystique of the Dreyfusard cause degenerate into the politics of Combisme, a generation that had been forced to live under the constant threat from Germany and had never been given the opportunity to avenge the humiliation that France had endured ever since the defeat of 1870.[57]

At a personal level Péguy's pride and ambition were affronted by the lack of proper recognition that he had received for his efforts. Despite an influential readership that included personalities like Jaurès, Millerand, Poincaré, Gide and Anatole France, despite the fact that many contributors to the Cahiers were willing to receive little or no payment and were content with the prestige of appearing in its pages, the financial viability of Péguy's magazine was always in doubt, especially since the loss of Socialist subscribers, offended by his increasingly Nationalist and Catholic stance after 1905, was not offset by corresponding gains amongst the Catholics, who were appalled by the violence of his anti-clericalism. In terms of literary recognition, too, Péguy had to endure many disappointments. Despite the fact that there was fairly widespread agreement that his achievement was remarkable, the extraordinary length, and the even more extraordinary repetitiveness, of his poetry discouraged even his most sympathetic readers, while the archaic, biblical aspects of much of his work were hardly likely to endear him to the avant-garde.

Yet another source of distress to him was his private life, which was wretched. He was made miserable by the incompatability between himself and his wife: in his poem 'Eve' there are thinly disguised criticisms of his mother and his wife for incarnating woman's desire to submit man to discipline, order, and the philosophy of 'getting on', criticisms that are reminiscent at times of those of D.H. Lawrence, to whom Péguy had on occasion more than a passing resemblance. He also felt guilty towards his wife's family, who had provided so much of the original capital for his publishing activities and who bitterly disapproved of the Catholic orientation of his thought after 1905. Then there was the complicating factor of his love for a young Jewish girl, Blanche Raphael. It was a love affair that could not be consummated because of his Catholicism and his sense of obligation towards his family, but it continued to torment him, particularly after he encouraged the girl into a marriage with someone else, a marriage in which she was not happy.

All these frustrations help to explain the bitterness that is apparent in the closing years of Péguy's life. They also undoubtedly increased his desire that if a war between France and Germany was sooner or later inevitable, it should break out in the near future before he was too old to seek glory and perhaps martyrdom in it. In 1912 he wrote to Millerand, who had just become Minister of War, 'Puissions-nous avoir, sous vous, cette guerre qui, depuis 1905, est notre seule pensée'[58] ('Let us hope that in your time we will have that war that has been our one thought since 1905'). In 'Eve' in 1913 there appeared the famous lines that have been quoted so often as his own most fitting epitaph:

> Heureux ceux qui sont morts pour la terre charnelle,
> Mais pourvu que ce fût dans une juste guerre.
> Heureux ceux qui sont morts pour quatre coins de terre.
> Heureux ceux qui sont morts d'une mort solonelle.[59]

> (Happy are those who have died for the carnal earth,
> Provided they died in a war that was just.

Happy are those who have died for four handfuls of earth.
Happy are those who died a ritual death.)

And already in 1910, at the beginning of the crisis over Blanche Raphael, he had proclaimed that the experience of war was one of mankind's basic necessities:

Quand une grande guerre éclate . . .c'est qu'un grand peuple, une grande race a besoin de sortir; qu'elle en a assez; notamment qu'elle en a assez de la paix. C'est . . . un violent besoin, un grand, un profond besoin . . . de gloire, de guerre, d'histoire, qui à un moment donné saisit tout un peuple, toute une race, et lui fait faire une explosion, une éruption.[60]

(When a major war breaks out . . . it is because a great people, a great race needs to break out; because it has had enough; principally because it has had enough of peace. It is a violent, a great, a profound need . . . for glory, for war, for history, a need which, at a given moment, takes hold of a whole people, a whole race, and leads it to explode, to erupt.)

The element of psychological and sexual anguish behind these lines is unmistakable.

All these accumulated frustrations contributed, too, to his pathological hatred of Jaurès, a hatred that increased as the threat of war came nearer and nearer. While Barrès admired the Socialist leader, and while Maurras's hatred of Jaurès was fanatical, but cold and impersonal in its nature, Péguy's resentment had all the bitterness of the friend and admirer who had been deceived. To Péguy Jaurès was the great corrupter of Dreyfusism, the man who had transformed the robust patriotism of the Jacobin tradition into a vague and vicious form of cosmopolitanism. In Péguy's fevered imagination Jaurès represented nothingness, 'le néant', a form of emptiness that was capable of betraying everybody, even of betraying the traitors themselves. To Péguy, Jaurès was a capitulator, a servant of Imperial Germany, a pan-German agent, bent on seducing the French masses with his fraudulent rhetoric. If Péguy looked forward with hope to the coming war and to the possibility of a heroic death in that war as the crowning glory of his career, he was determined that there must be no defeatists and traitors left behind. Already in 1913, when French politics were dominated by the quarrel over the three-year military service law, he was looking

forward with anticipation to the time when it would be necessary to
ensure that Jaurès's influence was eliminated:

En temps de guerre, il n'y a plus qu'une politique, et c'est la politique de la
Convention Nationale. Mais il ne faut pas se dissimuler que la politique de la
Convention Nationale, c'est Jaurès dans une charrette et un roulement de
tambour pour couvrir cette grande voix.[61]

(In time of war there is only one policy, that of the National Convention. But
one must not disguise the fact that the policy of the National Convention
means Jaurès in a tumbril and a roll of drums to drown that powerful voice.)

And in 1914, on receiving the news of Jaurès assassination, Péguy's
response was one of savage exultation.

To posterity this is an appalling reaction. But at the time Péguy's
obsession was with the defence of France. The war he had long
predicted had come, and his own moment had arrived. It was in an
exalted state of mind, therefore, that he made his farewells –
including farewells to those on the Left like Léon Blum, whom he had
offended in the past and to whom he did not repeat his attacks on
Jaurès. On 17 August he wrote to a friend from the Front:

Si je ne reviens pas, vous me garderez une fidélité sans deuil. Je vis dans cet
enchantement d'avoir quitté Paris les mains pures. Vingt ans d'écume et de
barbouillage ont été lavés instantanément.[62]

(If I do not come back, be faithful to my memory but do not mourn for me. I
live in the happiness of knowing that I leave Paris with clean hands. Twenty
years of scribbling and of dross have been washed away instantaneously.)

Like his one-time bosom friend Ernest Psichari, like Rupert Brooke in
England, like Richard Dehmel in Germany and Rilke in Austria, like
so many others in all the nations that went to war in 1914, Péguy
regarded the conflict as an act of purification.

Just under three weeks after writing this letter he was dead, and in
the course of the next four years the France that both he and Jaurès so
passionately loved was to suffer wounds that proved to be almost
mortal. If Tragedy is, as Aristotle defined it, a representation of an
action that is weighty, complete and of a due magnitude, effecting
through pity and terror a purgation of the spectators' emotions, it is
difficult to resist the conclusion that the quarrel that Péguy had with

Jaurès – this is an inaccurate way of describing it, for Jaurès never replied to the attacks[63] – can only be described as tragic. Here one is confronted with two heroic but flawed protagonists, two patriots, two saviours of France, two men of prophetic stature, doomed to an irreconcilable conflict and eventual death.

In themselves the ironies of the story can exercise a considerable fascination, but in the international situation of today they possibly have added point. For arguments similar to those of Péguy and Jaurès are the everyday currency of national and international debate. To one school of thought the defence of liberty is the supreme objective, and the threat of war, even of a nuclear war, is a guarantee of this liberty. To others the existence of massive armaments will eventually lead to an inevitable catastrophe unless action is taken to break out of this situation. Whatever the outcome of present debates, debates which take place in an era in which the stakes are so much higher than they were in 1914, it may be that what Jaurès and Péguy demonstrated so many years ago is the folly of either side in the controversy maintaining that they have a monopoly of truth, or believing that what confronts them is a clear-cut choice between right and wrong.

— 3 —

Ernest Psichari: the call of arms

One sign of the growing expectation in France that a war with Germany was sooner or later inevitable was indicated by the increasing respect accorded to the army in the years immediately before 1914. Vilified for its role during the Dreyfus Affair and then further demoralised by General André's manipulation of the promotion system in the aftermath of the Affair, the French army had seen its prestige seriously eroded in the course of the first decade of the century.

By the time of the Second Moroccan Crisis, however, the period of attrition was over. The seriousness with which Péguy undertook his duties as a lieutenant in the reserve was one sign of the times. And when the intellectuals opposed the three-year military service law in 1913, it was Péguy again who was one of the leaders of the counter-attack:

Que la Sorbonne le veuille donc ou non, c'est le soldat français qui lui mesure la terre . . . C'est le soldat qui fait qu'on parle français à Paris.[1]

(Whether the Sorbonne likes it or not, it is the French soldier who determines the disposal of its land . . . it is the soldier who determines that French is spoken in Paris.)

But there were other indications, too, that the army was now looked upon with greater favour. There was the rise in the number of recruits offering themselves to the military academy at St Cyr (where the annual intake had dropped from 1920 in 1897 to 982 in 1907).[2] There was also the appearance of a number of novels in which – in sharp contrast to earlier works by disillusioned conscripts, like Abel Hermant's *Le Cavalier Miserey* and Lucien Descave's *Sous-offs* – the army was glorified as the supreme symbol of national regeneration.

86

Foremost in this latter genre was *L'Appel des armes* by Ernest Psichari, which appeared in 1913. It tells the story of Maurice Vincent, a teacher's son who revolts against the values of his anti-militarist and anti-clerical father. Under the influence of Captain Nangès, a guru-type figure, Maurice enlists in the colonial army and is initiated by Nangès into the rites and the mystique of the military spirit. From Nangès Maurice learns that the army is superior to the French nation, for, whereas the latter is at the mercy of the forces of 'progress', the army is the incarnation of the eternal France, the France that remains while régimes come and go. Within the army, he is told, it is the colonial regiments that form the true *corps d'élite*, a force undiluted by reluctant and potentially disaffected conscripts, a body of professionals who have the solemn duty of impressing on the peoples of the Empire the power and the splendour of France.

The scene then switches to North Africa, where Maurice experiences the excitement of battle when he is involved in a conflict with rebellious Moors, a conflict in which he is wounded and which leads eventually to his being invalided out of the army. This engagement forms the highlight of *L'Appel des armes* and the reflections of Nangès after the battle contain the essence of the novel's message:

A mesure qu'il s'efforçait à s'approfondir, une résonance lointaine lui revenait, qui roulait de toute une profondeur mystérieuse: 'La guerre est divine.' Et il s'apercevait que, vraiment, de toutes les choses divines qui nous restent, celle-là est la plus divine, la plus marquée du sceau divin. Et elle est la plus inaccessible dans son essence, et aussi elle est la plus voisine des puissances cachées qui nous mènent.[3]

(As he tried to examine himself more deeply, a distant resonance came back to him, that reverberated from a great and mysterious depth: 'War is divine.' And he realised that, truly of all the divine things that remain to us, it is war that is the most divine, the most clearly marked with the hallmark of the divine. Of all these things, war is the most inaccessible in its essence, and thus it is the most real to us of all the forces that control us.)

The story ends with Maurice as a civilian, intensely aware that the most significant period of his life is now over.

L'Appel des armes is far from being a work of particular

profundity: it is possible to argue that it would never have been singled out for particular attention had France not been convulsed by the quarrels over the three-year military service law at the time of its publication, and had Psichari himself not been a member of one of the great families of Republican France. Nevertheless, the novel remains of considerable historical interest, offering as it does an insight into some of the more extreme pressures that were at work within the Nationalist and Catholic revivals, movements that were to inspire so many young men who, like Psichari himself, were to meet their death in the course of the coming war.

Ernest Psichari was born in 1883. His father, Jean Psichari, was Professor of Greek philology at the Ecole Pratique des Hautes Etudes in Paris, a distinguished academic, whose principal claim to fame lies in the fact that he was one of the leading champions of demotic Greek, the cause that was ultimately to triumph in the great debate on the future of the language that took place in Greece in the course of the nineteenth century. Ernest's mother, Noémi, to whom he was devoted, was the daughter of Ernest Renan, the writer and biblical scholar, whose loss of religious faith as a seminarian, whose investigations into the nature of the historical Jesus and whose *L'Avenir du science* had made him into one of the most famous figures in the intellectual life of nineteenth-century France. In his later years, by his championship of the spirit of rational inquiry and by his slow conversion to democratic ideals, Renan came to be regarded as one of the father-figures of the Republican and anti-clerical traditions in France. He died when Ernest Psichari was only nine years old, but his influence was in one way or another to pervade his grandson's life.

Like his great friend and contemporary Jacques Maritain (the grandson of Jules Favre, one of the heroes of the Republican opposition to Napoleon III) Psichari came from the Republican and intellectual purple, therefore, a social stratum that had some resemblance to that of the great Cambridge dynasties that contributed so much to the intellectual and artistic life of England in the nineteenth and twentieth centuries. It almost goes without saying that both the Psichari and Maritain clans played a prominent role in the Dreyfus Affair and were active in the movement for workers' education – the Universités Populaires – that was one of the offshoots of the Affair.

The high-minded and liberal Bloomsbury-like atmosphere in which they moved did not completely satisfy the members of the younger generation, however. In England, the revolt of the young, of men like Julian Bell, against the ethos of the intellectual haute bourgeoisie came in the 1930s. In France it came a generation earlier. The impact of Barrès and his 'Culte du Moi' were extremely powerful influences on Ernest Psichari (even though he bitterly resented Barrès's attacks on his family for their cosmopolitan background and their Dreyfusard sympathies), and various incidents from his youth indicate the fascination exerted on his generation by Symbolism. On one occasion Ernest and Jacques Maritain composed six sonnets entitled 'Ciels', and signed them with the joint initials of their surnames, MP.[4] On another Ernest read some of his poems to his family, and then burnt them, depositing the ashes in an urn.[5]

According to Henriette Psichari Maritain was the more cerebral and decisive personality, while her brother was more passionate and more inclined to dreams. Perhaps the latter was already being affected by the identity crisis that had its roots in his family situation. The fact is that in many ways his parents were temperamentally incompatible. Jean Psichari resented Noémi's tendency to monopolize the affections of the children, and was further angered by the way in which she subordinated the interests of her family to the wishes of the Renans. He complained frequently that his children had the particular distinction of not having a father, only a grandfather, and a maternal grandfather at that.[6] And behind these tensions there was also a fundamental clash in cultures, with Noémi having the advantage of being able to bring up her family in her own country. The discord between the two did not actually lead to a break-up of the marriage until shortly before the outbreak of the First World War, but there can be little doubt that Ernest's constant search for order, for stability and for identity was profoundly influenced by this background of family strife.

His own crisis, when it came, was dramatic and violent. At the age of eighteen he fell passionately in love with Maritain's sister Jeanne, who was seven years older than himself and about to be married to another man. She rejected his advances. On the night before her marriage Psichari walked disconsolately up and down outside her home until dawn. After the marriage ceremony had taken place he entered a friend's flat to which he had a key and took an overdose of drugs. His friend, Maurice Reclus, returned to the flat and helped to revive him. Psichari then took out a revolver to shoot himself, but Reclus struggled with him and the weapon discharged itself harmlessly. For some days afterwards Psichari wandered the streets of Paris seeking hard manual work and staying in seedy lodgings. Eventually his family rescued him and sent him to the country to recuperate.

From that point he began to pull himself together. Abandoning the idea of university studies for the moment, he decided that his best plan of action was to complete his period of compulsory military service. Having discovered in the army the discipline he so desperately needed, he then scandalized his friends by re-engaging as a regular in the 51st infantry regiment in 1904, eventually becoming a sergeant. Impatient with the placid routine of life in the garrison towns of metropolitan France, he got himself transferred to the colonial army as a gunner. He soon became an NCO and did a tour of duty in the Congo in 1907, under the command of Commandant Lenfant, an officer he came to idolize. He returned to France in 1908 and it was in that year that he published his first book, *Terres de soleil et de sommeil*, an account of his experiences in Africa.

Psichari had long been intent on a literary career, and in writing of his adventures in the Empire he had found a subject that had not hitherto been very much exploited in France. Admittedly Loti had evoked the sensuousness of the South Seas and the omnipresence of death in the tropics, but he had not focussed his attention primarily on France's imperial mission. Indeed, one of the major reasons why Kipling enjoyed such a vogue in France from the 1890s onwards was that by drawing attention to the splendours and responsibilities of empire he was bringing something new to the French public as well as to that of Britain. For many years French expansion overseas was bitterly attacked not only by the Left but also by elements on the Right like Maurras, who argued that the country's energies were being diverted from the major task of preparing for an eventual confrontation with Germany. It was only in the years after 1905 that

pride in the achievements of the Empire became widespread in
France, and from that point of view the timing of the publication of
Terres de soleil et de sommeil was particularly apt.

Psichari was not primarily a novelist of Empire, however. In all his
writing the territories that he visited provided little more than
primitive local colour. His primary interest was in his own response
to events, in recording the stages of his own intellectual and spiritual
progress, and *Terres de soleil et de sommeil* is no exception to this. The
influence of Loti is clearly discernible in the many passages devoted
to the lushness of the vegetation and the barbaric splendour of the
forests of the Congo, but this is little more than décor. Like Barrès
Psichari was only interested in landscape to the extent that it could
reveal to him aspects of his own soul, and *Terres de soleil et de sommeil*
is far more of an exercise in autobiography than a work of travel,
reportage or adventure. Its central theme is Psichari's search for an
enduring identity for himself and his fellow Frenchmen in the
modern world:

Du haut des collines de la Mambéré, d'où l'œil dominait un horizon infini de
désolation, il m'arrivait souvent de penser plus à la France lointaine qu'à la
terre d'Afrique où nous marchions. Je contemplais ce pays vierge, non
comme la patrie des Bayas, mais comme une patrie française, où des Français
nous avaient envoyés, et j'essayais de comprendre la conscience de ma race,
aussi obscure, aussi complexe que celle des peuples noirs que nous croisions
sur notre route.

A ces moments, comme j'étais fier de garder en moi cette petite lampe de
l'héroisme, si vacillante aujourd'hui, et de retrouver, dans la partie la plus
repliée de mon âme, un peu de l'antique passion des dominateurs et des
conquérants! . . . Nous venons ici pour faire un peu de bien à ces terres
maudites. Mais nous venons aussi pour nous faire du bien à nous-mêmes.
Nous voulons que la grande aventure serve à notre santé morale, à notre
perfectionnement. L'Afrique est un des derniers refuges de l'énergie
nationale, un des derniers endroits où nos meilleurs sentiments peuvent
encore s'affirmer, où les dernières consciences fortes ont l'espoir de trouver
un champ à leur activité tendue.[7]

(On top of the Mambéré hills, from which one can see a limitless horizon of
desolation, it was often the case that I thought more about faraway France
than about the land of Africa across which we were marching. I looked on
this virgin landscape not as the homeland of the Bayas, but as a homeland of

France to which the French people had sent us, and I tried to understand the consciousness of my race, a consciousness that is as complicated and as impenetrable as that of the black people that we came across on our journey.

How proud I was in those moments to realise that within myself there was that little flame of heroism, a flame that is flickering so much today, and to rediscover in the innermost part of my being a little of the spirit of the rulers and conquerors of old! . . . We come here to do a little good for these wretched lands. But we also come to benefit ourselves. We need adventures for our moral well-being, for our improvement. Africa is one of the last refuges of national energy, one of the last places where we can still affirm our noblest feelings, where the last bold spirits have scope to extend themselves.)

For a man as divided as Psichari was by his conflicting French and Greek parentage, the value of the Empire was that it enabled him to feel completely and wholly French. It also enabled the French to rediscover their self-confidence, their belief in their own strength:

Je sais que je dois me croire supérieur aux pauvres Bayas de la Mambéré. Je sais que je dois avoir l'orgueil de mon sang. Lorsqu'un homme supérieur cesse de se croire supérieur, il cesse effectivement d'être supérieur . . . C'est parce que l'Empire romain était grand et fort, que le citoyen de Rome pouvait dire avec orgueil: Civis romanus sum. Mais c'est bien un peu aussi parce qu'il disait cela, parce qu'il le criait, parce qu'il emplissait le monde du bruit de ces trois mots glorieux, c'est bien un peu pour cela que l'empire était grand et fort.

Jamais, plus qu'aux belles heures de marche sous le soleil du Tropique, je n'ai éprouvé de joie à me répéter à moi-même cette phrase si simple et si bienfaisante: 'Je suis soldat français.' Ces mots-là, c'était comme le refrain forcé, la prosodie de toute l'Afrique. Chaque objet me les suggérait et semblait les approuver. Comment s'étonner que cette lumière qui me venait tout à coup m'intéressât plus que les paysages de ma route et les rencontres de mon voyage?[8]

(I know that I must feel myself to be superior to the poor Bayas of Mambéré. I know I must have pride in my blood. When a superior man ceases to believe that he is superior, he effectively ceases to be superior . . . It is because the Roman Empire was large and strong that the Roman citizen could say with pride: Civis romanus sum. But it is partly the case also that, as a result of saying that, of affirming that, of proclaiming aloud to the world these three glorious words, the empire itself was large and strong.

Never have I felt greater joy than I did when, during the happy hours of marching under the tropical sun, I repeated to myself the so simple and consoling phrase: 'I am a French soldier.' These words were the refrain that was forced out of me, the prosody that I experienced everywhere in Africa. These words were prompted and confirmed by everything that I saw. How could it surprise anyone that this sudden illumination that I experienced interested me far more than the landscapes on the way and the things that I met with on my journey?

The influence of Barrès is unmistakable. Nationalism is Psichari's cure for a fragmented ego, the therapy for a French nation in danger of decline and disintegration. It is the great virtue of the Empire that it recalls the French to a sense of their greatness. It is the great virtue of Africa that it reminds the French that they must learn again to be a war-like people:

Maintenant, il nous faut venir prendre conseil chez des sauvages . . . Il est un moment où l'esprit trop guerrier s'affine et s'adoucit; la violence révolte comme une injustice; la bonté féconde remplace la haine stérile. Progrès normal et légitime, mais qui n'est pas le terme de notre évolution. Il vient une heure où la violence n'est plus de l'injustice . . . Alors la guerre n'est plus qu'un indicible poème de sang et de beauté . . . Dans ma patrie, on aime la guerre, et secrètement on la désire. Nous avons toujours fait la guerre. Non pour conquérir une province. Non pour exterminer une nation. Non pour régler un conflit d'intérêts. Ces causes existaient assurément, mais elles étaient peu de choses. Elles étaient secondaires et adventices. En vérité, nous faisions la guerre pour faire la guerre. Sans nulle autre idée. Pour l'amour de l'art. La guerre pour la guerre. Nous faisions la guerre, par un naturel besoin de nous dépenser et de nous imposer, parce que c'était notre loi, notre raison secrète, notre foi.[9]

(We must now learn from the savages . . . There is a moment when the excessive concentration on war begins to slacken; violence becomes offensive as an injustice; good will replace sterile hatred. This is a natural and legitimate form of Progress, but it is not the end of evolution. There comes a time when violence is no longer a form of injustice . . . At that point war is nothing other than an indescribable poem of blood and beauty . . . In my country we love war and secretly desire it. We have always made war. Not in order to conquer a province. Not in order to exterminate a nation. Not in order to find a solution to a conflict of interests. These reasons were certainly there, but they counted for little. They were secondary and accidental. The truth of the matter was that we made war for its own sake. Without any other idea. For the love of the thing. War for the sake of war. We made war fulfilling a normal desire to spend ourselves, to tax ourselves because that was our law, our secret reason, our faith.)

'La terre me violente avec délices et me ravit de douleur mâle'[10] ('The land assails me with delights and enraptures me with its masculine harshness'), Psichari wrote of the Congo, and it is clear that a further important factor that contributed to his insecurities, a further element behind his devotion to the camaraderie of the army, his slighting references to women, behind all his talk of power, submission and the search for wholeness, was the unmistakable element of homo-eroticism that is to be found in many of his writings. The product of an era that was still largely innocent of Freud, Psichari himself may not have been fully aware of this element in his make-up, and it is one to which his contemporaries make no open references, but there seems little doubt that it was this ingredient above all that was to give the particular edge and extremism to his work.

Certainly in his glorification of violence and war he was in the process of leaving his masters far behind. Like Barrès, who was generous in his praise of his work, Psichari sought in Nationalism an escape from the isolation of the 'Moi', but compared with Psichari's first-hand accounts of adventure and empire the former's National-ist writings looked like so much salon confectionery. Like Péguy, with whom his relations were close, Psichari had abandoned the anti-militarism of his youth and had come to venerate the role of the army, but even Péguy's hymns to war were usually qualified by the assertion that the war that had to be fought must be legitimate and just. Now in Psichari's work all the restraints are cast aside. At his birth the sceptical and ironic Renan had wondered what kind of future the poor child would see and what kind of France his new grandson would have as a country.[11] Now, a quarter of a century later, that grandson was emerging as one of the idols of the younger generation of the Nationalist Right.

This position was confirmed by the publication of *L'Appel des armes*, which was based on the further developments that had taken place in his career since the appearance of *Terres de soleil et de sommeil*. After his return from the Congo in 1908 Psichari had spent a

year at the military academy at Versailles, where he was commis-
sioned. In the autumn of 1909 he left France as a sub-lieutenant and
sailed for Mauritania, where he remained for the next three years.
Before his departure he expressed some anxiety that the heroic
period in North Africa might now be nearly over since the area was
almost completely pacified. What he was seeking was action, and
already somewhat earlier in his career he had confessed to his friends
that if his future in the colonial army meant that he was condemned
to vegetate in France, Hanoi, Saigon or Martinique, it would be of
little interest to him.

His fears that he would be bored by the work that he would be
called upon to do in North Africa proved to be groundless, however.
He was fascinated by the landscape and people of Mauritania, the
starkness and austerity of the desert, the simplicity and dignity of
the Moors, the directness and fevour of their Islamic faith. To a far
greater degree than the Congo, North Africa was to influence him
profoundly. It was there, too, that he had his first taste of battle
when, on an expedition into the interior, he was involved in a
skirmish with rebellious tribesmen in which two of his men were
killed. All these experiences went into *L'Appel des armes*, which
appeared the year after his return to France in 1912.

To the present-day observer it must appear that for Psichari to base a
panegyric of war in general on his experience of a trivial engagement
with a small group of dissident Moors is more than ironical in view of
the events that were to take place in France between 1914 and 1918.
But *L'Appel des armes* is no more an exercise in realism than *Terres de
soleil et de sommeil*. Even as portrait of the colonial army in the years
before the outbreak of the war, the novel is open to considerable
criticism. Psichari did not pay much attention to the kind of routine
work of administration to which a man like Lyautey devoted his life.
Nor was he interested in the latter's concern to overcome the divorce
between the professional officer corps and the rest of French society.
Seen against this background *L'Appel des armes* is far more a further
instalment in Psichari's autobiography than an accurate rendering of
the situation of the army in the modern world.

But this in no way affected the reception of the book when it
appeared. By 1913 the influence of the Nationalist revival was

reaching its peak. After the tension of the Second Moroccan Crisis, when France had been forced to hand over to Germany parts of the Congo (including areas that Psichari had served in and written about), there was a determination that this would be the last concession that France would make. In 1913 Poincaré became President of the Republic, and French politics were dominated by the issue of the three year military service law. Meanwhile, various investigations into the opinions of French students, notably that of 'Agathon', indicated that there was now a general feeling that war with Germany was, sooner or later, inevitable, that the virtues of action and commitment were those that the young now prized most highly, and that personalities like Psichari who incarnated these virtues were particularly to be admired.

In these circumstances the success of *L'Appel des armes* was assured. Jaurès might be sufficiently disturbed by 'Agathon's' findings to appeal to French youth to divert their fervour for war into an energetic pursuit of peace. The Socialists in general might be appalled by *L'Appel des armes* – not least by the passage in which a working-class soldier is praised for his willingness to obey orders to fire on striking relatives. But to many Frenchmen Psichari was expressing the popular mood. Barrès, Galliéni and Lyautey praised the novel. Péguy, to whom *L'Appel des armes* was dedicated, hailed 'le grand Ernest' as a soldier who ensured peace by the sword, the only kind of peace 'qui compte'[12] (that counts). Maurras spoke of Psichari's 'curieux et fort roman'[13] (unusual and powerful novel), while Bergson stressed its educational value:

Il me semble que vous obtenez de votre lecteur – au moins pendant qu'il vous lit – une simplification de lui-même, un rejet de certaines émotions déprimantes qu'il croyait naturelles et qui apparaissent alors comme artificielles, enfin une reprise de contact avec ce qu'il y a en lui de plus sain et de plus viril. Ou je me trompe beaucoup, ou le livre contribuera à créer une atmosphère morale nouvelle – celle dont nous avons besoin.[14]

(It seems to me that the effect you have on your reader – at least while he is reading your work – is to force him to simplify himself, to discard certain depressing ideas that he had taken to be normal and now realises to be artificial, and to make contact again with what is healthy and virile in himself. Either I am very much mistaken, or the book will help to create a new moral atmosphere, something that we badly need.)

The Left might hate the novel, and the present-day reader may be intrigued by the enthusiastic reception awarded it by the *bien-pensant* press (which seemed to be unaware of the ambiguities in the relationship depicted between Maurice and Nangès, particularly the passage in which the latter, who is bored by his mistress, imagines his young disciple in bed with her), but, on the whole, there was no doubt that *L'Appel des armes* was a resounding success.

To be fair to Psichari, he himself was less overwhelmed by the reception accorded to his book than might have been the case a few years earlier. It might be flattering to be hero-worshipped by the readers of the 'Agathon' generation, but he was concerned that their cult of action and distrust of reason could easily degenerate into a kind of 'mindless Rooseveltism'.[15] He was worried, too, by the extent to which the success of his novel was due to his name. There were many on the Right who considered Psichari's evolution to be a form of judgement on the long-dead Renan, and Psichari himself was fully aware of this. 'Entre nous, mon vieux,' he wrote to Jean Dietz, 'tu crois qu'ils feraient tout ce bruit si je n'étais pas le petit-fils de bon-papa?'[16] ('Between ourselves, old friend, do you think they would have made so much commotion if I had not been the grandson of grand-papa?').

The irony of the whole situation, however, was that the main reason for his sense of dissatisfaction with *L'Appel des armes* was that it did not reflect the further development that had taken place in his life since he had written it, a development that was bound to give even further aid and comfort to his grandfather's enemies – his conversion to Catholicism.

In many ways this latest development was a predictable outcome to events. At his birth his paternal grandmother had insisted that he be baptised according to the rites of the Greek Orthodox Church, and from an early age it was quite clear that Psichari was possessed of a naturally religious temperament that could never be satisfied with the rarified agnosticism of his parents' background. It is also clear that he was influenced over the years by the evolution of his friends: the dramatic conversion of Jacques Maritain and his wife, Raïssa, after a period of despair when they had contemplated suicide by drowning themselves in the Seine, was obviously important; and the slow return of Péguy to the faith of his childhood was not without its effect, too. But it can hardly be doubted that it was his encounter with Mauritania that was the decisive factor in Psichari's progress towards religion.

Like so many of his contemporaries who went to North Africa Psichari was profoundly influenced by the experience. The starkness of the desert, the simple piety of the Moslems, the contrast between the vitality of Islam and the state of the Church in France – all had their effect on him. Time and again – in his letters, in *Les Voix qui crient dans le désert* (the journal of his North African years) and finally in *Le Voyage du Centurion*, the novel about his conversion, which he wrote in the spring of 1914 and which was posthumously published in 1915 – he returned to these basic themes. 'Nous sommes de ceux qui brûlent de se soumettre pour être libres'[17] ('We are numbered amongst those who are consumed by the desire to submit themselves in order to be free'), he noted on one occasion, and the land of Africa, 'terre de soumission et pas de révolte' ('land of submission and not of revolt'), was the natural setting for spiritual meditation. The desert might be the most inhospitable place in the world, but it was there that he came in contact with a mysticism and a faith which were still flourishing in the twentieth century. No, the people of Africa did not ridicule religion, *they* would never be sceptics,[18] he wrote in *Le Voyage du Centurion*, and there and in his other writings he told the story of what he came to regard as the decisive experience of his life. This was a conversation that he held with a North African Moslem to whom he had remarked that the Moors were mad to resist a nation as rich and as powerful as the French, to which the Moslem replied:

Oui, vous autres Français, vous avez le royaume de la terre, mais nous, Maures, nous avons le royaume du ciel.[19]

(Yes, you French possess the Kingdom of this world, but we Moors have the Kingdom of Heaven.)

At a stroke Psichari's attempt to find wholeness and unity through his cult of the army was exposed as hollow and unconvincing. Like Father Foucauld, who was also impressed by the fidelity of the Moslems of North Africa, his knowledge of Islam was never more than fragmentary, and he could never regard the Moslems as anything other than a colonial people; it is typical of him that he should have started arguing that Islam was all very well for the Moors but that Christianity was a superior faith and the natural religion for Frenchmen. And yet, despite all this, the role played by Islam, a militant as well as a mystical faith, in influencing him in his conversion to Catholicism – he was received into the Church in the early months of 1913 – can hardly be exaggerated.

The Catholics were, of course, delighted, and there was further talk of the inscrutable ways of Providence that had led the grandson of Renan back to the true faith. For Psichari himself, the remaining eighteen months of his life were not to be without their complications, however. On the one hand everything was now simple, and it was with his customary extremism that he now embraced Catholicism. On the other hand his zealotry could be a stumbling-block in his relationship with others. It was, for example, to put under strain and eventually to rupture one of his most important friendships, that with Péguy. Psichari, the convert, could no longer approve of the latter's anti-clericalism and refusal to take the sacraments, and relations were not improved by incidents like the one that happened one day when the two were at lunch with Maritain's mother, Madame Favre, who remained a staunch free-thinker. On this occasion Psichari exclaimed that he would like to have cancer so that he could go to Lourdes to seek a cure, to which Péguy replied that he was waiting for the day when someone would go to Lourdes in order to be made ill.[20] This boded ill for the future, but in any case by this time Jacques Maritain had already broken with Péguy, and Psichari's rejection of his former mentor was not to be long delayed. 'Je l'ai beaucoup aimé,' Psichari explained, 'mais je me suis détourné de lui. Il a un manque de logique en raison duquel son influence ne peut pas être sans danger'[21] ('I loved him very much, but I have turned against him. There is a lack of logic in him that can make his influence dangerous'). For his part Péguy was appalled that Psichari should have been so completely taken over by the curés. 'Nous devons prendre le deuil d'Ernest,' he lamented to Madame Favre, 'il est perdu pour nous'[22] ('We should go into mourning for Ernest. He is lost to us').

The break with Péguy was distressing enough, but Psichari had more immediate worries to face in these closing months of his life. He was tortured by the thought that, whereas he had sought for and been granted the gift of faith, the other members of his family, with the exception of his brother Michel, stubbornly refused to follow his example. He was particularly anxious about and solicitous towards his mother, who had recently been deserted by his father. There was the further complicating factor of the reappearance of Maritain's sister in his life, for, after an unhappy marriage, she had been divorced and now was clearly in love with him. In normal circumstances they could have been married in a civil ceremony, but the situation was now made difficult by the fact that in the years that had elapsed since their first encounter they had both become ardent Catholics. It is more than likely that her love for him was now greater than his love for her, but they agreed to wait on events. Meanwhile Psichari had already been exploring the possibility of becoming a priest, but had contented himself with becoming a tertiary in the Dominican order after deciding that for the time being he could be of most service to the Church by remaining within the army.

It was at this point that the First World War broke out. Suddenly all the complications disappeared and his duty was clear. As a regular army officer stationed in France he was immediately sent to the Front. 'Nous ne sommes pas prêts,' he told a priest, 'mais j'ai confiance dans le Sacré-Cœur'[23] ('We are not ready, but I have faith in the Sacred Heart'). To his mother two days before his death he was more reassuring:

Nous allons certainement à de grandes victoires et je me repens moins que jamais d'avoir désiré la guerre qui était nécessaire à la grandeur de la France.[24]

(Without a doubt we are going to achieve great victories and I am less repentant than ever for having wanted the war that was necessary for the greatness of France.)

Years earlier he had written to Péguy that he hoped that historians would not have to say of the period in which they lived merely that, 'de 1890 à 19 . . ., le commerce et l'industrie prospérèrent'[25] ('from 1890 to 19 . . ., commerce and industry flourished'). Now both of them had their wish. Both of them left for the war convinced that France would come out of her ordeal rejuvenated and regenerated. On 22 August, less than three weeks after the outbreak of the conflict, Psichari's artillery battery was overwhelmed by the German advance in the north east of France, and, after a fierce rearguard action, he was killed.

His younger brother Michel, suffering from typhoid in an army hospital, fainted when he saw a copy of *Le Petit Parisien* with the caption 'The grandson of Renan killed by the enemy'.[26] Michel, who had been married to the daughter of Anatole France, a marriage that had ended in divorce, was the one member of the family who followed Ernest's example in moving from the left-wing sympathies of his youth to a growing identification with Nationalism and Catholicism in his later years. After recovering from his illness in 1914, he went through the battle of Verdun, an experience that shattered many of the illusions that he had entertained about the war at the beginning of the conflict. He was killed in Champagne in 1917.

Two years earlier *Le Voyage du Centurion* had been published. Once again a work by Ernest Psichari was hailed as a masterpiece. Not everyone was impressed, it is true: when Paul Bourget nearly burst into tears whilst reading passages from the book aloud to Edith Wharton and Gide, the latter maliciously reported that neither of them knew what to wonder at more, Bourget's emotion or the mediocrity of the pages.[27] But still the plaudits continued. Such was the resonance of the family name that it was, perhaps, inevitable that Psichari's memory should have been annexed by the Right in the years after 1914. For the same reason it was hardly surprising that many should have followed Barrès in claiming that by his death Psichari had atoned for the sins of his grandfather.[28]

This was not a situation that could be relished by the surviving members of his family (especially his sister Henriette) who remained faithful to the Left, but they were obliged to live with it, and to witness the spectacle of his memory forming part of the battleground between warring groups of his Catholic friends. After the Papal condemnation of the Action Française in 1926, for example, Psichari's friend and biographer, Henri Massis, who remained faithful to Maurras, continued to portray Psichari as a hero of the Maurrassian tradition, while the Maritains believed that, had he survived, Psichari would not only have followed them in breaking with Maurras but would have prevailed on Massis to do the same.[29] Throughout all these debates and controversies, controversies that became even more acute during the Second World War when the Maritains, now in the USA, supported de Gaulle, while Massis in France became one of the speech-writers of Pétain, Henriette Psichari did whatever she could to defend the integrity of her brother's reputation. But she had other troubles, too. In November 1942 one of her sons, an officer in the French submarine force, was killed off Oran whilst obeying Vichy's orders to resist the Anglo-American invasion of North Africa, at a time when Admiral Darlan was in clandestine negotiations with the invading armies, negotiations which finally resulted in an Allied take-over.

A few years later, however, she had her revenge. Like a figure from Greek tragedy, and speaking in the name of the mothers of France, she made an electrifying intervention at the trial of Pétain in 1945, recounting the circumstances of her son's death and concluding her indictment of Vichy with the words, 'Gentlemen, that is why our children died. They died, I am grieved and ashamed to say, in the service of Germany.'[30]

At the end of this speech few in the courtroom in Paris in 1945 could have doubted that what they had just heard was the cry of a sister as well as of a mother. With characteristic passion, the Psichari drama, a family drama that had its origins in the conflicts that had divided Frenchmen in the years before 1914, was played out to the end.

— PART II —

For ever England

Sir William Orpen (1878–1931), *Poilu and Tommy*

'But the thing's absurd. Why *should* Germany attack France?'

H.G. Wells, *Mr Britling Sees it Through* (1916), p. 76

— 4 —

Rupert Brooke: the soldier

Although the full horror of the First World War was something that could hardly be anticipated by any of the combatant nations, there can be little doubt that the shock of actually being engaged in a major war was greater in England than in any of the other embattled Great Powers in 1914. The continental countries, after all, possessed long military traditions and long traditions of conscription, and, although there had been no major conflict between the great European powers since that between France and Prussia in 1870, the possibility of war was an idea that was deeply ingrained in the European conscious-ness, a possibility that seemed to be turning into an increasing probability in the years before 1914. Seen against this background it is not surprising that every one of the Frenchmen whose careers are examined in this book had an acute sense of the threat of war and invasion, and that two of them, Péguy and Psichari, should have been killed in the early weeks of the conflict.

In England there was no such long period of psychological preparation for the battle. Admittedly there *were* memories and portents of the horrors of warfare: there was the ancestral memory of the battlefields of Waterloo and the Crimea, and there was the painful reminder of more recent ordeals during the Boer War. And there *had* been recent moments of tension with Germany, particularly at the time of the Second Moroccan Crisis. Indeed, the expansion that had taken place in the German navy since the 1890s had convinced a number of Englishmen that war was, sooner or later, inevitable. In the world of fiction, for example, the possibility of a German invasion of England had been openly raised on a number of occasions before 1914, notably in *The Riddle of the Sands* by Erskine Childers which appeared in 1903, in William Le Queux's novel *The Invasion of 1910*, and in Saki's *When William Came*, which was published in 1913.

Already in 1902 in his poem 'The Islanders', which attacked the complacency that had led to the long string of British disasters in the Boer War, Kipling had queried whether the English would ever realise the dangers of the world in which they lived until it was too late:

> Do ye wait for the spattered shrapnel
> 'ere ye learn how a gun is laid?
> For the low, red glare to southward
> when the raided coast towns burn?
> (Light ye shall have on that lesson,
> but little time to learn)

But for the majority of the English the possibility of a major European conflict breaking out in which they themselves would be involved seemed remote.

All the greater, then, was the shock of August 1914, and all the more inevitable was it that, once the conflict had started, the English response to battle should have been articulated by civilians in uniform. Julian Grenfell, a professional army officer, was very much an exception to this general rule. The other poets of the war were young men who carried with them into the conflict all the innocence of a civilisation that, far more than most, had little knowledge or experience of the realities of mass slaughter.

In view of all this it was only natural that the English public should long ago have decided that, of all the poets of the early years of the war, it should be Rupert Brooke who should be the recipient of their most intense admiration. For who could articulate the sentiments of 1914 more convincingly than this golden youth, this darling of Cambridge and London society, this idealist who wrote the celebrated war sonnets and then died on the way to the Dardanelles?

The acclaim has never been universal, of course. During the war itself there were complaints from fellow poets like Charles Sorley and Isaac Rosenberg, who disliked the posturing and the attitudinising that they detected in Brooke's work. And, as the years have passed and more evidence has come to light, the myth of the 'chevalier sans peur et sans reproche' largely created by Winston Churchill, Edward Marsh and Henry James has effectively been demolished.

This seems in no way to have affected Brooke's enduring appeal, however. The reasons for this continuing indulgence must remain speculative, but, in his contacts with the English during the war, Barrès noticed that puritanism and a love of gardens and the countryside were two of the outstanding characteristics of an English civilisation that was so heavily industrialised, and there can be no doubt that both elements were present in Brooke's work. It is possible that English readers have always been aware of the deep uncertainty and vulnerability that lay behind Brooke's façade of self-assurance. Certainly they have never failed to respond to the love of England that is manifest in his work, a love affair in which he was always sincere, a passion which provides perhaps the only unifying element in a personality that was otherwise characterised by an extraordinary elusiveness.

The contradictions that were to mark his career were stamped on him early in his life. He was born in 1887, the son of a house-master at Rugby School. His father seems to have been an ineffectual personality, and Brooke probably had his father in mind when he spoke in a paper delivered to a society at Cambridge many years later of a schoolmaster whom he called George Rump, who considered that his main duty was 'to turn a blind eye to sodomy and to prepare the lads for confirmation'.[1] Brooke's mother was a much more formidable personality, a Scottish puritan, Liberal in politics, towards whom his attitude was one of mingled respect and terror. Brooke's later career can largely be seen in terms of rebellion against and acceptance of his mother's values. The fact that he was physically so handsome, with a beauty that appealed to both sexes, only enhanced the problem of identity that he had to face in later years.

At Rugby his position must have been not without difficulties, given the close proximity of his parents, but he managed to distance himself from them sufficiently to win the confidence of his contemporaries, whilst excelling as a scholar and as an athlete. In 1906 he went up to King's College Cambridge with a scholarship in classics. At school he had written a quantity of poetry that was heavily influenced by the Pre-Raphaelites and the Decadents, and a letter that he wrote at the age of seventeen reveals an aestheticism that seems like a more playful, more 'English', version of that of the young Ernest Psichari:

I am writing a book. There will only be one copy. It will be inscribed in
crimson ink on green paper. It will consist of fifteen small poems, each as
beautiful, as perfect, and as meaningless, as a rose-petal or a dewdrop. When
the book is prepared I shall read it once a day for seven days; then I shall
burn the book – and die.[2]

The theatrical manner was never to desert him, but at Cambridge he
was to discover a whole variety of different ideas and life-styles that
were to leave him deeply perplexed for the rest of his life.

In terms of worldly success it might seem that he coped with life
superbly well. He soon made his mark at the university, joining the
burgeoning Fabian Group and becoming president of the Fabian
Society in 1910, playing a prominent role in university dramatic
circles, appearing as the Herald in a production of the Eumenides,
and taking a leading part in the formation of the Marlowe Society. He
also secured election to the Apostles, the self-selecting intellectual
élite of the university, where he came into contact with men like
Maynard Keynes and Lytton Strachey.

His academic work suffered somewhat from these activities, but,
after a disappointing result in his Tripos examination, he switched
from classics to English. He also moved out of college to Grantchester
where he worked hard and completed a dissertation on the work of
the dramatist John Webster, a dissertation that at the second attempt
secured him a fellowship at King's in 1913. Already in 1911 he had
published his first volume of poetry, and in 1912 he was prominently
featured in the first volume of *Georgian Poetry* edited by his friend
and fellow-Apostle Edward Marsh. After a world tour to North
America and the Pacific he returned to England a few weeks before
the outbreak of the war. By now, his poetry, his beauty and his
contacts had made him famous. Marsh introduced him to a whole
galaxy of talent, both political and literary: Churchill, Asquith,
Henry James, Barrie, Granville Barker, Shaw, Yeats, Chesterton, Paul
Nash, W.H. Davies and Siegfried Sassoon. Already before the
outbreak of the war and his subsequent apotheosis Brooke had
secured quite a number of the world's glittering prizes.

And yet there was another side to the picture. He once confessed to
Geoffrey Keynes that 'even more than yourself I attempt to be all
things to all men; rather "cultured" among the cultured, faintly
athletic among athletes, a little blasphemous amongst blasphemers,

slightly insincere to myself'.[3] The fact is that, while Brooke fitted
with apparent ease into so many groups and societies, he did not feel
completely at home in any of them.

His interest in the Fabian Society, for example, was undoubtedly
sincere. He applauded their good intentions, and in the summer
vacation of 1910 he expended considerable energy in touring the
west country in a caravan. proclaiming his support for Beatrice
Webb's Minority Report for the Royal Commission on the Poor Law,
in which she had attacked the old system for the humiliation that it
inflicted on the poor. On the other hand, the dullness and the
philistinism that were to characterise so many of the activities of the
Fabians were features of their work to which Brooke could not
instinctively respond. In a letter of December 1907 he wrote:

> Socialism is making great advances at Oxford and Cambridge just now, but
> its upholders are too apt to make it seem to others and to themselves a selfish
> scheme of economics. They confound the means with the end; and think that
> a Compulsory Living Wage is the end, instead of a good beginning. Bernard
> Shaw came down last term and made a speech that was enthusiastically
> received, in which he advised a state of things in which each 'class' had its
> own party in Parliament fighting for its own hand. The whole thing was
> based on selfishness. It was not inspiring.[4]

Beatrice Webb, with her customary acerbity, soon came to the
conclusion that Brooke was unsatisfactory material. Commenting on
the behaviour of some of the Cambridge contingent at the 1910
Fabian school at Llanbedr, she wrote:

> 'They won't come, unless they know who they are going to meet' sums up
> Rupert Brooke . . . They don't want to learn, they don't think they have
> anything to learn . . . The egotism of the young university man is colossal.[5]

But with many of the Apostles, too, Brooke's relations were to be
far from harmonious. He was excited to join them (and tended from
now on to discard Fabian friends like Hugh Dalton who were not
elected to this most select of societies), but, like all such groups, their
understanding of people outside their inner circle was far narrower
than they imagined. Their intensity could also be alarming. Maynard
Keynes wrote to Duncan Grant on 19 January 1909:

On Sunday at breakfast Sheppard delivered an indictment on poor Rupert for admiring Mr. Wells and thinking truth beauty, and beauty truth. Norton and Lytton took up the attack and even James and Gerald (who was there) stabbed him in the back. Lytton, enraged at Rupert's defences, thoroughly lost his temper and delivered a violent personal attack.[6]

Above all, there was the problem of the homosexual influence within the Apostles. This was a factor that had certainly facilitated Brooke's early election to the group, but in this respect, too, he did not properly fit in – he appears to have had homosexual experience at Rugby and on at least one occasion afterwards, but his fundamental disposition was heterosexual.

Even in his relationship with women, however, Brooke's experience was not happy. As Paul Delany has shown, the neo-Pagan group of young people, over which Brooke was the presiding spirit, may have revolted against the stuffiness of some of the older generation of Fabians, but they themselves were often deeply inhibited in sexual matters. Whilst repudiating the industrialisation, the materialism and the puritanism of English society, whilst subscribing in theory to the appeals of gurus like Edward Carpenter, Wells, Orage and Eric Gill, for sexual liberation and indulging themselves in mild versions of naturism and nude bathing, they remained basically innocent in the realm of love and sex. Brooke, in particular, behaved like an adolescent in these matters until his death.

To attempt a detailed investigation of this aspect of his career would be beyond the scope of this present study, but the basic facts are now well known. After falling in love with Ka Cox in the course of 1911 he suffered a serious nervous breakdown after the notorious incident at Lulworth during the Christmas vacation of that year when he suspected (wrongly, it seems) that Lytton Strachey was manipulating affairs to involve Ka with the painter Henry Lamb, thus leaving Brooke free for overtures from the homosexual fraternity. Taking pity on Brooke after his breakdown, Ka Cox met up with him in Germany, where for a period in 1912 they lived together. As a result of this affair Ka gave birth to a still-born child, but, to her great distress, Brooke's ardour had long since cooled.

Although his behaviour was by any reckoning deplorable, the whole incident scarred both of them deeply: on a number of occasions he talked wildly of suicide and many of his friends were convinced that he never made a total recovery. Although the main purpose of his trip round the world in 1913–14 was to put the affair behind him, and despite the fact that he found sexual fulfilment in the uncomplicated society of the South Seas in the company of Taata Mata, an affectionate Tahitian girl who obviously lacked the inhibitions and neuroses of the West and who inspired his love poem 'Tiare Tahiti', henceforth his attitude towards women was guarded. He professed an interest in the actress Cathleen Nesbitt, but behaved towards her in a patronising way – 'child' was one of the most common forms of endearment that he used in his letters to her – and objected to her desire to carry on with her career after they became unofficially engaged.

His love poetry might at first give the appearance of wide experience and worldly sophistication, but basically Brooke was far more brittle than appearances might suggest. Throughout his correspondence after his breakdown in the early months of 1912 there are many passages which suggest that behind the charm there was a latent hysteria. It is, perhaps, typical of him that, feeling lonely at Liverpool as he set off on his tour round the world, he devised a piece of theatre:

Everybody else seemed to have people to see them off. So I went back on shore and found a dirty little boy, who was unoccupied, and said his name was William 'Will you wave to me if I give you sixpence, William?' I said. 'Why, yes', said William. So I gave him sixpence, and went back on board. And when the time came he leaned over his railing on the landing-stage, and waved. And now and then he shouted indistinct messages in a shrill voice. And as we slid away, the last object I looked at was a small dot waving a white handkerchief, or nearly white, faithfully. So I got my sixpenn'orth and my farewell – Dear William.[7]

The incident is both trivial and revealing.

In view of the turmoil of his private life it may seem surprising that he should have been able to accomplish as much as he did in the years before 1914. But his self-centredness was a source of strength as well as of weakness. Repudiating the Bloomsbury circle because of the role that he believed they had played in the Lulworth affair, he now transferred his loyalties to Edward Marsh, who, as well as providing him with the emotional support and admiration that he needed without the sexual complications that were inevitable in any relationship with the Stracheys, was already embarked on his remarkable career as patron of the arts and confidant of men of power.

At the same time, despite all his troubles in the spring of 1912, Brooke was still able to insulate himself from them sufficiently to produce what is, perhaps, his most famous poem, 'The Old Vicarage, Grantchester'. This won him a prize from the *Poetry Review* for the best poem published in 1912, and the committee which made this award by a 'decided majority' represented a fair cross-section of the English literary scene at the time, including as it did Henry Newbolt, Ernest Rhys, Edward Thomas, Edward Marsh, T.E. Hulme and Harold Monro. Later on in 1912 it was with this poem and 'Dining-Room Tea' that he made his appearance in the first volume of *Georgian Poetry*. Brooke himself played a leading role in encouraging Marsh to embark on this anthology, and was indefatigable in his endeavours to promote it, suggesting favourable reviewers, spreading the word that something remarkable was afoot, contacting booksellers so that ample supplies would be available. All these labours bore impressive fruit on the day of publication when the Prime Minister's car was seen outside Bumpus's shop in Oxford Street waiting for it to open.

For many years after the First World War the various Georgian anthologies that were published after 1912 were decried by the literary avant-garde, but, as C.K. Stead demonstrated some years ago, Marsh's aim in publishing these volumes had been to demonstrate that English poetry had something new and fresh to offer other than imitations of the fin-de-siècle and the strident Imperial verse produced by Newbolt and Kipling.[8] The third and fourth volumes of the series may have betrayed a marked decline in Marsh's ability to discern new trends in poetry – and both the Sitwells and the supporters of T.S. Eliot were to be prominent in the attack that was made on the bucolic commonplaces produced by the poets surrounding J.C. Squire that appeared in the volumes in the 1920s – but the failure of nerve that took place in the aftermath of the First World War could not be foreseen in 1912, and certainly at the beginning the enterprise performed a valuable service in purifying the language of the tribe.

It could be argued, in fact, that without the pioneering work of the Georgians before 1914 the subsequent achievement of the 'war poets' would have been impossible. The 'little England' sympathies of the Georgians may have left them open to the charge of insularity, but it was this element, together with the importance they attached to the depiction of the details of everyday life, that enabled poets like Sassoon and Owen to express the bitter disillusionments of the war with verse that was both direct and poignant. In France, by contrast, the inheritance of Symbolism and the Symbolist belief in the alchemy of language made it difficult for many poets to respond to the war, while an irrepressible Modernist like Apollinaire tended to glory in the emotional intensities that derived from battle. Romain Rolland was one of those who constantly lamented the excessively urbanised character of French literature, its lack of contact with the world of nature. Whatever the defects of Georgian poetry in the eyes of the sophisticated, its pastoral emphasis enabled the war poet to contrast the devastation of war with the beauty and continuity of the natural world to powerful effect. The same possibilities did not exist in France. There was plenty of 'war poetry' in France, but it was patriotic verse: the tradition of Béranger and Déroulède was important; the influence of the hypnotic rhetoric of Hugo and Péguy was potent; and the baroque exuberance of a Claudel could not be restrained by artificial conventions. But it did not take long before such verse began to appear hollow and unconvincing, and the characteristic form of anti-war protest in France lay in variations on – and mutations of – the naturalistic novel, whether it was Barbusse's *Le Feu*, which was published in 1916, *Les Croix de bois* by Roland Dorgelès, which came out in 1919, or Céline's hallucinatory *Voyage au bout de la nuit*, which appeared much later in 1932. In England this function was performed by poetry. It was a function that would have been almost unthinkable before 1912.

If the importance of 'Georgian Poetry' in the history of modern English literature is secure – and, with the decline of Modernism in England in the years since the Second World War, it has become increasingly clear that it is the Georgians, together with Thomas Hardy, Edward Thomas and D.H. Lawrence, who represented the mainstream of the English tradition – so, too, is the value of the role played by Brooke. Quite apart from his skills as a literary entrepre-

neur, his own poetry is marked by a freedom and a lack of reverence
that made a significant contribution to the task of aerating the
atmosphere of the English literary world in the years before 1914. It
may well be the case that he only really excelled in 'light' verse, but
Brooke was that very English phenomenon, the professional disguised as an amateur, the attention that he paid to the example of
Donne was far from wasted, and the skill and poise that he
demonstrated in the later poems of his first volume of verse in 1911
were exhibited to even greater effect in 'The Old Vicarage,
Grantchester', an extended exercise in *fausse naïveté*, a quality that
Brooke wanted to emphasise by his first choice of title, 'The
Sentimental Exile'.

The poem is also important in that it demonstrates to the full that
passionate love of England that was to characterise so much Georgian
poetry, a love that was to form the central theme of Brooke's later
work. Indeed, as Timothy Rogers has pointed out, one of the many
debts that Brooke owed to the example of Donne is a gift for dramatic
distancing, and it may be no accident that, just as the latter's songs
and sonnets were written on his visit to the continent, so nearly all
Brooke's most notable poems were written when he was outside
England or contemplating the prospect of exile from England.[9]

Highly intelligent, and responsive as he was towards develop-
ments in art and music on the continent – the Blaue Reiter painters in
Munich, the Post-Impressionists in France, the operas of Richard
Strauss, the brilliance of Diaghilev's Ballets Russes – European
literature apart from Ibsen meant comparatively little to Brooke,
which was perhaps a further factor that alienated him from the
Francophiles of Bloomsbury like Lytton Strachey. Away from
England he soon suffered from intense feelings of homesickness. The
Grantchester poem, for example, celebrates England from the
vantage point of the Café des Westens, the stronghold of the
Expressionists, in Berlin in May 1912:

> Here am I, sweating, sick and hot,
> And there the shadowed waters fresh
> Lean up to embrace the naked flesh.
> *Temperamentvoll* German Jews
> Drink beer around; and there the dews
> Are soft beneath a morn of gold.

Here tulips bloom as they are told;
Unkempt about those hedges blows
An English unofficial rose;
And there the unregulated sun
Slopes down to rest when day is done,
And wakes a vague unpunctual star,
A slippered Hesper; and there are
Meads towards Haslingfield and Coton
Where *das Betreten*'s not *verboten*.

While there is no mistaking the vividness of recall, the nostalgia for a
Platonic vision of England and for more temperate climes, in 'The
Great Lover' that was written in Tahiti:

These I have loved:
White plates and cups, clean-gleaming,
Ringed with blue lines; and feathery, faery dust;
Wet roofs, beneath the lamp lights; the strong crust of friendly bread; and
many tasting food;
Rainbows; and the blue bitter smoke of wood;
And radiant raindrops couching in cool flowers;
And flowers themselves, that sway through sunny hours,
Dreaming of moths that drink them under the moon;
Then, the cool kindliness of sheets, that soon
Smooth away trouble . . .

'The Great Lover' was written in the early months of 1914. Later
on in the year there was even greater cause to celebrate an idealised
England when the long years of her peace were shattered by the
onset of the First World War.

Despite his concentration on the practicalities of a career, and despite
the multiple distractions of his private life, Brooke had not entirely
ignored the danger of a major European conflict in the years before
1914. His friendship with Marsh, who was private secretary to
Churchill at the Admiralty, meant that he was well informed on the
realities of British naval policy and the threat from Germany, and in
his letters he made clear his support for Churchill's endeavours to
build up British naval power to match this threat. The possibility of a
war breaking out between Austria and Russia over the Balkans is
another theme in his correspondence, and in March 1913 he spoke of

the possibility of becoming a war correspondent in the Second Balkan War.

Like the vast majority of his contemporaries Brooke does not seem to have seriously entertained the possibility of British involvement in a major European conflict, however, and his initial reaction to the outbreak of the First World War was one of shocked disbelief. On 1 August 1914, three days before the British declaration of war, he wrote to his French friend Jacques Raverat:

Everything's just the wrong way round. I want Germany to smash Russia to fragments, and then France to break Germany. Instead of which I'm afraid Germany will badly smash France, and then be wiped out by Russia. France and England are the only countries that ought to have any power. Prussia is a devil. And Russia means the end of Europe and any decency.[10]

His Liberal and Fabian inheritance meant that his first response to the war was to regard it as a conflict between competing imperialisms, and in the early days of August he had a violent quarrel with Raverat, who was understandably concerned by the German threat to France.

Even after Britain had actually entered the war Brooke's reaction was not entirely untroubled, as is shown by his article 'An Unusual Young Man' that was published in *The New Statesman* soon after the start of the conflict. In the essay, the 'unusual young man' – who is obviously a transparent disguise for Brooke himself – seems at first lukewarm in his attitude: 'Well, if Armageddon's *on*, I suppose one should be there.'[11] The Germans themselves did not provoke Brooke's hostility at this point: in the article he recalls the visits that he had paid to Germany before the war, reminisces about the pleasures that he had experienced in Munich and Berlin, and speaks of 'that air of comfortable kindness which Germany had always signified for him.' A little later in the article Brooke's mood abruptly changes, however. It is a change of mood with which the reader will by now be familiar:

But as he thought 'England and Germany', the word 'England' seemed to flash like a line of foam. With a sudden tightening of his heart, he realised that there might be a raid on the English coast. He didn't imagine any possibility of it *succeeding*, but only of enemies and warfare on English soil. The idea sickened him. He was immensely surprised to perceive that the actual earth of England held for him a quality which he found in A–, and in a friend's honour, and scarcely anywhere else, a quality which, if he'd been sentimental enough to use the word, he'd have called 'holiness'.[12]

Having resolved his doubts in this manner, Brooke now applied himself with his customary energy to securing a suitable occupation in time of war. Unsuccessful in his efforts to become a war-correspondent, he now pulled strings to secure a commission – much to the disgust of some of his Fabian friends like Ben Keeling, who remained in the ranks until he was killed. Given the contacts that he already possessed the task was not too difficult, and he soon found himself as an officer in the highly select band of men who were recruited by Churchill into the Royal Naval Division, a force which the latter regarded as his own private army.

In October 1914 Churchill ordered the division to go to Antwerp in a vain attempt to prevent the port falling into the hands of the Germans. As matters turned out they were sent in too late, and, in the chaos of the final hours of the German onslaught, many of the marines were left behind, either to make their way to neutral Holland – like the future novelist Charles Morgan – where they were to be interned, or to be picked up by the enemy and sent to prisoner-of-war camps. Although the Antwerp expedition can be defended on the grounds that it delayed the enemy advance and helped to save the Channel ports falling to the Germans, the whole operation was severely criticised in the House of Commons, where, inevitably, it was added to the catalogue of blunders for which Churchill was held to be responsible by the band of enemies who were eventually to secure his downfall following the débâcle of Gallipoli.

For Brooke, however, the brief experience of the Antwerp affair was decisive. The terror of a town under bombardment, the misery of the refugees, the rumours of atrocities committed by the German army after the fall of the city, transformed him from the hesitant patriot of August into the self-righteous Germanophobe that makes its appearance in his correspondence (if not, to be fair, in his poetry) later on in the year. On 5 November he rebuffed Edward J. Dent, the eminent Cambridge musicologist, when the latter asked him to help someone who was suffering from tuberculosis to move to the warm dry climate of Los Angeles. In his reply Brooke cited the case of a girl he knew, whose doctor had said she would not survive the winter, but who had decided to stay in England to help the war-effort.[13]

At the same time his letters were full of his anxiety that the English literary fraternity should be seen to be supporting the war in the same way as their counterparts in France. In one letter he noted that 'Péguy, the poet is killed. Also various other poets. I am envious of our good name.'[14] He returned to the subject in another letter to Jacques Raverat on 21 December: 'And why isn't Gide at the front? And is Péguy a good poet?'[15] On 10 November he explained to Cathleen Nesbitt that the main ambition of his life, 'the aim and end of it now, the thing God wants of me, is to get good at beating Germans. That's sure.'[16] The war had provided him with a clear purpose. The conflicts and torments of earlier years had been forgotten, and it was in a mood of newly-born serenity that he set to work on his war sonnets in the closing months of 1914. Like Péguy and Psichari Brooke celebrates the war as the opportunity for self-purification. The world of Ka Cox and the Stracheys is left far behind:

> Now, God be thanked Who has matched us with His hour,
>   And caught our youth, and wakened us from sleeping,
> With hand made sure, clear eye, and sharpened power,
>   To turn, as swimmers into cleanness leaping,
> Glad from a world grown old and cold and weary,
>   Leave the sick hearts that honour could not move,
> And half-men, and their dirty songs and dreary,
>   And all the little emptiness of love!

The Platonic idea of Englishness in which he had sought refuge in the era before the war was now something to be embodied and defended, something which even Death could not annihilate:

> If I should die, think only this of me:
>   That there's some corner of a foreign field
> That is for ever England. There shall be
>   In that rich earth a richer dust concealed;
> A dust which England bore, shaped, made aware,
>   Gave, once, her flowers to love, her ways to roam,
> A body of England's, breathing English air,
>   Washed by the rivers, blest by suns of home.

The sentiments that he expressed in these poems are, obviously, the common currency of the period before the full horror of the conflict was made clear. And whatever may be thought of them in retrospect, his reactions to the war, especially after the Antwerp affair, are entirely understandable in the context of the widespread revulsion in England against German behaviour in Belgium and the upwelling of English national sentiment that accompanied these developments. What distinguishes Brooke from his contemporaries, however, is the extremism of his response. Mercurial as always, he swung violently away from the irony and self-mockery that had characterised so much of his earlier poetry – the semi-serious nature of 'The Old Vicarage, Grantchester' and the satire on religion in 'Heaven', for example – to a portentous and self-regarding patriotism.

The whole thing was done with great skill, of course, and his sincerity cannot be placed in doubt, but it is not surprising that a number of those who had known him well in earlier years found the transformation distressing. It was only to be expected that Blooms-bury should be deeply offended by the way in which he celebrated the fact that the war had liberated him from 'the sick hearts that honour could not move', the 'half-men and their dirty songs and dreary'. But others, too, found his new position distasteful. Later on in the war Isaac Rosenberg was to express his disapproval of Brooke's 'begloried sonnets',[17] while Charles Sorley, who enlisted in 1914 and was to be killed in the battle of Loos in the following year, was repelled by the narcissism that underlay Brooke's attitudes:

[Brooke] is far too obsessed with his own sacrifice, regarding the going to war of himself (and others) as a highly intense, remarkable and sacrificial exploit, whereas it is merely the conduct demanded of him (and others) by the turn of circumstances, where non-compliance with the demand would have made life intolerable . . . He has clothed his attitude in fine words, but he has taken the sentimental attitude.[18]

Had he survived, he could not have persisted in the same vein. His own younger brother Alfred, who enlisted in the Post Office Rifles, and was killed only two months after Brooke's death, told his mother not to believe the sentiments that Rupert had expressed in his poetry and that war was horrible. And it is fascinating to speculate what his own response to the war might have been in later years.

It seems safe to assume that his love of England would still have featured prominently, but already in the 1914 sonnets and in the

fragmentary 'ode-threnody on England' that he worked on in the last
months before his death he was making clear that disdain for the
civilians, that identification of the real England with the soldiers,
that was to be carried much further in the course of the war by poets
like Wilfred Owen. There were also signs from his last drafts that he
was moving towards a concern for others as well as for himself. This
is particularly the case with 'I strayed about the deck, an hour,
tonight', a fragment that admirably illustrates his extraordinary
virtuosity, a virtuosity that led Pound to declare later that Brooke
had been 'the best of all that Georgian group'. This uncompleted
poem was written on board ship shortly before his death:

> I would have thought of them
> – Heedless, within a week of battle – in pity,
> Pride in their strength and in the weight and firmness
> And link'd beauty of bodies, and pity that
> This gay machine of splendour'ld soon be broken,
> Thought little of, pashed, scattered . . .
>
> Only, always,
> I could but see them – against the lamplight – pass
> Like coloured shadows, thinner than filmy glass,
> Slight bubbles, fainter than the wave's faint light,
> That broke to phosphorus out in the night,
> Perishing things and strange ghosts – soon to die
> To other ghosts – this one, or that, or I.

In yet another fragment the later satirical mode of Sassoon and Owen
is anticipated:

> 'When Nobby tried', the stokers say
> 'To stop a shrapnel with his belly
> He   away
> He left a lump of bleeding jelly.'
> But *he* went out, did Nobby Clark
> Upon the illimitable dark,
> Out of the fields where soldiers stray,
> Beyond parades, beyond reveille.

If he had lived, then, there is sufficient evidence to suggest that
Brooke had the potential to be a quite different war poet from the one

we know now. But in the last analysis such conjectures are only of very limited value. Some commentators have wondered whether he might have abandoned poetry for a political career, a career that might have seen him ending up as Prime Minister, but if he possessed the ruthlessness and determination essential for a career in high politics, it is doubtful whether he was endowed with the nervous and physical stamina necessary for political success. 'One can smell death in Rupert', wrote D.H. Lawrence, with his usual disturbing insight, to Lady Cynthia Asquith in 1918,[19] and it is possible to imagine a Brooke who, surviving the holocaust that was to overtake so many of his comrades at Gallipoli, would have been doomed to linger on as one of the 'broken men', once of great promise, who were to be so familiar on the English scene in the years that followed the First World War.

Fate decreed otherwise, however. He died of blood-poisoning on 23 April 1915, and the war sonnets, to which Dean Inge had drawn attention in a sermon preached at St Paul's only a few days before Brooke's death, now secured his passage to immortality. Like T.E. Lawrence he had contributed to his own myth with an unerring instinct for self-promotion, and his death, on the way to liberate Constantinople from the Turks, had a profound symbolic significance for an England that was still dominated by the public school ethos and a reverence for the classics. 'Figure me celebrating the First Holy Mass in St. Sophia since 1453', he had written to his friend Dudley Ward as he set out for the Mediterranean.[20] To a public that was to be sickened by the reality of Gallipoli and Flanders this was the stuff of High Romance.

The circumstances of the First World War help to explain the mushrooming of his reputation in 1915. They do not explain why, three-quarters of a century after his death, the myth still endures. Perhaps its potency is due to his charm, a quality that is apparent in so many of his letters, despite their egocentricity. Perhaps it is due to his miseries and uncertainties, the revelation of which seems to have enhanced and not diminished his reputation, for the English will forgive sins of the flesh provided that the sin is accompanied by suffering.

But perhaps it is due, above all, to his continuing ability to tap deep wells of nostalgia within the English psyche, a nostalgia for the unspoiled, innocent (and, despite the slums, the strikes, the Irish problem, the decline of British agriculture, still not entirely fictitious) land that existed before 1914. Perhaps Brooke's lasting reputation is due to the fact that he articulates that secret regret that haunts the English, a regret for an England where the clock yet stands at ten to three, where the war has not yet broken out, and where the horrors of the twentieth century have not yet made themselves manifest.

— 5 —

H.G. Wells, Bernard Shaw: prophecy and heartbreak

'Ours is an essentially tragic age . . . The cataclysm has happened, we are among the ruins'.[1] It is possible that the opening words of D.H. Lawrence's *Lady Chatterley's Lover*, which was first published in 1928, provide the most succinct explanation why both H.G. Wells and Bernard Shaw lost ground in the years that followed the First World War. Both of them remained phenomenally productive in the years after 1918 and both, indeed, were to enjoy major successes in the 1920s, with works like Wells's *The Outline of History* and Shaw's *St Joan*, but their reputations never really recovered from the effects of the war.

It is easy to see why this should have been the case. While neither of them can be accused of a facile optimism or of being unaware of the tragic nature of the conflict, their work in the years after the war continued to proclaim the possibility of and the necessity for progress, if necessary, in the teeth of disaster. To the men who survived the trenches, however, their solutions to the problems of the world no longer carried the same conviction. To the post-war generation both Wells and Shaw had been rendered irrelevant by a catastrophe that had exposed the hollowness of their message, a catastrophe, moreover, that neither of them had foreseen.

In some way it is surprising that H.G. Wells should have been unprepared for the catastrophe, for his was an imagination that lent itself easily to the chiliastic. Despite the popularity of Wells's work in France, Jules Verne once pointed out the radical differences between his own achievement and that of his English counterpart:

I do not see the possibility of comparison between his work and mine . . . his stories do not repose on very scientific bases . . . I make use of physics. He invents.

123

Whereas Verne reflects the optimism of the middle years of the nineteenth century, the pessimism of Wells was fed by both his mother's brand of Calvinistic religion and by the gloom of men like T.H. Huxley about some of the implications of the theory of evolution. The results of all this can be clearly seen in many of the novels which he produced before 1914 in which mankind is faced with the possibility of disaster. In *The Time Machine* in 1895, for example, he explored some of the consequences that might flow from the running-down of the universe. The next year, in *The Island of Dr Moreau*, Wells imagined the terrible results of a misapplied science, which had led to the creation of beasts made half-human by the application of surgery.

From 1898 onwards he was also increasingly excited by the idea of war. In *The War of the Worlds* of that year England is invaded by Martians who are eventually destroyed by the earth's bacteria. *In the Days of the Comet* (1906) has a scenario that is very similar in a number of respects to the crisis that developed in the Europe of 1914, with the difference that in the novel the opposing armies are brought to a halt by the arrival of a wandering comet whose trail of gas induces mankind to return to the ways of peace. A more pessimistic vision dominates *The War in the Air* (1908), in which the Germans attack New York city from the air, leaving the survivors to exist at subsistence level. But of all Wells's excursions into the future before the outbreak of the war perhaps it is *The World Set Free*, which appeared in serial form between December 1913 and May 1914, which is the most striking. In this novel he describes a conflict between the free nations and the central powers taking place in 1958 and 1959, in which mankind eventually repudiates warfare after atomic bombs dropped from the air have caused terrible devastation in most of the major cities of the world.

To the unsuspecting reader, then, it might appear from all this as if Wells was already so resigned to the idea of a major cataclysm that the outbreak of the First World War came as no great shock to him. But this was far from being the case. As he himself admitted many years later:

I will confess I was taken by surprise by the Great War. Yet I saw long ahead how it would happen, and wove fantastic stories about it. I let my imagination play about it, but at the bottom of my heart I could not feel it would really be let happen.[2]

In saying this Wells, like Jaurès in France, was reflecting the essential optimism and innocence of western Europe before 1914, an optimism and innocence that was particularly characteristic of Edwardian England. After the deep pessimism of many of his scientific romances of the 1890s, a pessimism which accorded well in certain respects with the mood of the fin-de-siècle, Wells had moved on in the early years of the new century to more positive and more affirmative themes. Whilst in no way abandoning his apocalypticism and his intuitions of long-term disaster in novels like *The War in the Air* and *The World Set Free*, his bubbling energy and sheer high spirits could not be repressed indefinitely, and, with increasing popularity and success as a further incentive, a far more hopeful outlook characterised much of his other work after 1900.

These were the years of *Anticipations* (1902) and *A Modern Utopia* (1905), in which he called for old conventions and taboos to be swept away, an era in which he championed the cause of sexual emancipation and called for the creation of a new kind of Samurai, an élite of scientists and engineers who would work to free mankind from hunger and poverty and devote themselves to the creation of the World State. For a time he was hopeful that the Fabian Society might be the instrument for the transformation of existing society, a society whose shapelessness, drift and profligate waste he depicted so vividly in *Tono-Bungay* (1909). And even after Shaw and the old guard of the Fabians, alarmed by his exuberance, defeated his attempt to energise and expand the Society his hopes for the future remained undiminished. At the end of *Tono-Bungay* there is a striking evocation of the boundless possibilities that still seemed open to mankind in the years before 1914, when George Ponderevo, free at last from his uncle's megalomania, finds himself in a destroyer sailing down the Thames out to the open sea:

Light after light goes down. England and the Kingdom, Britain and the Empire, the old prides and the old devotions glide abeam, astern, sink down upon the horizon, pass – pass. The river passes – London passes. England passes.[3]

There is a sense of liberation and of exhilaration in this passage. There is also a sense of doom and of menace, but perhaps this is an ambivalence that affects the modern reader more than it did Wells and his contemporaries. For, despite his astonishing intuitions concerning the future, there was throughout his work in the years before 1914 an almost complete divorce between the world of his speculative imagination and his sense of everyday reality. This can be seen in the contrast between his visions of catastrophe and utopia on the one hand and the universe inhabited by his petit-bourgeois heroes – the naïf Kipps, the resigned Mr Lewisham and the oppressed Mr Polly (until Polly's escape from his marriage and his shop, the 'Beastly, Silly Weeze of a hole') – on the other. It can also be seen in the paradox that while Wells spent a great deal of time thinking – often with great foresight – about a future conflict, he was still shocked when this conflict became a reality in 1914.

Quite apart from his prophecies of future wars in his novels, Wells did, in fact, devote considerable attention to the nature of modern warfare in his other writings in the years before 1914. Already in the short story 'The Land Ironclads', published in 1903, he had predicted the use of armoured tanks:

They were essentially long, narrow, and very strong steel frameworks carrying the engines, and borne upon eight pairs of big pedrail wheels, each about ten feet in diameter, each a driving wheel and set upon long axles free to swivel round a common axis. This gave them the maximum of adaptability to the contours of the ground. They crawled level along the ground with one foot high upon a hillock and another deep in a depression, and they would hold themselves erect and steady sideways upon even a steep hillside.[4]

Wells imagined that the bulk of the tank's fire-power would come from riflemen operating from port-holes, but his basic idea is convincing, and the theme of 'The Land Ironclads' – that victory would be won by the side that was prepared to utilise to the full the resources of science and technology – was one to which he returned on a number of occasions in the years before the outbreak of the First World War. In *Anticipations*, where his vision of the future was influenced by the work of the Polish Jewish banker I.S. Bloch (who predicted that the next war would be a war of trenches, that ten million men would be involved in it and that it would last a minimum of two years),[5] Wells further developed the idea that mankind was moving towards a new kind of 'total war' in which scientific expertise and economic power would be more important than individual acts of heroism.

Inevitably some of his prophecies were not borne out by events. On the war at sea he predicted that the era of battleships was over, but dismissed the idea that there was a major role for the submarine. On land he foresaw the obsolescence of cavalry and anticipated the development of trench warfare, but his claim that the chaos of the battlefield would be reduced by the use of balloons and artillery was not to be the experience of 1914–18, and he did not foresee either the duration of the coming conflict or the scale of the slaughter in the murderous mass offensives of the war:

It will be evident that such warfare as this inevitable precision of gun and rifle forces upon humanity will become less and less dramatic as a whole, more and more as a whole a monstrous thrust and pressure of people against people. No dramatic little general spouting his troops into the proper hysterics for charging, no prancing merely brave officers, no reckless gallantry or invincible stubbornness of men will suffice . . . In the place of hundreds and thousands of more or less drunken and untrained young men marching into battle – muddle-headed, sentimental, dangerous and futile hobbledehoys – there will be thousands of sober men braced up to their highest possibilities, intensely doing their best; in the place of charging battalions, shattering impacts of squadrons and wide harvest fields of death, there will be hundreds of little rifle battles fought up to the hilt . . .[6]

Clearly he expected a far more professional and a far more scientifically proficient war than the bloody shambles that actually occurred. He also seriously underestimated the role of the machine gun in perpetuating the static warfare of the trenches. And yet, on the whole, Wells the civilian, like Jaurès the civilian, saw some of the features of the coming conflict more clearly than a majority of the military specialists, with the exception of the enigmatic Kitchener.

But whether Wells, having foreseen all this, really believed that such a war would break out in the future is another matter. I.S. Bloch himself was a pacifist who thought that the conflict he prophesied so vividly was unlikely to occur because of the disastrous political and economic consequences it would bring. And, despite the fact that elements in the British press were excited from time to time by the possibility of war with Germany in the years before 1914, Wells himself seems to have remained undisturbed. In 1913 he published a series of articles in Northcliffe's *Daily Mail* (which had played an important part in fanning the fear of a German invasion) in which he put forward his personal views on the danger of war. The striking feature about these articles is that, while recapitulating many of the views on the nature of a future war that he had already expressed in *Anticipations*, he considered conflict with Germany to be unlikely:

For a decade or more all Western Europe has been threatened by German truculence; The German, inflamed by the victories of 1870 and 1871, has poured out his energy in preparation for war by sea and land, and it has been the difficult task of France and England to keep the peace with him. The German has been the provocator and leader of all modern armaments. But that is not going on. It is already more than half over. If we can avert war with Germany for twenty years, we shall never have to fight Germany. In twenty years' time we shall be talking no more of sending troops to fight side by side on the frontier of France; we shall be talking of sending troops to fight side by side with French and Germans on the frontier of Poland.

And the justification of that policy is a perfectly plain one. The German has filled up his country, his birth-rate falls, and the very vigour of his military and naval preparations, by raising the cost of living, hurries it down. His birth-rate falls as ours and the Frenchman's falls, because he is nearing the maximum of his population. It is an inevitable consequence of his geographical conditions. But eastward of him, from his eastern boundaries to the Pacific, is a country already too populous to conquer, but with possibilities of further expansion that are gigantic. The Slav will be free to increase and multiply for another hundred years. Eastward and southward bristle the Slavs, and behind the Slavs are the colonial possibilities of Asia.[7]

Why Germany should be converted to the cause of peace because its birth-rate was falling, why the Germans should be content to sit and watch the inevitable growth of Russian power in the East without attempting to nip the process in the bud – these are questions that Wells neither raised nor attempted to answer.

Right down until the German demand for unrestricted right of passage through Belgium, two days before Britain's declaration of war on Germany on 4 August 1914, in fact, Wells found it impossible to believe that the two countries would be involved in a major conflict with each other. Throughout the first half of 1914 he was far more concerned with the possibility of a civil war resulting from the Irish problem than from any hostilities in Europe, and although Anthony West in his biography of his father notes the fact that Wells told R.D. Blumenfeld, the editor of the *Daily Express*, that there would be a big war as a result of the assassination of the Archduke Franz Ferdinand at Sarajevo,[8] he still did not yet believe that this was a war in which Britain herself would necessarily be involved. In *Mr Britling Sees it Through*, a novel that Wells produced during the war but one that accurately records his own changing responses to the crisis of 1914, Mr Britling comforts himself with the thought that, since the second Moroccan Crisis had not led to general war, neither would a crisis in Serbia.

They may fight in the Balkans still; in many ways the Balkan states are in the very rear of civilization, but to imagine decent countries like this or Germany going back to bloodshed! No . . .[9]

All the greater was Wells's sense of excitement and of shock, therefore, when the crisis of 1914 escalated into a general European war.

His first response to the crisis was that he must devote himself to some kind of practical service. As he explained in a letter to *The Times* on 8 August, nobody 'wants to be a non-combatant in a war of this sort', and in accordance with this he advocated a system of volunteering for men over the age of military service so that they could form a defence corps while the younger men went overseas. Amidst the frantic activity and dislocation of 1914 the British government was intent on far more important concerns than the frustrations of middle-aged men, however, and Wells had to be content with his continuing role as a publicist.

In this capacity, of course, his gifts were far more effectively employed than they would have been in some kind of Home Guard. In September 1914 he was one of the group of authors (a group that included Bennett, Bridges, Hardy, Barrie, Chesterton, Belloc, Galsworthy and Masefield) who attended the first meeting of the War Propaganda Bureau set up under the aegis of the Cabinet Minister Charles Masterman. And already in a series of newspaper articles

published in August 1914, he had helped to coin the phrase
describing the present conflict as 'the war that will end war':

We cannot simply put the Germans back over the Belgian border and tell
them not to do it again . . . There can be no diplomatic settlement that will
leave German Imperialism free to explain away its failure to its people and
start new preparations. We have to go on until we are absolutely done for, or
until the Germans as a people know that they are beaten, and are convinced
that they have had enough of war.[10]

At this stage he was insistent that, while the British might be
fighting Germany, they were not fighting with any hatred of the
German people and did not intend to destroy their freedom or unity.
The war was being fought ultimately for peace and disarmament.
Admittedly, there was the Russian danger, but Wells was hopeful
that by forcing Russia to modernise her society, the war would help
to civilise the backward region of the East. In any case he was
convinced that within three months the Tricolour would be flying
over the Rhine:

The German is not naturally a good soldier; he is orderly and obedient, but
he is not nimble or quick-witted; since his sole considerable military
achievement, his not very lengthy march to Paris in 1870 and '71, the
conditions of modern warfare have been almost completely revolutionised
and in a direction that subordinates the masses of unintelligent men to the
rapid initiative of individualised soldiers. And, on the other hand, since
those years of disaster, the Frenchman has learnt the lesson of humility; he is
prepared more sombrely for a sombre struggle; his is the gravity that
precedes astonishing victories.[11]

This, of course, was wishful thinking, for, although Wells was
correct in thinking that the strength of the modern defensive
strategy and 'the stinging power of an intelligent enemy in retreat'[12]
(which was to be demonstrated superbly by the French at the Marne)
would prevent the Germans from taking Paris, his overall view that
there would be a speedy conclusion to the war was not to be borne
out by subsequent events. Increasingly frustrated by the failure of
the war to come to an end, therefore, and appalled and infuriated by
the news now reaching England of German atrocities in Belgium –
atrocities which were greatly magnified in the public imagination
and uncritically accepted by the committee of inquiry led by Lord

Bryce, but were based on the realities of German military ruthlessness – Wells's attitude now became increasingly bellicose. By the
autumn of 1914 his views on Germany were verging on the
hysterical. He now demanded that unlimited annexations should be
made of German territory at the end of the war, and that Berlin
should be looted. Inflamed by the notorious manifesto of ninety-
three German intellectuals who defended the German invasion of
Belgium and denied the truth of any atrocities, he now claimed that
German literature was without merit, and that anything that was any
good in it had been written by Jews.[13]

At the same time he rounded on the doubters and pacifists at home.
When his old colleague and rival, Bernard Shaw, expressed his
reservations about the competence of British foreign policy before
1914 in his *Commonsense About the War* and satirised the hypocrisy
of Britain's concern for 'gallant little Belgium', Wells counter-
attacked with that mixture of exasperation and vitriol that only an
old acquaintance can deploy:

> It is almost as if there was nothing happening in Flanders. It is almost as if
> there was no pain in the world . . . All through the war we shall have this
> Shavian accompaniment going on like an idiot child screaming in a hospital,
> discrediting, confusing. He is at present . . . an almost unendurable
> nuisance.[14]

Against this background, and against the background of Wells's
brilliantly malicious attack on the aestheticism of Henry James in
Boon, that was to be published the next year, it is not surprising that
literary circles hostile to the war such as Bloomsbury, which had
already come to the conclusion that Wells was in the process of
abandoning literature for propaganda, now broke their bridges with
him.

In the course of 1915, however, Wells regained something of his
balance. The more he reflected on things, the more he became
convinced that the Germans were not alone in promoting Nationalism and Imperialism. Racialism could be found in the work of the
Frenchman Gobineau and the English historian J.R. Green. And if the
war must end with the removal of the Hohenzollerns, it should also
put an end to the monarchy in England. It was no good for the
English to imagine that they could carry on in the same old lazy and

anti-intellectual way. What England needed was a more progressive version of the mental and spiritual discipline that prevailed in Germany. This preoccupation is clear in Wells's account of the conversation of the dying novelist in *Boon*, the novel that reveals so many of Wells's inner conflicts, the mixture of aggression and self-doubt in his approach to literature, his awareness that his view of the world owed more to the strength of his own will than to the disciplines of science, the battle that now raged within him between his instinctive bellicosity and his increasing sense of the stupidity of war:

'While this great strong wickedness has developed in Germany what thought have we had in our English-speaking community? What does our world of letters amount to? Clowns and dons and prigs, cults of the precious and cults of style, a few squeaking author-journalists and such time-serving scoundrels as I, with my Bathwick filter, my twenty editions, and my thousands a year. None of us with any sense of a whole community or a common purpose! Where is our strength to go against that strength of the heavy German mind? Where is the Mind of the Race?'
He looked at me with tired eyes.
'It has been a joke with us' he said . . .
He sat up in his bed; his eyes were bright and he had little red spots in his cheeks.
'At least the Germans stand for something. It may be brutal, stupid, intolerable, but there it is – a definite intention, a scheme of living, an order, Germanic Kultur. But what the devil do *we* stand for?'[15]

And the same theme appears in his major novel of the war, the semi-autobiographical *Mr Britling Sees it Through*, which was written in the second half of 1915 and published in 1916.

Mr Britling is, of course, a thinly disguised self-portrait. Mr Britling's house in Essex, his family, his marital problems, are all those of Wells himself. So, too, are the changing attitudes of Mr Britling towards the First World War. At the opening of the book he is far more concerned by the Irish crisis than by events in the Balkans, but then the war breaks out and he reacts with great excitement, producing a pamphlet entitled *And Now War Ends*. He is appalled by German atrocities in Belgium, and goes through a period of violent Germanophobia, but then comes to a realisation that the war is not simply a struggle between different states but the product of a more deep-seated crisis within European civilisation as a whole.

Personal tragedy reinforces this conviction when he is faced by the death in battle of his son, Hugh, and then hears the news that his children's former German tutor Heinrich (a character based on Karl Büttow, who had fulfilled the same function for the Wells family) has also been killed in the war. Overwhelmed by the waste and madness of the conflict, Mr Britling attempts to sketch out the draft of a highly emotional letter to Heinrich's parents in Germany:

Let us make ourselves watchers and guardians of the order of the world . . . If only for love of our dead . . . Let us pledge ourselves to service. Let us set ourselves with all our minds and all our hearts to the perfecting and working out of the methods of democracy and the ending for ever of the Kings and emperors and priestcrafts and the bands of adventurers, traders and owners and forestallers who have betrayed mankind into this morass of waste and blood – in which our sons are lost – in which we flounder still.[16]

The death of their sons, he concludes, can only be given meaning if everyone begins to work for a new political order under the aegis of God, the Master, the Captain of Mankind.

Published in 1916, a year that was marked by numerous setbacks to the Allied cause, *Mr Britling Sees it Through* was widely welcomed as a token of the spiritual rededication that was necessary if victory was to be won. Inevitably there was a great deal of speculation amongst clergymen and others that Wells, the arch-sceptic and anti-clerical, might be returning to the Christian fold, but it soon became clear that, whilst he was attracted by religious terminology, all his talk of 'God, the Invisible King' in 1916 and 1917 was little more than a somewhat portentous relabelling of the force that he had earlier described as the collective Mind of the Race. Still, Wells could not but welcome the attention the book received – unlikely though it may seem in retrospect, Gide and his friends read it aloud to each other in France – and an even more flattering form of tribute to his literary powers was the multitude of letters of condolence that he received from readers who imagined (wrongly) that the depth of Mr Britling's grief for a son killed in the war would only have been written by an author who had suffered a similar loss himself.

On one of the key points in *Mr Britling Sees it Through* he was to be disappointed, however. The end of the war was not imminent, as he indicated in the novel and as he was to proclaim on further occasions in 1916 and 1917. Instead, it was to drag on for over another two years. Wells himself faced this possibility in *What is Coming*, a collection of newspaper articles that he published early in 1916, in which he admitted that I.S. Bloch's prophecies had been even more impressive than he had realised, that the Germans had not smashed themselves to pieces in the course of their initial offensive in the west as he had anticipated in 1914, and that it was now possible that the war of attrition might last until 1918 or 1919.[17] But he still believed that it was the Central Powers who would be the first to crack, and it was to the task of encompassing their downfall that he continued to devote his best energies. Politically he advocated that the Hohenzollern system must be undermined by propaganda portraying the conflict as a war to liberate Germany from Prussian rule, as a stage towards the creation of a League of All Nations, and the eventual World State. On the military front he bombarded the War Office with suggestions for the adaptation of his Land Ironclads so that the stalemate of the trenches could be broken. Another of his ideas to hasten the end of the war – a proposal for a system of conveyor belts to transport equipment to the trenches – got as far as a successful working model before it finally succumbed to bureaucratic inertia.[18]

And yet, if Wells's resourcefulness and fertility of imagination, his fizz and his sparkle, constantly amaze the student of his career, on the central issue of the war by 1916, the suffering of the men at the Front, he had relatively little to say – an omission that was to do incalculable damage to his reputation in the course of the conflict. In August 1916 he paid an official visit to sections of the French and Italian Front, but on any reckoning the reports that he brought back were meagre and inadequate:

If I were to be tied down to one word for my impression of this war, I should say that this war is Queer. It is not like anything in a really waking world, but like something in a dream . . . It is a gigantic, dusty, muddy, weedy, bloodstained silliness . . .[19]

During his time at the front, he explained, he had had many glimpses of death and had seen many wounded, but he had not felt any sense of real horror:

That side of the war has, I think, been overwritten. The thing that haunts me most is the impression of a prevalent relapse into extreme untidiness, of a universal discomfort, of fields and ruined houses treated disregardfully . . . The real horror of modern war, when all is said and done, is the boredom.[20]

In fairness it must be said that his lack of awareness of the appalling slaughter that was taking place on the Somme during his visit was due to the fact that his tour had taken place under official auspices, and that, even if he had known anything about the realities of the situation, he would not have made too much of the horror for fear of undermining British morale. In further justice to Wells it should also be pointed out that during his tour of the British sector he was accompanied by someone who inspired trust, C.E. Montague, the former theatre critic of the *Manchester Guardian*, who had dyed his hair and falsified his age in order to enlist, and Montague, who, ironically enough, in 1922 was to publish *Disenchantment*, one of the most impressive indictments of the role played by the war correspondents in suppressing the truth about the trenches, seems at the time to have followed the official line of supplying visiting dignitaries with only highly selective accounts of what was really happening in the combat zone. Even so, Wells did not simply minimise the horror of the Front in the summer of 1916, but went on repeating these impressions for some months to come, thus indicating that a real insensitivity lay at the root of his approach to this matter.

One explanation for this failure of imagination has been advanced by Jean-Pierre Vernier, who has argued that Wells was never fundamentally interested in the fact of individual human misery.[21] Certainly there is a quality that is both antiseptic and ultimately chilling in the claim that the latter made in his *War and the Future*, published after his trip to the Front, that 'the war is nothing more than a gigantic and heroic effort in sanitary engineering; an effort to remove German militarism from the life and regions it has invaded'.[22] And in *Joan and Peter*, which he published in 1918, when his eyes had been opened to the true cost of the war, it was the waste and incompetence of the military effort that appalled him as much as the suffering of the soldiers. On the other hand, Wells had shown himself to be capable of eloquent personal grief in *Mr Britling Sees it Through*, and perhaps the truth is that, for someone who was possessed by such a powerful mythopoeic imagination, reality was always an inferior substitute for his own visions and nightmares.

Whatever the reasons for the content of Wells's reports from the front, however, there is no doubt that from now on his ability to communicate with the younger generation on their own terms was severely impaired. In *Goodbye to All That* Robert Graves paints a satirical picture of Wells pontificating about the war to himself and Siegfried Sassoon in the warmth and comfort of the Reform Club,[23] while Wilfred Owen recorded Sassoon's annoyance that Wells was far more interested in pumping information out of Dr Rivers (one of the specialists in the Craiglockhart military hospital near Edinburgh where both Owen and Sassoon had spent periods of convalescence from shell-shock) to secure confirmation of his theories on God, the Invisible King, than in enquiring about Sassoon's own experiences at the Front.[24]

But if Wells's preference for fantasy over reality was to cost him dear in the long run, he was for the moment far too wrapped up in his dreams for the future to pay much attention. More and more he was looking beyond the war to the kind of peace that must be established at the end of the conflict. In 1917 he intensified his campaign for a League of Free Nations, and for a few weeks in 1918 he held a government post under Lord Northcliffe, devising propaganda to convince the Central Powers of the necessity for peace and world reconstruction. Admittedly, this was an intensely disillusioning experience in which he came to realise that British policy was not primarily concerned with a future League of Nations but with the necessity for crushing the Central Powers and securing the future of the British Empire. But for a time he was hopeful that the idealism of President Wilson might prevail against the old-style imperialism and *realpolitik* of England and France. All the greater, then, was his sense of outrage and shock when the terms of the Treaty of Versailles were promulgated in the summer of 1919, a shock, he was later to admit, that was equal to that which he had experienced in 1914.

What, then, could one do in this situation? In September 1920 he visited the Soviet Union and was genuinely impressed by the efforts of the Bolsheviks to overcome the devastation that had been caused by the war, the Revolution and the civil war. But he had never been sympathetic towards the Marxist emphasis on the primacy of the class struggle, and, when he urged on Lenin the necessity of creating a managerial élite recruited from all sections of Russian society, the latter was not impressed – 'Ugh! What a narrow petit bourgeois! Ugh! What a Philistine!' was Lenin's verdict.[25] Having failed to win the Bolsheviks to his cause, and disenchanted as he was by the short-sightedness of the Western powers and the fraudulent nature of the

League of Nations that had emerged from the Peace Settlement, Wells was left for the next twenty years as a lone crusader for the World State.

It would be beyond the scope of this present study to go into the details of the many campaigns to realise his dream in which he was involved in the course of the next twenty years: his valiant attempts to produce a twentieth-century version of the educational achievements of the French encyclopaedists in *The Outline of History* (1921), *The Science of Life* (1929) and *The Work, Wealth and Happiness of Mankind* (1932), the support that he gave for a time in 1919 and 1920 to Barbusse's Clarté movement, which attempted to unite the intellectuals of the world behind the cause of rationalism and Socialism (a movement which eventually collapsed because of Barbusse's increasing involvement with Communism), his efforts in *The Open Conspiracy* (1928) to involve the leading men of business and science throughout the world in the creation of the World State, and the work that led to the setting up in 1940 of the Sankey committee which was instrumental in drawing up a Declaration of Human Rights. What all his activities demonstrated, however, was the insularity and irascibility of Wells as a World Citizen, his tendency to become involved in frequent (and sometimes hilarious) quarrels with his collaborators, and the fact that all the hopes that he invested in his campaigns were eventually doomed to disappointment. Instead of greater understanding between the nations of the world there was an intensification of nationalism. Instead of universal co-operation to conquer famine, disease and poverty, there was the rise of totalitarian systems that were intent on plunging the world into chaos and war.

Meanwhile Wells's reputation went into a sharp decline. The world of serious literature had written him off many years ago, while to many of his former admirers his arguments seemed to be increasingly repetitive, old-fashioned and simplistic. Writing in *The New Republic* in 1934 Malcolm Cowley was still respectful, likening Wells to 'a survivor of a prehistoric time, a warm, ponderous, innocent creature, ill adapted to the Ice Age in which we live, and yet overshadowing the smaller animals that shiver behind the rock, without ever venturing into the open'.[26] But Orwell, in his 'Wells, Hitler and the World State' published in 1941, was far more cruel.

He opened his essay by quoting newspaper articles written by

Wells in the early months of 1940 which repudiated the notion that
Hitler was about to deliver a knock-out blow in the spring, claiming
that Hitler's resources were 'ebbing and dispersed' and maintaining
that German air power had been 'largely spent'. After pointing out
that events had demonstrated that each of these assertions was false,
Orwell then moved on to consider Wells's solutions to the problems
of mankind:

What is the use of saying that we need federal world control of the air? The
whole question is how we are to get it. What is the use of pointing out that a
World State is desirable? What matters is that not one of the five great
military powers would think of submitting to such as they. All sensible men
for decades past have been substantially in agreement with what Mr. Wells
says; but the sensible men have no power and, in many cases, no disposition
to sacrifice themselves.[27]

Because of his commonsense, his nineteenth-century attitudes and
his essentially civilian and hedonistic world view, Wells was totally
unfitted to understand the world of dictators.

In some ways this was an unfair attack. In his Englishness, in the
pugnacity of his style, in his choice of petit-bourgeois heroes like
George Bowling in *Coming Up for Air*, in his conception of the role of
the writer as social commentator, Orwell himself owed an immeasur-
able debt to Wells's example, and, despite his criticisms, he was
forced to admit that between 1900 and 1920 Wells had been a major
liberating force in English life. In his reply to Orwell – 'the Trotskyist
with big feet', as he called him privately – Wells was perfectly
justified in complaining that the former had overlooked his basic
pessimism, the fear that he had expressed throughout his career that
the triumph of science and reason was neither inevitable nor
conclusive, a fear that he had expressed in his scientific romances of
the 1890s, in *Mr Blettsworthy on Rampole Island* in 1928, and again as
recently as 1939 in *The Fate of Homo Sapiens*, where he had depicted
the world relapsing into barbarism and war. And, in further justice
to Wells, it must be pointed out that he was fully aware that he was
now a back number. In *The Bulpington of Blup*, published in 1932, for
example, whilst revealing only too clearly his sense of jealousy at
Ford Madox Ford's reputation as a war veteran and as a guru of the

younger members of the literary avant-garde, he had included himself, together with Shaw, Kipling and others, in Bulpington's (Ford's) attack on the old reputations who after the war stood up like great empty hulls that had served their purpose:

They had said what they had to say; they were finished . . . They were pre-war. They ought to have gone onto the bonfires of Armistice Day . . .[28]

Much can be forgiven to a man capable of such self-mockery.

Nevertheless, once all these qualifications have been made, there can be little doubt that Orwell had put his finger on the essential escapism that, despite all his visions of catastrophe, lay at the heart of Wells's achievement. The latter's abilities as a fantasist had not always been a source of weakness. If they tended to foster the carelessness of his writing in his later years, if they went with an increasing disregard for evidence that did not fit in with his preconceived theories, so that he could dismiss 'Great Men' (and evil 'Great Men' like Hitler) as being of little importance in the onward march of mankind, they had also helped to fuel the imaginative universe of his scientific romances of the 1890s – *The Time Machine*, *The Island of Dr Moreau* and *The War of the Worlds*, which are now widely regarded as the summit of his literary achievement – and, allied with his memories of his impoverished youth, they had inspired those indelible portraits of frustrated idealism that are the strength of *Love and Mr Lewisham, Kipps* and *The History of Mr Polly*. The temptations that lay in wait for Wells, however, were those of taking imaginative short-cuts and searching for quick solutions to the problems of the world, and it was to these temptations that he eventually succumbed. In the quarrel that took place between Wells and Henry James in the closing years of the latter's life, the basic issue, despite what the participants said, was not really the question of art versus journalism, but whether Wells really had the patience to exploit his considerable abilities as an artist to realise as successfully as possible the kind of novels that he wanted to write. Unfortunately it became clear in the long run that Wells was increasingly unwilling to submit himself to the constant test of art and of reality.

This impatience, this inability simply to endure the miseries of the human condition as they are *now*, can be illustrated by many examples taken from every phase of Wells's life (both public and private), but, inevitably, it was in the years after 1918 that this element became most apparent in his work. Of his later novels only *Mr Blettsworthy on Rampole Island* is really successful, partly, no doubt, because he had a definite aim in mind, to come to terms at last with the savagery and horror of the First World War. As for the rest of his achievement, apart from his *Experiment in Autobiography* (1934) when he was able to recreate brilliantly the years of his youth, the marks of impatience and a kind of intellectual somnambulism are only too obvious. *The Outline of History* is an amazing tour de force, one which it may seem churlish for academic historians to criticise, but, quite apart from its manifold inaccuracies and preposterous generalisations, it is vitiated by an anti-historical and propagandist obsession with the necessity for the World State. In *The Shape of Things to Come* (1933) Wells describes in graphic and prophetic detail a terrible war breaking out as a result of a dispute between Germany and Poland over Danzig, a war that leaves the world in ruins. But the force of the novel is considerably diminished by the transformation scene which operates at the end of the conflict in which the airmen who have reduced the world to chaos now league together to impose the World State on mankind. Even at the time of the later and intensely pessimistic *Mind at the End of its Tether* Wells seems to have baulked at the idea of finishing his career on a note of unrelieved gloom. As his son G.P. Wells has shown, not only was that optimistic account of his dreams, *The Happy Turning*, written at the same time as *Mind at the End of its Tether*, the latter book itself is a conflation of two different texts with two very different messages.[29] In the first part Wells confesses that his lifelong hope that science might be able to halt mankind's urge towards mass suicide had now been exposed as an illusion. In the latter portion he holds out the possibility that a small élite might be able to salvage something from the wreck, even though this élite will cease to be human in the formerly accepted meaning of the term.

Towards the end of his life, however, Wells's messianic impulses seem finally to have been stilled. In August 1945, a year before his death and eight months after he produced the last draft of *Mind at the End of its Tether*, the atomic bombs were dropped on Hiroshima and Nagasaki. Faced with this situation Wells issued a public statement claiming that it had been obvious to the clear-sighted for half a century that the human situation was grave and tragic, but he now urged Man to face his culminating destiny with dignity, mutual aid and charity, without hysteria, meanness and idiotic misrepresentation.[30]

More than thirty years earlier Wells had expressed the hope that after the devastation caused by the atomic bomb mankind would come to its senses and revolt against war. But *The World Set Free* had been published in 1914, before two world wars had demonstrated that the world was far too complicated and far too recalcitrant for any Wellsian solution to its problems. Instead, mankind would continue to muddle through in its own way, towards either survival or self-destruction.

It is not difficult to see the reasons why the decline in the reputation of Shaw was less spectacular than that of Wells in the years that followed the First World War. The latter was completely immersed in his ideas and, although his enthusiasms might change, his commitment to them was total. In the case of the former, the reader is immediately aware that, behind any statement that Shaw might make about his current position, there was always a mocking, disinterested and disabused intelligence, the poise of an experienced controversialist, completely prepared for any opposition that he might encounter.

Shaw's determination to address the world behind the protection of a mask may have been the result of an early sense of desperation, a result of his strange and disturbing childhood spent with an alcoholic father and an unmaternal mother who was fascinated by the charlatan singing-teacher Vandeleur Lee. His determination to hide his emotions may have been further strengthened by the many struggles that he was forced to endure before he was accepted as a writer and personality of note. Once established, however, the persona of 'G.B.S.', the licensed jester of the British public, the never-failing provider of witty and memorable copy for journalists, allied to Shaw's very considerable abilities as a dramatist, seemed to render him immune to the adversities that afflict the rest of mankind.

In reality, of course, Shaw himself was a far more sensitive and far more vulnerable personality than his public image might suggest. This can obviously be detected in his private life, about which so much has been written, but it can also be seen in his reactions to the First World War, an event that he had not anticipated, a tragedy with which he was never able fully to come to terms, a catastrophe that destroyed his world just as surely as it did that of Wells.

With the outbreak of the First World War, in fact, Shaw himself was forced to recognise that he and his fellow-Fabians had been blind to the real dangers that faced the world in the epoch before 1914. In the years after the Boer War (a war, incidentally, that he had supported on the grounds that the British Empire was potentially an engine for greater efficiency than the outmoded patriarchal society of the Afrikaners) the Fabians, he confessed, had concentrated far too much on internal British affairs and had seriously underestimated the possibility of a major European conflict.

This did not mean that he had entirely overlooked the danger of a major European war in an age of rival imperialisms, and on several occasions before 1914 he had tried to avert the possibility of conflict. His most important initiative was an attempt in 1913 to follow the lead of foreign progressives like Count Harry Kessler in Germany, who openly called for the policy that Jaurès and the Socialists favoured, a non-aggression pact between London, Paris and Berlin that could avert a war between the three most highly-developed societies of Europe – England, France and Germany.[31] Shaw supported this line on the grounds that the alliance system in Europe was nonsensical in moral terms and that the Balkan quarrels of a Habsburg Empire in decline and reactionary Tsarist Russia were of no concern to civilised Europe.

As matters turned out, Shaw could not find any convincing support for these proposals in England, since he coupled them with a statement that Britain should welcome Germany's naval expansion and recognise that it did not necessarily represent any threat to her, and perhaps this illustrates the basic weakness of his approach to the problem of peace and war. For, like Jaurès and Wells, he could not really believe that mankind would be so foolish as to embark on a major conflict. Praising Wells's *The World Set Free* when it appeared early in 1914, Shaw commented that the right line to take about war was to treat it neither as calamity nor as glory, but simply as 'an unbearable piece of damned nonsense'.[32]

Unfortunately the fear and suspicion that poisoned the atmosphere of international relations could hardly be conjured away by arguments like this, and, despite the easy intercourse that existed between nations before 1914, illustrated by the fact that the premières of *Pygmalion* in Berlin and Vienna took place before that in London in 1914, all Shaw's efforts to prevent war came to naught. After all his troubles with Mrs Patrick Campbell and Beerbohm Tree, and the latter's attempt to give a romantic ending to the saga of Professor Higgins and Eliza Doolittle in the London production of the play, he was now confronted with an even greater disaster, a war between England and Germany in which England and France were allied with that power universally detested by European Socialists, Tsarist Russia, ostensibly to defend the semi-barbarous Serbs and the holy grail of Belgian neutrality.

It was essential that the cause of this débâcle should be understood. Soon after the outbreak of the war, Shaw retired to the Hydro Hotel at Torquay, therefore, taking with him all the government publications that came to hand. There he produced his provocatively entitled pamphlet *Commonsense about the War*, which was first published as an eighty-page supplement to the *New Statesman* on 14 November 1914.[33]

It was the way in which British public opinion seized on the German violation of Belgian neutrality as a pretext for coming into the war that particularly infuriated him. It must be remembered that Britain had no formal alliance with either France or Russia in 1914. The Ententes were, at least officially, only understandings, and not alliances. Unofficially, of course, the Anglo-French Entente had matured to the extent that military conversations and undertakings about naval dispositions had already been entered into before 1914. But the extent of these commitments was not known by the country at large, and the majority of the Cabinet itself was not informed about them (and then not in every detail) until 1912. For an agonising period on 3 August 1914, following the German declaration of war on Russia and France, the French ambassador in London, Paul Cambon, waited anxiously to see whether Britain would come into the conflict on France's side. It was only the German invasion of Belgium that provided the British government with an immediately convincing and morally elevated reason for involving the nation in the war, and, predictably, it was against this mixture of moralism, sentimentality and self-interest, so dear to the Anglo-Saxon character, that Shaw, the Irishman, concentrated his polemic.

In his *Commonsense about the War*, then, it is the complacency and indecisiveness, as well as the hypocrisy, of British foreign policy that Shaw attacks. In the years before 1914, he argued, Asquith and Grey (for whom he had little regard after the latter had refused to order an investigation into the hanging of four Egyptian fellaheen who had protested at British officers shooting their pigeons at Denshawi in 1909)[34] had pursued a policy of drift, envying the Germans for their growing industrial power and their increasing naval strength, but hoping that the balance of power might maintain itself in Europe and that Britain might never have to honour the secret obligations that she had entered into with the French. Meanwhile, the permanent officials of the Foreign Office had so manoeuvred affairs that Germany would have to take the initiative if she wanted to break out of the encirclement policies of the Ententes. Had the non-aggression pact between England, France and Germany that Shaw had advocated before the war been achieved, there would have been no war in the West. Had England openly allied herself with France and made it clear that she, too, would immediately enter a European war in the event of hostilities, Germany might have hesitated. But England had done nothing, so making the war inevitable.

Once the war between the major continental powers had broken out, however, the Germans played into the hands of the British government by violating the neutrality of Belgium in accordance with the necessities of the Schlieffen plan. Had the British been seriously concerned over the plight of the Belgian people, Shaw maintains, they would have urged the Belgian government to grant right of passage to the German army under protest whilst encouraging the Belgians to appeal to the public opinion of the world, particularly that of the United States, to sustain their protest. But the British were only interested in providing themselves with a moral justification for a war that was in reality a war between competing imperialisms. Accordingly the British encouraged the Belgians to resist and themselves declared war on Germany.

These indeed were unpopular truths, or perhaps half-truths, to present to British public opinion in 1914. Shaw can, of course, be criticised for some of the details of his attack on British policy: the Schlieffen plan assumed, and then discounted, the effect of a British entry into the war; the Belgians decided to resist invasion quite independently of British pressure; and, after Arnold Bennett protested at Shaw's implication that Britain deliberately enticed Germany into the war, an implication that the German propaganda machine was quick to exploit, Shaw himself admitted that British policy before 1914 had been characterised more by muddle than by Machiavelli. Even so, these were unpalatable issues to raise amidst the war hysteria and hatred of everything German that were manifested in Britain and France in 1914. Predictably, Shaw brought down on himself considerable unpopularity. In France, where his plays had never been popular (in striking contrast to the situation in central Europe), and where his wit had always been regarded as cold, arrogant and mechanical, and lacking the real courage of that of Voltaire, his reaction to the war was contrasted unfavourably with the patriotic response of their own satirist, Anatole France. Shaw could have replied that the French estimate of his talents tallied exactly with his own assessment of the state of much of the French theatre, but in England, too, he was under fierce attack. He was subjected to public and private abuse; he was ostracised in polite society; and the charge that he was relentlessly chasing publicity was continually revived. Prominent personalities joined the fray: the vitriolic attack by H.G. Wells has already been noticed, while Asquith said privately that Shaw deserved to be shot.[35]

Reactions such as these are considerable tributes to Shaw's formidable powers as an irritant and gadfly. One further example of Shaw at work, a few months after the publication of *Commonsense About the War*, indicates the degree to which he was prepared to court unpopularity. Who but he would have dared to provoke the outburst of public anger that inevitably followed his open mocking at the outrage expressed in Britain at the death of nearly 1,200 'innocent victims' of the sinking of the Lusitania? Hundreds of thousands of equally innocent human beings, he pointed out, were being sent to their deaths on the Western Front and at Gallipoli, the only difference being that they were not millionaires and saloon passengers, but misled khaki.[36]

And yet, having acknowledged to the full Shaw's capacity to get under the skin of the *bien-pensants*, having paid all due respect to his hatred of the inhumanity of the conflict, to his campaign for a just and equitable peace, to his later denunciation of the Treaty of

Versailles for its injustices and hypocrisies, what else is there to say? The fact is that, once Britain – rightly or wrongly – was involved in the war, Shaw supported British endeavours whilst attempting to ennoble them. He did this partly on the typically cynical and Shavian grounds that, if the war was the result of rival imperialisms, he might as well support the British pirate fleet rather than the pirate fleet on the other side. But there were deeper motives and deeper contradictions at work here.

Perhaps it was Lenin who saw further than anyone else ever did into Shaw when he described him to Arthur Ransome as 'a good man fallen amongst Fabians'.[37] For, while Shaw's intellect was radical and revolutionary, his instincts preached realism and caution. It is possible that it is this very conflict between the two opposing sides of his nature that made him so successful as a playwright. Certainly it is a conflict that diminished and ultimately paralysed his effectiveness as a public figure. Shaw criticised the war, but in the last analysis gave it his support. Holding forth in general terms in *Commonsense About the War* he said that the heroic remedy for the soldiers of all the combatant nations to adopt would be for them to shoot their officers, to return home to gather in the harvests and then to make revolution in the towns. But while Lenin turned this sentiment into an effective, if a monumentally brutal, policy, Shaw clearly did not feel that this was realistic. In any case he made it clear later on in the course of the pamphlet that, despite all his attacks, he still believed that the British pirate fleet represented something more worthy of support than the naked force worshipped by Imperial Germany. The moral superiority of the Allied cause might very well be compromised by their alliance with Tsarist Russia, and a victory unattainable without Russian aid would undoubtedly be a defeat for the liberal forces in western Europe. But in his view that was all the more reason why England and France must strive to defeat Germany by their own efforts.

In fact as a Fabian Shaw believed that the war should be prosecuted efficiently, and as a private individual he had been in favour of some kind of military training for all in the period before 1914. During the conflict itself he made it clear that he did not agree with the position of the conscientious objectors. Perhaps the most spectacular demonstration of his ambivalent attitude towards the war came in 1917, when the collapse of Russia gave Germany an opportunity for seeking victory in the west. To Maxim Gorki Shaw wrote in 1917 that while the downfall of Tsarism was, of course, to be welcomed, the provisional government must stay in the war to ensure the defeat of the Central Powers.[38] And to his French translator, Augustin Hamon, he expressed his horror at talk of disaffection in the French armies:

Every other nation can talk peace because they have not German soldiers on their soil, but France must hear of nothing but driving them off it.[39]

It was in 1917, too, that he received and accepted one of those invitations that were extended by the British army to prominent literary men to visit the Front as an official observer. Clad in a khaki tunic and a pair of breeches Shaw duly crossed over to France, where he was accompanied round the trenches by the inevitable C.E. Montague. The sophistication of those responsible for this invitation almost induces one to revise one's opinions about the general competence of British military policy in 1917, for Shaw's response, however wayward, was fundamentally a tacit endorsement of the status quo.

Privately, of course, and as the decent human being that he was, he abhorred what was going on at the Front, an abhorrence that was enhanced when he was entertained by the British commander, Sir Douglas Haig, who gave him the impression that the war could be prosecuted for another thirty years with the same lack of concern for human lives that had characterised it in the past. Publicly, Shaw's performance – if his articles for the *Daily Chronicle* are to be taken at their face value – was one of an almost intolerable archness. Like Wells, Shaw minimised the horror of the war and made much play of the boredom that the troops experienced between bombardments. Unlike Wells, Shaw attempted to turn the whole event into comedy. The title that he gave to his articles, 'Joy-Riding at the Front', is one sign of this. A further indication is supplied by Shaw's comments to the effect that the devastation inflicted by the war on areas subjected to industrial blight was not to be universally deplored:

The tragedy of the Somme district began for me in some of the villages that have not been demolished, not in those which have. A comparison with what the Germans have done to Albert with what I would like to do to London and Manchester would make the Kaiser seem a veritable Angel of the Passover beside me.[40]

There is not much one can say as a commentary on this kind of thing, except to suggest that Shaw's relentless cheerfulness was not due primarily to his desire to get his material past the censor, but to his realisation that by accepting the army's invitation he had landed himself in a false position; it is no accident that when he was invited to inspect the Italian Front later on in the same year he turned the invitation down. No doubt he was indulging himself, too, in his favourite sport of saying the opposite of what everybody else was saying, and was underlining once again his contempt for English sentimentality.

Once all these factors have been taken into account, however, it is still difficult to acquit Shaw of an extraordinary frivolity in his reportage from the Front. Throughout his career he was open to the charge that he was out to secure the best of all possible worlds, whether Socialist or capitalist, that he ran with the hare but also hunted with the hounds. And it is undeniable, too, that throughout his life he rearranged reality to suit his convenience, diverting attention from his contradictions by paradoxes and clowning. But on this occasion at least, silence in the face of human misery would have been preferable to Shavian comedy, and, like H.G. Wells, he was to pay dearly for this kind of monumental insensitivity in later years.

Still, if 'G.B.S.' was at times a heartless and cruel monster, Shaw himself was no monster. His seeming callousness, his fear of expressing elemental feelings of grief and sorrow, emotions that he undoubtedly felt, were far too deeply rooted in the experience of his early years for him to change course now. His élitism and contempt for the opinions of the majority of mankind were also legacies from his youth, for, like Yeats, he was a product of the rigid caste system that characterised the Anglo-Irish Protestant Ascendancy. Shaw's remoteness was enhanced by his personal puritanism, his authoritarianism by his belief that only the Superman could save society from the ruin that awaited it. And yet in spite of all this, in spite of all his posturings, his emotional inhibitions, his sophistries, he was possessed of an enormous, if largely concealed, generosity of spirit. This can be seen in *Commonsense About the War*, where he proclaimed that by far the greatest calamity wrought by the war had been the death of Jaurès, to whom he paid tribute as a man 'worth more to France and to Europe than ten army corps and a hundred archdukes'.[41] The same spirit was at work in his dealings with H.G. Wells, who had attacked him so bitterly in 1914 but whose more moderate tone by 1916 enabled him to effect a reconciliation in which he praised *Mr Britling Sees it Through* as 'a very fine book'.[42] Above all, it can be seen in his pain and distress at the cruelty and waste of the war, distress that led him to write the bitter farce *Heartbreak House*, which he began in March 1916 and finished in May 1917, a play that was disregarded by the public when it was first performed in 1921 but is now regarded by many critics as Shaw's most impressive achievement in the theatre.

It is not difficult, of course, to see why audience made relatively little of *Heartbreak House* when it was first produced. Shaw called it in the sub-title *A Fantasia in the Russian Manner on English Themes* and in the long and important Preface to the play (in which he denounced the war-hysteria of the early years of the conflict and recapitulated some of the themes of *Commonsense About the War*) he explained that it was a portrait of 'cultured, leisured Europe before the war'. But the public can perhaps be forgiven for the bewilderment they experienced at witnessing this strange mixture of tragedy, farce and Chekhovian irony. It is a play in which Shavian debates on money, marriage and morality are punctuated by the aged Captain Shotover's tirades against the folly of the educated and intelligent classes in opting out of the responsibilities of political power. Periodically the action is halted while Shotover disappears from the scene to fill himself up again with rum. He then returns to resume the argument and to predict the imminent collapse of society. At the end of the play an air-raid destroys Shotover's principal antagonist, the ruthless business magnate Boss Mangan – a character based on Lord Devonport, whom Lloyd George appointed as Food Minister at the end of 1916, a personality whom Shaw destested – who is sheltering in a gravel pit where the Captain has stored dynamite. The heroine, Ellie Dunn, one of the inmates of 'this silly house, this strangely happy house, this agonizing house', celebrates with Hesione Hushabye the activity of the zeppelins in shattering the greed and boredom of pre-war society. 'It's splendid,' says the latter, 'it's like an orchestra: it's like Beethoven.'

Coming so soon after the events that it described, *Heartbreak*

House was condemned at the time of its first performance for its lack of 'realism', its arbitrariness, its seemingly wild and disordered atmosphere. But now that the First World War has passed into history, the richly poetic and symbolic aspects of the play have a powerful impact, Now that a theatre audience has some knowledge of the cultured, leisured world of the Bloomsbury group and Ottoline Morrell, the behaviour of the denizens of *Heartbreak House* in the first part of the play before the arrival of the zeppelins no longer seems as bizarre as it must have done in 1921. And now that the tragedy of the First World War and its consequences can be fully appreciated, the madness and eccentricity of Shotover become more explicable. Against this background the surrealistic absurdities of the play no longer bewilder the spectator, while Shaw's gift for buffoonery – a gift that can on occasions be so irritating – tends only to heighten the effect of this extraordinary piece of theatre.

Heartbreak House has never been without its critics. For some observers the mixture of genres remains extremely disconcerting, while Desmond MacCarthy denied that it possessed a genuinely tragic dimension:

Mr. Shaw does not know what heartbreak is. He conceives it as a sudden disillusionment . . . as a sharp pain, but not as a maiming misery.[43]

On the other hand it can be argued that Shaw, like many Irishmen, found it difficult to regard tragedy and comedy as two separate responses to life, and that, far from being regarded as something of an oddity in Shaw's *œuvre, Heartbreak House*, unlike the flippant war reportage of *Joy-Riding at the Front*, should be seen as part of an Irish tradition that combines the tragic and the comic, a tradition that manifests itself in different ways in the work of Swift, Joyce, O'Casey and Beckett, a tradition that has immeasurably enriched English literature. The structure of Shaw's play may remain too conventional and the dialogue too prolix for it really to be regarded as a specimen of the Theatre of the Absurd. And yet its significance in illustrating the decline of the purely tragic mode as a means of coming to terms with the problems of the twentieth century is considerable.

Seen in retrospect, in fact, it becomes clear that *Heartbreak House* represented the summit of Shaw's achievement and that after this, despite the popular success of *St Joan* – the one play of his which for obvious reasons was a major success in France – there could only be decline. In *St Joan* 'G.B.S.' was very much back in charge, emptying the subject of much of its Catholic and medieval content in order to present us with a portrait of a historically progressive Protestant and Nationalist Shavian woman. In *Heartbreak House*, by contrast, we feel that the mask has slipped temporarily and that Shaw, in his anger at the war, is for once no longer in complete control. The world of the cultivated bourgeoisie in *Heartbreak House* was Shaw's own world. When that world was undermined, Shaw himself was undermined.

In the long period of life that was left to him he still attempted to take a positive and affirmative view of human affairs. At one point in *Heartbreak House* Hesione's husband, Hector, enquires of Shotover what his duty as an Englishman might be to prevent the English ship being driven on the rocks, to which the latter's reply is, 'Navigation. Learn it and live, or leave it and be damned.' But the English showed little desire to entrust their fate to Shaw's own increasingly erratic sense of navigation in the years that followed the First World War. It was easy to follow him in his denunciations of the folly of the war, the cruelties caused by the continuation of the Allied blockade of Germany after the Armistice, the indefensible nature of the Versailles Peace Treaty, the absurdity of a financial system that led to the Wall Street crash and the Great Depression of the 1930s. It was less easy to approve of some of his other responses to the situation that had been created by the political and economic failures of Western liberalism in the inter-war years: his worship of men of power and the kind words that he was prepared to lavish on Mussolini, Hitler and Stalin; his claim that the Bolsheviks had 'taken the advice' of himself and his fellow-Fabians in eschewing the idea of world revolution and concentrating on domestic realities and large-scale economic planning; the statement that he made on the notorious trip that he made to the Soviet Union with his violently anti-Communist friend Lady Astor in 1931 that Stalin could not be regarded as a tyrant because he could be dismissed by the Politburo 'in ten minutes'; his sympathy for Germany at the time of the Anschluss and the Czech Crisis;[44] his description of Hitler's attack on Poland in 1939 as a 'reconquest';[45] and, finally, his hope that Hitler might be allowed to live in retirement in Ireland at the end of the Second World War.

In *Back to Methuselah*, which he had finished in 1921, Shaw's anger at the appalling folly and tragedy of the war had led him to argue, in yet another variation on the theme of reverence for the life force and the possibility of creative evolution, that the only hope for the human race lay in extending the lifespan so that mankind could acquire greater wisdom. After reviewing some of the activities of the aged Shaw a detached observer might wonder whether there was indeed an automatic connection between sagacity and longevity and might perhaps conclude that there was a greater degree of wisdom in the Lear-like Shotover's observation that 'Old men are dangerous: it doesn't matter to them what is going to happen to the world.'

The comedy had to be played out to the end, however:

I am by nature and destiny a preacher, I am the new Ecclesiastes. But I have no Bible, no creed: the war has shot both out of my hands . . . I must have affirmations to preach. Without them the young will not listen to me; for even the young grow tired of denials . . . I am ignorant; I have lost my nerve and am intimidated; all I know is that I must find the way of life, for myself and all of us, or we shall surely perish. And meanwhile my gift has possession of me: I must preach and preach and preach no matter how late the hour and how short the day, no matter whether I have nothing to say.

Shaw vigorously repudiated the idea that these lines from Aubrey's final speech in *Too True to be Good* had autobiographical overtones, declaring that Aubrey's despair 'is not my despair' and that he had never lost his optimism: 'I affirm, on the contrary, that never during my life-time has the lot of mankind seemed so hopeful.'[46] But perhaps he protested too much. It is interesting to note that the play was written in 1932, the same year that Wells said that men like himself and Shaw should have been thrown on the bonfire on Armistice Day. And as the 1930s progressed Shaw became increasingly isolated. There would still be admiration for his wit and verve as a dramatist, for his unfailing skill and resource as a public entertainer, but, as for his 'message', that had ceased to be credible many years ago.

6

Rudyard Kipling: stoicism and empire

'I had spent some of the afternoon in looking through reports of submarine work in the Sea of Marmora. They read like the diaries of energetic weasels in an over-crowded chicken-run, and the results for each boat were tabulated something like a cricket score. There were no maiden overs.'[1] These lines from Kipling's war journalism, reprinted in *The Fringes of the Fleet* in 1915, go a long way towards explaining why he was so detested by liberal opinion in the years that followed the First World War. Progressives had long been alienated by his stridency, his jingoism and his schoolboy sadism, but the ardour of his support of British imperialism and the virulence of his hatred of Britain's opponents during the war finally convinced them that he should now be cast out into the darkness. When Kipling publicly warned of the dangers to the British Empire that emanated from a resurgent Germany in the early 1930s, therefore, his statements were largely received either with indifference or with active hostility. His warnings against Germany were regarded as being in the nature of self-fulfilling prophecies. The rise of National Socialism, it was argued, was a product of the iniquities of the Treaty of Versailles at the end of the war, and, since it was Kipling and men like him who had whipped up the hatreds that had led to the Peace Settlement, it was they who were to blame for the present state of affairs. Since the English do not take literary personalities as seriously as do the French, Kipling's critics did not push matters to the cruelty of a mock trial as the Dadaists did with Barrès. Instead, it became part of the accepted wisdom that no advice that he gave to the nation now could be of any value.

In response to all this admirers of Kipling could only point to the ironies of the situation. In the years before 1914 he had warned of the German danger, and that danger had duly materialised. Now in the

1930s he was giving the same warnings. Should the new German threat be treated seriously? The events of 1939, three years after his death, were to prove a conclusive answer.

It was at an early age that Kipling acquired that sense of menace that was never to desert him. After an idyllic early childhood in India he and his sister were sent to England to avoid the danger of their 'going native'. They ended up in the notorious 'House of Desolation' at Southsea where they were boarded with the family of a retired sea captain. The persecution that Kipling endured at the hands of the captain's wife and son is recorded in poignant and terrible detail in his short story 'Baa Baa Black Sheep', and he returned to the subject in his autobiography *Something of Myself* that he was working on at the time of his death, over sixty years later. The whole experience was something that he could never forget: when he and his wife visited Southsea much later in his life, his fame as a world figure could not prevent the misery that he had experienced between the ages of six and twelve reasserting its hold.

There has been a tendency in recent years to play down the importance of this period in his life on the grounds that some of the facts that he records in his autobiography do not seem to have been completely accurate, but it is difficult to refute the basic veracity of Kipling's own testimony, and the essential truth of Edmund Wilson's claim that these years were of cardinal importance for Kipling's future development is hard to dismiss.[2] Like Dickens in the blacking factory, Kipling at Southsea felt superior to his environment, but also felt rejected by his parents and abandoned by mankind. In both cases a highly sensitive and imaginative child – a child already half-consciously aware of the latent powers within him – was thrust into a situation in which he rapidly acquired bitter experience of the cruel and arbitrary nature of the world. The reader of Kipling is constantly aware of the many conflicting elements in his character – his exaggerated respect for the realities and practicalities of life, his extraordinary capacity for hatred, his intermittent but deep compassion for those injured and abandoned by the world, his sense of wonder, and sometimes of terror, in the face of the mysterious and irrational nature of human experience. It is clear that many of these tensions and contradictions had their origin in the hidden wounds that he had received in his early years.

The blustering, hectoring tone that Kipling was to affect so often in later life was clearly a form of psychological compensation for the deep inner securities that he had experienced in his childhood, and the stoicism that he cultivated in his dealings with the outside world can be traced back to the same source. But in his adolescence and early manhood his animal high spirits carried him successfully through the years of his stay at the cut-price, extremely minor, public school at Westward Ho! (where any bullying that occurred seems to have been gleefully magnified in *Stalky and Co*) and then out to India. It was there, at the age of seventeen in 1882, that he was reunited with his parents, and it was there that he learnt his trade as a journalist on the *Civil and Military Gazette* of Lahore and later on *The Pioneer* at Allahabad. It was while working on these newspapers that he started writing the short stories that were later collected in *Plain Tales from the Hills*. This volume, together with the poems in *Barrack Room Ballads*, were to bring him fame when they were published in England in 1890.

It is not difficult to see why Kipling's work should have had the enthusiastic reception that it did. In 1890 England was entering into a decade in which imperial expansion and the problems and ideologies of empire were to become the burning issues of the day. The fact that British power had already passed its zenith – that Britain was in the process of being overtaken and surpassed by Germany's economic expansion, and that Imperialists influenced by Social Darwinism, such as Joseph Chamberlain, were coming round to the view that in the coming era of the super-states the British Empire must federate or perish – only enhanced the urgency and immediacy of Kipling's message.

Kipling's fame was, in any case, solidly based in a real achievement. Even his most vehement critics could never deny that in literary terms he was a master craftsman, with a talent for encapsulating in a few pages the essence of the romance, the challenge, the colour – and terror – of empire. It was a talent, moreover, that was reinforced and enhanced by a systematic exploitation of the popular culture of the day – the language and rhythms of a secularised Evangelical Christianity, the vividness and bite of music-hall songs. In Kipling's hands, the ideals of imperialism were transformed and transmuted. No longer was the Empire seen simply as an affair confined to the Establishment and to exceptional heroes. Kipling's portrayal of India is focussed not on the grandees of empire, but on the toiling district officers and subalterns, and, beneath them, on the common soldiers immortalised in *Soldiers Three*. Mulvaney, Ortheris and Learoyd owe an obvious debt to Dumas, and, like many of Kipling's characters drawn from the other ranks, no longer convey the same authenticity and conviction that they seemed to possess in their heyday, but, in attempting to convey the pride and stoicism of the despised nineteenth-century British army, Kipling was a pioneer in exploring territory that had not previously been exploited in literature. In every possible way he was superbly equipped to attract a mass readership, a readership whose numbers had been swelled by the extension of public education and popular journalism that had taken place in the closing decades of the nineteenth century.

His extraordinary success did not pass by without adverse comment, however. Robert Buchanan's attack on Kipling as 'The Voice of the Hooligan' and his description of the schoolboys in *Stalky and Co* as 'hideous little men'[3] are rightly famous, while Oscar Wilde's remark that as one turned the pages of *Plain Tales from the Hills* one felt as if one 'were seated under a palm tree reading life by superb flashes of vulgarity',[4] indicates that the success of Kipling's work, like that of the early romances of H.G. Wells, owed something to the desire for shock and sensation that was characteristic of the fin-de-siècle. In this situation it is not surprising that Kipling's popularity with the sophisticated, like that of Wells, did not last for very long. By the end of the decade the London literary world felt that they had the measure of Kipling, that they had him effectively 'placed': he had enormous natural gifts, but he was squandering them in the service of right-wing causes; he had elements of the genius within him, but he was in the process of selling himself out to the authoritarianism, anti-intellectualism and philistinism that were endemic in English society. This was to be the burden of Max Beerbohm's attacks in the years before 1914. It was a charge that was to be taken up and partially rebutted by Orwell in his famous essay published during the years of the Second World War.

It is a charge to which in many ways Kipling must be adjudged guilty. 'India's full of Stalkies', he wrote at the end of 'Stalky and Co', 'Cheltenham and Haileybury and Marlborough chaps – that we don't know anything about, and the surprises will begin when there's really a big row on . . . Just imagine Stalky let loose on the South side of Europe with a sufficiency of Sikhs and a reasonable prospect of loot – consider it quietly.'[5] The strong must dominate the weak. This was a theme that recurred constantly in Kipling's career. On a visit to the United States, shortly after the Spanish American War and his exhortations to the Americans to take up the 'White Man's burden', he urged on the writer Israel Zangwill the importance of making the Filipinos work for their liberators:

Nothing is gained by coddling weak and primitive men. The law of survival applies to races as well as to species of animals. It is pure sentimental bosh to say that Africa belongs to a lot of naked blacks. It belongs to the race that can make best use of it. I am for the white man and the English race.[6]

To which the gentle Zangwill made what was perhaps the only effective reply, 'Why, Kipling, you're almost Hebraic.'

And yet there was another side to all this. One part of Kipling pandered to popular taste in England; another part responded to the sophistication of French literature and the tradition of Balzac, Maupassant and the 'conte'. The Kipling who admired Cecil Rhodes, the Kipling who wrote his famous poem 'If' in honour of, of all people, Rhodes's henchman, Dr Jameson – of the notorious 'Jameson Raid' into Boer territory to support the voting rights of the white 'Uitlanders', an action which made the Boer War virtually inevitable – was also the creator of 'Kim' and the *Jungle Books*, a writer of high intelligence with an extraordinary empathy for the primitive and the child-like. T.S. Eliot spoke of Kipling's 'queer gift of second sight, transmitting messages from elsewhere, a gift so disconcerting when we are made aware of it that henceforth we are never sure when it is *not* present'.[7] Perhaps this is why he wrote so well on India, a civilisation of infinite complexity and diversity, a culture that ranges from the most elemental to the most sophisticated, its powers of assimilation enabling it to embrace all kinds of contradictions. Both sides of Kipling – the worshipper of efficiency and the writer sensitive to the irrational – can be found in 'The Bridge Builders', one of the most subtle and profound of his Indian parables, where his respect for the British man of action – Findlayson, the engineer, who is responsible for building a bridge over the mighty Ganges – is balanced by his sense of the anger of the Indian gods. In the long run Kipling sees both British imperialism and the gods themselves doomed by the inevitable advent of the world of technology. There is no doubt, however, that Indian civilisation will survive.

Despite his role as unofficial laureate of the British Empire, in fact, Kipling could never find complete fulfilment in English values or in an English environment where he could not find either the colour and mystery of India, the finesse of France, or the energy of the United States (where his attempt to settle in the early 1890s was made impossible by a series of absurd quarrels with his brother-in-law). Constantly he complained that England was not worthy of her empire: her upper classes, symbolised by Balfour, were languid and effete; her working classes were guilty of selfishness and a reluctance to work. And constantly the spirit of his Methodist ancestors can be heard in the exhortations that he addressed to his countrymen. In 'The English Flag' they are told that they must venture abroad and discover their empire:

> Winds of the World, give answer! They are whimpering to and fro
> And what should they know of England who only England know?

Above all, in the famous lines that he wrote at the time of the Diamond Jubilee in 1897 he warned the English against complacency:

> If drunk with sight of power, we loose
> Wild tongues that have not Thee in awe,
> Such boastings as the Gentiles use
> Or lesser breeds without the law –
> Lord God of Hosts, be with us yet.

'Recessional' was widely admired at the time, and has been widely admired since (by Orwell amongst others) on the grounds of its humility. But Kipling was not pleading for excessive modesty:

if we aren't very civilised, we're about the one power with a glimmering of civilisation in us . . . my objection to that hymn is that it may be quoted as an excuse for lying down abjectly at all times and seasons and taking what any other country may think fit to give us. What I wanted to say was – 'Don't gas but be ready to give people snuff' – and I only covered the first part of the notion.[8]

All this bravado was soon to be put to the test in the Boer War.

This was a conflict in which Kipling played an active role. His poem 'The Absent-Minded Beggar' was set to music and the proceeds were devoted to army charities. He himself went out to South Africa, where for a short time he helped to edit *The Friend*, a newspaper for the troops, and, in the course of sixteen days of active service away from the Cape, he was excited to come under fire for the first time in his life. The battle in which he was involved at Karee Siding was an anti-climactic affair, however, in which, after inflicting 180 casualties on the British, the Boers melted away on their ponies.

But this disappointment was only a foretaste of the greater disappointment and disillusionment that Kipling was to experience during the war, for it was a conflict in which the incompetence of the British army was revealed at all levels, a conflict that was redeemed, not by the Stalkies and the subalterns, not by the common people of England in the third-class carriages on whom Kipling at one time had pinned his hopes, but by the volunteers from the Dominions who were used to the terrain and were superb marksmen. In 'The Lesson', published in *The Times* on 29 July 1901, Kipling admitted that 'We have had an Imperial lesson; it may make us an Empire yet.' And in another poem, 'The Islanders', there appeared his famous indictment of English amateurism, of 'the flannelled fools at the wicket' and the 'muddied oafs at the goals'.

In place of all this his hopes for the future were outlined in 'The Army of a Dream', which was published in *The Morning Post* in 1904. Here Kipling proposed that the strength of the professional army should be supplemented by a system of military service in which the principle of compulsion did not figure (except that men who refused to volunteer lost their right to vote). In his view this system would not only bring Britain into line with the other European powers, which had long conscripted its young men for a period of military service followed by a period in the reserve, but there was also the further advantage that the working classes would have their horizons broadened by means of further education, trade-training and foreign travel. At one point in his exposition of the scheme Kipling dreamed of a situation in which a harmful miners' strike would be broken by the men being called up to act as stokers on naval manoeuvres taking place between Land's End and Gibraltar.

But these were only dreams, and his hopes were to be shattered by the landslide victory of the Liberals in the general election in 1906. After the frustrations and expense of the Boer War the country was tired of imperialism and impervious to the proposals of men like Joseph Chamberlain (whom Kipling deeply admired) who argued in favour of imperial protection and imperial federation. This was something that the Dominions themselves did not want. It was also anathema to that other England of which Kipling was so ignorant, the England of the industrial masses, the England of social idealists, Home-Rulers and pro-Boers, that now had its triumph.

From now on until the outbreak of the First World War Kipling was forced to witness with impotent fury the dismantling of everything in which he believed. In domestic affairs the Liberals ignored the doctrine of self-help and laid the foundations of the welfare state. In the Empire they granted self-government to the conquered Boers, thus destroying Milner's ideal of a South Africa in which the Afrikaner element would not be preponderant, and took the first hesitant steps in putting India on the road to eventual self-government with the Morley-Minto reforms. Nearer home they attempted to grant Home Rule to Ireland, thus threatening the unity and integrity of the British Isles themselves.

During these years of the Liberal ascendancy Kipling did what he could to salvage something from the wreck. If events in South Africa culminating in the defeat of Jameson as Prime Minister of Cape Province were a cruel disappointment, if he now felt obliged to stop wintering at the Cape in the house that Rhodes had had specially built for him, he attempted to find a substitute country of the future in Canada where he made an extensive tour in 1907. If Lord Roberts's campaigns for compulsory military service were unsuccessful (the result of Tory indifference as well as of Liberal hostility) Kipling found some consolation in moving away from the army to praising the British navy in the *Pyecroft Stories*. Meanwhile there was the development of Baden-Powell's scouting movement, which borrowed heavily from Kipling's work to alert the youth of England to the excitement and responsibilities of empire. And in *Puck of Pook's Hill* and *Rewards and Fairies* Kipling formulated his own, highly idiosyncratic interpretation of English history, warning the younger generation of the mutability of things in poems like 'Cities and

Thrones and Powers', and pointing to the example of the centurions on Hadrian's Wall, who endured the boredom and the cold in order to defend civilisation against the barbarians.

The relevance of all this to contemporary events was unmistakable as Kipling contemplated with gloom the disintegration of Britain and her empire in the years before 1914. During this period his domestic targets were legion: the activities of the suffragettes, the influence of syndicalist ideas within the unions, the involvement of Cabinet Ministers in the Marconi scandal, Lloyd George and his budget, the Liberal attack on the powers of the House of Lords that culminated in the Parliament Act of 1911. Increasingly, however, it was the Irish question that came to dominate his thoughts. Needless to say he was in total support of the Ulster cause and was a signatory to the Covenant which pledged resistance to Irish Home Rule. At the time of the Curragh mutiny he supported the army officers who baulked at the idea that they might be ordered to put down Unionist opposition to the Home Rule bill by force. And in a speech at Tunbridge Wells in May 1914 all Kipling's pent-up emotions found release. He accused the Liberal cabinet of behaving as they did for monetary gain and bribing back-benchers to support them by introducing the principle of payment of members of Parliament. On the Irish question he warned:

Civil war is inevitable unless our rulers can be brought to realise that even now, they must submit these grave matters to the judgement of a free people.[9]

In the event, however, it was not Ireland and the threat of civil war that were to dominate events in 1914. On 4 August he made a characteristically laconic note in his diary, 'Incidentally Armageddon begins.'

Despite his preoccupation with the Irish problem in the years immediately before 1914 Kipling never forgot that over-riding all the domestic and imperial issues that concerned him was the threat of a European war and the challenge of Germany. Unlike Shaw and Wells, who were surprised and shocked by the events of 1914, he could take a certain grim satisfaction in the fact that the threat he had long predicted had now materialised.

The defence and security of the Empire had obsessed him ever since he had observed in India the degree to which the external and internal well-being of an entire sub-continent depended in the last resort on the principle of military force. It is typical of him that on his departure from India to England in 1889 he had wondered whether a Russian man-of-war might intercept his steamer. On arriving in San Francisco he caused some offence to his American hosts by commenting on the vulnerability of that great city to attack from the sea:

When the 'City of Peking' steamed through the Golden Gate I saw with great joy that the blockhouse which guarded the mouth of 'the finest harbour in the world, Sir', could be silenced by two gunboats from Hong Kong with safety, comfort and despatch.[10]

And throughout the 1890s, he was intensely aware that British power was jealously regarded by her two traditional rivals, Russia and France.

His fear of Russia had obvious roots in the politics of the North West Frontier, and in the constant struggle for supremacy that took place in Afghanistan and Persia. The danger from France had surfaced at the time of the Fashoda Crisis and had again become clear at the time of the Boer War, when Britain had found herself almost totally isolated. But it also became apparent by the late 1890s that it was Germany that was now the major threat to the British Empire. It was Germany that gave encouragement to Krüger in the years before the Boer War. It was Germany that embarked on *Weltpolitik* in the course of the decade and rebuffed Chamberlain's attempts to come to an understanding with her. And it was Germany that ignored the grandiose dreams of Cecil Rhodes for a great Anglo-Saxon alliance of Britain, Germany and the United States to dominate the world, and initiated a programme of naval expansion that constituted a mortal threat to Britain's command of the seas.

However immersed he became in the crises that dominated English politics in the years before 1914, therefore, Kipling could never forget that beyond all these domestic problems there remained the threat of war with the Wilhelminian Reich. In 1910 he wrote to his friend H.A. Gwynne, later to be editor of *The Morning Post*:

Meanwhile the Teuton has his large cold eye on us, and prepares to give us toko when he feels good and ready. We ought to see in a few years now.[11]

It was not simply the dynamism of Germany that Kipling resented. Like Maurras, he was repelled by the *Masslosigkeit*, the unrestrained romanticism, the power of the irrational in German culture – things that he, like Maurras, always feared and tried to restrain within himself. By contrast the harmonious nature of French civilisation, its formalism, its austerity, its emphasis on what Maurras once called 'la belle notion du fini', made a great appeal to the craftsman and the peasant within him. With one part of himself Kipling took pride in the empirical and piecemeal approach of the British, exemplified by the almost accidental way in which they had acquired so much of their empire. Another part of him responded with enthusiasm to the French concern with 'savoir' and 'intelligence pure'.

This admiration of Kipling for France was reciprocated. His work was always well received there, despite a temporary period of unpopularity during the Fashoda Crisis and the Boer War when the Tharaud brothers satirised him in their novel *Dingley*. With the conclusion of the Anglo-French entente and the strengthening of understanding between the two nations in the years before 1914 Kipling became a frequent and welcome visitor to France and made a number of important friendships with personalities like Clemenceau.

As he embarked on the new delights of touring provincial France by automobile Kipling came more and more to appreciate the frugality and realism of French civilisation, the lessons that England could learn from her nearest continental neighbour:

We came to a village where a line of young men, linking hands, swept the public square dancing. Their faces were very clear in that unearthly light and the tricolour ribbons in their caps rattled in the mistral. An infantry soldier leaned against a shop door and watched them with an elder brother's instructed smile. 'What's this circus?' said my friend as they shouted round us. 'Those are conscripts,' I replied, 'Young men drawn for service in the Army for the next three years.' But he was frankly contemptuous, and the lounging infantryman only impressed him as slovenly and ungainly. 'But there are three-quarters of a million of them', I said. 'They have to take over each other's clothes and equipment and wear them out – like monks. Very little is wasted in this country'. All the English in him revolted at the

apparent meanness, but the splendour of the sacrifice was hid. As a
Frenchman once said to me, 'We Continentals are more separated from your
world by our compulsory service than by anything else. How can you
English understand our minds if you do not realise those years of service –
those years of service for us all? When we come to talk to you about life it is
like talking about death to children.'[12]

In 1913 Poincaré paid a state visit to England and Kipling
celebrated the occasion with a poem in praise of his country:

> Broke to every known mischance, lifted over all
> By the light sane joy of life, the buckler of the Gaul,
> Famous in luxury, merciless in toil,
> Terrible with strength that draws from her tireless soil;
> Strictest judge of her own worth gentlest of man's mind,
> First to follow Truth and last to leave old Truths behind
> France, beloved of every soul that loves its fellow-kind!

In later years he recalled that a few months before this visit he had
been dining at a French officers' mess. Sitting next to him was a
French colonel who insisted that war with Germany was imminent.
'It is coming. It is certain to come and come soon. The question is,
what will England do?' 'Then', said Kipling, 'I made the plunge.' 'We
are going to take over your left wing.'[13] It was with the memory of
that conversation that the poem 'France' was born, and it was with
the memory of incidents like these that he watched events unfold in
1914.

It is sometimes said that Kipling glorified war, and evidence to
substantiate this charge can be found in many parts of his work. But
on the whole after the Boer War his attitude became more sombre. In
an interview that was published at the end of 1913 he declared that
there was 'no more romance or glamour' in war, and explained that
he had gone out to South Africa anticipating excitement and danger,
but that modern warfare was very different from what he had
expected:

And all this method and precision and application of modern efficiency ideas
makes the carnage that follows all the more ghastly. You don't know in
advance just what is going to happen. You don't know how it happened; you
just look at the dreadful dead men and the shrieking wounded men, and
they seem to you like innocent bystanders who have got in the way of some
great civil-engineering scheme and been torn and blown up.[14]

Like the great majority of his contemporaries he had little idea of
what the reality of the trenches would be, but he had few illusions
that the coming struggle would be easy, and the mood of his famous
poem published in *The Times* in September 1914 is not one of light-
heartedness:

> For all we have and are,
> For all our children's fate,
> Stand up and take the war,
> The Hun is at the gate!
> Our world has passed away
> In wantonness o'erthrown
> There is nothing left today
> But steel and fire and stone!

Once the war had started, of course, Kipling became deeply
immersed in a host of activites. There were innumerable articles to be
written and dignitaries to be met. There were visits to the Front:

The French officers seem as mother keen on their men as their men are
mother fond of them. Maybe the possessive form of address 'mon général',
'mon capitaine', helps the idea, which our men cloak in other and curter
phrases.[15]

The French reported that they had no doubt that their experience
with Moroccan troops was the same that the British experienced with
the martial races of India:

We get our best recruits from the tribes we have fought. These men are
children. They make no trouble. They only want to go where the cartridges
are burnt. They are of the few races to whom fighting is a pleasure.[16]

He made a tour of the camps of Kitchener's volunteer New Armies
that were being trained in England to replace the old regular forces
that had been almost annihilated in stemming the initial German
onrush in 1914 and noted:

There is a gulf already opening between those who have joined and those
who have not; but we shall not know the width and depth of that gulf till the
war is over.[17]

He also made a number of recruiting speeches, although he made it
quite clear that he did this reluctantly, believing that conscription
was the only real solution to the situation.

Creative work was largely laid aside while Kipling devoted himself to the war effort, and even the few short stories that he completed during this period were deeply affected – 'warped' might perhaps be a better word – by the demands of the moment. His anger at the activity of German submarines and the failure of the United States to enter the war, for example, was reflected in 'Sea-Constables', written in early 1915, which is concerned with four naval reserve captains reminiscing after a long period of active service. In the course of the story it emerges that one of them, after pursuing a neutral ship that was trading with the enemy while relying on the protection of the British navy, had refused to help the owner of the ship when he became ill, leaving him to die of bronchial pneumonia.

From the same period came the notorious 'Mary Postgate', which was obviously influenced by the German air-raids on Britain which started in January 1915. Mary Postgate, the principal character of the story, refuses to help a wounded German airman who has crashed on a bombing mission in which children have been killed, and leaves him to die. Apologists for Kipling have rightly pointed out that there is far more to the story than this, that it is with great economy and subtlety that he indicates the limited horizons and emotional frustrations of his principal character and the sexual excitement that she experiences as a result of abandoning the airman to his fate. But this only enhances the horror of this deeply disturbing minor masterpiece, and Kipling did not indicate any disapproval of Mary Postgate's behaviour. Indeed, the story was published in American magazines, no doubt to enlist sympathy for the British cause. To underline the moral Kipling added an epitaph that was clearly intended as his riposte to Ernst Lissauer's notorious 'Hassgesang gegen England' that had appeared in 1914:

> It was not suddenly bred
> It will not swiftly abate,
> Through the chill years ahead,
> When Time shall count from the date
> That the English began to hate.

A year later he wrote in *The Daily Express*:

One thing we must get into our thick heads is that wherever the German man or woman gets a suitable culture to thrive in he or she means death and loss to civilised people, precisely as germs of any disease . . . mean death or loss to mankind. There is no hate or danger or excitement in the matter, any more than there is in flushing out sinks . . . as far as we are concerned the German is typhoid or plague – Pestio Teutonicus if you like.[18]

Statements like this have done massive and permanent damage to Kipling's reputation, and it is no exaggeration to say that in terms of verbal violence his outbursts against the Germans go much further than anything perpetrated by Barrès and Maurras and have points of resemblance, indeed, with Nazi attacks on the Jews. And yet it must be remembered that after the autumn of 1915 he had reason to feel a deep personal bitterness against Germany, for it was on 27 September, six days after his eighteenth birthday, that his son John was reported wounded and missing in the course of the battle of Loos. His body was never found.

Despite his youth John Kipling had been extremely anxious to get to the Front as soon as possible, and, despite his concern for his safety, his father had used his influence to secure him a commission in the Irish Guards. The letters that John sent from France helped to enlighten Kipling about the true conditions at the Front. To his father's suggestion that he should use rabbit netting to make his trench more secure, for example, John replied:

Many thanks for Dad's letter. His 'tips' for the trenches are rather quaint. Surely you know it is a standing order never to have anything on top of a trench, even rabbit wire. If the Bosch comes he has you like rabbits underneath.[19]

The light-hearted tone did not last for long, however, and, after a series of exhausting route marches, he pointed out to his father that 'You people at home don't realise how spoilt you are'.[20] A few days later he was dead. John was only one of the 20,000 British troops who were mown down by the German shells and machine guns at Loos, the first major test of Kitchener's New Armies, an offensive decided on by a reluctant Kitchener to aid Joffre despite the British inferiority in heavy artillery and shells. The result was a battle that hardly made a dent in the German line. Rider Haggard was told that John was last seen trying to fasten a field dressing round his shattered mouth. He was crying with the pain of the wound. Haggard did not forward this news to Kipling, knowing that it would cause him further distress.[21]

There is no doubt that John's death was a shattering blow to his parents. In one of his famous 'Epitaphs of War' Kipling raised the painful issue of responsibility:

> If any question why we died
> Tell them, because our fathers lied.

This points the finger of blame on those who had minimised the danger of war with Germany and had not prepared Britain for the magnitude of the ordeal to come, but whether, in addition to this, there was an element of personal guilt, because of the nature of his political beliefs and activities and the encouragement that he had given to John to enlist, is a question which cannot be answered. There can be no doubt, however, of the pain that Kipling and his wife now had to endure. Carrie began to suffer from depression and became at times almost intolerably possessive after the death of her son, while it seems likely that the deterioration that took place in Kipling's health – a duodenal ulcer was very belatedly diagnosed – had its origins in the strain, exhaustion and grief of the war. To an old friend, Julia Taufflieb, the American wife of a French general, who visited the Kiplings at Brown's Hotel soon after John's death, Kipling made no mention of him until he was seeing her into the car on her departure. Suddenly he pressed her hand so hard that it almost hurt and said, 'Down on your knees, Julia, and thank God you haven't a son.'[22]

But only a small group of intimate friends were allowed to see the full extent of his suffering. Outwardly he attempted to preserve an attitude of dignified stoicism. He remained calm and resolute after the collapse of Russia meant that France and Britain must prepare themselves to bear the full fury of a German attack, and in February 1918, soon after the signing of the Treaty of Brest Litovsk, he wrote to Rider Haggard:

I am sure our national unimaginativeness is going to be our salvation in the long run and, between ourselves, I look for peace by the end of the year – a bad peace for Germany too.[23]

Meanwhile in addition to all his other duties and responsibilities he played an important role in the work of the Imperial War Graves Commission and was responsible for the choice of many of the texts that were used on monuments to the fallen. A further act of piety towards the dead was shown by his decision to accept an invitation to write the official history of the Irish Guards during the First World War.

In the course of writing this history he derived a great deal of pain as well as pleasure from the fact that he came into contact with many of John's comrades – officers, NCOs and men. But there is no doubt that as a result of this he was able to come nearer than perhaps any other civilian writer could to understanding something of what the experience of the war had actually entailed. His efforts to grapple with the reality of war had already been clearly revealed in his attack on the incompetence that had led to the surrender of Kut in 'Mesopotamia', and in his attempt to come to terms with the truth of the conflict in the superb 'Gethsemane':

> The Garden called Gethsemane
>   In Picardy it was,
> And there the people came to see
>   The English soldiers pass.
> We used to pass – we used to pass
>   Or halt, as it might be
> And ship our masks in case of gas
>   Beyond Gethsemane
>
> The Garden called Gethsemane
>   It held a pretty lass
> But all the time she talked to me
>   I prayed my cup might pass.
> The officer sat on the chair
>   The men lay on the grass
> And all the time we halted there
>   I prayed my cup might pass
> It didn't pass – it didn't pass –
>   It didn't pass from me.
> I drank it when we met the gas
>   Beyond Gethsemane

And the after-effects of the front experience – trauma, shell-shock, guilt, grief – form the theme of many of the short stories that he wrote after the war. Compassion for human suffering had not been absent from Kipling's earlier work. Despite his distaste for the urban masses, in 'The Record of Badalia Herodsfoot' he told the story of the life and death of a generous and loyal girl from the slums of the east end of London with understanding, if with some sentimentality. In 'Without Benefit of Clergy', the ill-starred love affair between an English civilian and a Moslem girl is handled with great sympathy and tact. And the intensity of parental grief at the death of young children is powerfully conveyed in 'They'. But from the time of the First World War onwards this element becomes increasingly pronounced in his work.

This later phase of Kipling's achievement has been much admired by the critics, especially since the extreme concision that he now practised gives them plenty of opportunities for exegesis, but, however moving many of his later poems and short stories undoubtedly are, it may be felt that there was a freshness and an immediacy in his earlier work that was now lost forever. Reviewing Kipling's history of the Irish Guards during the First World War Edmund Blunden pointed out the inevitably second-hand nature of Kipling's account:

The fact is that Mr. Kipling appears not perfectly to understand the pandemonium and nerve-strain of war; it seldom surges up in his pages of that appalling misery which brought seasoned men down the shell-holes beyond Thiepval, as they went up to relieve the Schwaben Redoubt, crying and 'whacked to the wide'. He makes constant stern attempts at actuality; he constantly falls short in expressions merely strained, in sheer want of comprehension. To those who were in the line, his technical phraseology will seem incongruous now and then; but the deeper defects may be exemplified by such expressions as – touching pill-box fire –, 'the annoying fights and checks round the concreted machine gun post . . .'[24]

And the same kind of criticism can be made against the way in which he dealt with the war in much of his fiction. The truth of the situation seems to be that, however great were his efforts to penetrate to the heart of the war experience, the innermost reality often eluded him. His description of the efforts of a group of soldiers to cope with the strain of battle by means of code-words and phrases derived from the work of Jane Austen in 'The Janeites', for example, is ingenious but unconvincing. The same can be said of 'The Woman in His Life', in which a man is helped to recover from the after-effects of two years of activity as a sapper beneath the Messines Ridge by being obliged to climb down a badger set to rescue his dog. As for 'On the Gate', in which St Peter and the angels are seen working overtime to cope with the rush of souls waiting for admission to Heaven in the course of the war, and the much-lauded 'The Gardener', which appeared in 1926, in which an unmarried mother visiting the war graves is directed to the resting place of her son by a man she supposes to be a gardener but who is in reality Jesus Christ, the charge of sentimentality is one to which Kipling must surely plead guilty. This was literature written by a civilian in an attempt to comfort other civilians. Despite all his efforts, the experience of the trench generation, the experience of those who had truly been 'dans le bain', was one form of freemasonry in which Kipling could never fully participate.

In any case his preoccupation with themes of healing and redemption in his later work would have carried more conviction had he shown any willingness to extend his charity to those whom he had attacked in the past. But of this there was no sign. On the contrary, in his letters and conversations in the years after the war there was a constant stream of invective against all those groups that he considered to be enemies of Britain: the trade unions, the Labour party, the former 'conchies' who had now risen to the highest positions in the land, Gandhi and the Congress party, the Irish, the Bolsheviks, the 'Yids' (whose 'machinations' were behind 'our Russian troubles, and many others'),[25] and the Americans, who had made enormous profits before their late entry into the war and had then refused to ratify the Treaty of Versailles.

In fairness to Kipling it is possible to argue that on many of these issues the very diehard quality of his position was an indication of the fact that he himself realised that the cause was basically lost. And Maurice Bowra believed that behind the dogmatic assertions there were deep uncertainties as well. After talking with Bowra about the latter's war experiences (when it became clear that there were deficiencies in Kipling's knowledge of artillery matters) he turned the topic of conversation to some of his favourite *bêtes noires*:

He gave the impression that his views were formed less on reason than on rather hysterical emotions. Despite his courtesy there was a note of violence in what he said, and I felt that fundamentally he was less sure of his opinions than he liked us to believe and that his over-emphasis on certain matters was necessary to counter his chameleonic adaptability.[26]

But on one matter there was no hesitation: his unrelenting hatred of Germany and his conviction that there could be no peace in Europe until her power was destroyed.

Already during the war he had joined with other writers (including Wells) in denouncing as defeatist the well-intentioned, if somewhat utopian, proposals of Lord Lansdowne (one of the architects of the Anglo-French Entente of 1904), contained in a letter sent to the *Daily Telegraph* in November 1917, arguing for a compromise peace to save what was left of Western civilisation. At the same time his friendship with Theodore Roosevelt acquired added depth. In Kipling's eyes Roosevelt was the one American statesman who had been prepared to take up the White Man's Burden, the one American politician with whom he could identify. Together the two men attacked Wilson's delay in bringing America into the war on the side of England and France, and together they dismissed the 'mush' of Wilson's talk of self-determination and other impractical ideals. Four days before the Armistice Kipling was already complaining to Roosevelt:

The guts of Europe are sliding into our laps day by day but at the one moment when we Allies ought to have had our hands free to deal with a hemisphere in extremis we are tied up by his idiotic Fourteen Points.[27]

When the terms of the Treaty of Versailles were promulgated, therefore, Kipling was not surprised by their 'leniency'. As far as he was concerned the next war had started 'at a quarter past eleven on 11th November 1918'.[28] Whatever the attacks that he launched on other countries in the years after the war, Kipling never criticised his beloved France. On the contrary, ever conscious of the sacrifices she had made between 1914 and 1918, he ignored her failings, supported Poincaré's policy towards Germany and deplored the short-sightedness of the British in opposing him.

When Hitler began his ascent to power in Germany in the 1930s, then, Kipling's reaction could only be that his predictions were now being fulfilled. In 1932, the year in which the Nazis emerged as the strongest party within the Reichstag, he wrote 'The Storm Cone':

This is the midnight – let no star
Delude us – dawn is very far.
This is the tempest long foretold –
Slow to make head but sure to hold.

And three years later, at the time of George V's Silver Jubilee, he made a famous speech at a meeting of the Royal Society of St George on 6 May 1935, in which he lamented the illusion that had been created that the First World War had been a hideous mistake and had been fought over nothing. Referring to the brutalities of the Nazi and Bolshevik régimes that had developed out of the war, he emphasised the depth of their hatred of the West and the danger they now posed to Britain:

if the attack of the future is to be on the same swift all-in lines as our opponents' domestic administrations – it is possible that before we are aware, our country may have joined those submerged races of history who passed their children through fire to Moloch to win credit with the Gods.[29]

To counter the German threat he advocated rearmament, and supported the Stresa front, but was appalled when his own cousin, the Prime Minister Stanley Baldwin, went along with British public opinion and repudiated the Hoare–Laval pact that would have kept Mussolini (whom Kipling admired) in the anti-German front by making concessions to Italy over Abyssinia. The result of this, he predicted, would be that Mussolini would be thrown into the arms of Hitler, thus sealing the fate of Austria. Only a few days before his death on 18 January 1936 Kipling pointed out to one of his correspondents that Germany 'had been explaining what she is arming for for 5 or 6 years – as she did for 6 or 7 before the war. In these matters I have noticed that she keeps her word!'[30]

Few listened to his message, however. As the pacifist revulsion against the first World War intensified in the early 1930s, as the flood of autobiographies and memoirs denouncing the war now poured from the presses, as the old sweats' half-admiring stories of the methodical (and, therefore, predictable) nature of 'Fritz' as a fighter compared with the volatility of the French entered into the British folk memory, as the attention of the literary and left-wing young was increasingly focussed not on France but on Germany, the views of an unregenerate imperialist, Francophile and Germanophobe like Kipling carried little weight. Many believed that Nazism was a product of the harshness of the Versailles settlement that Kipling had denounced for its softness. Many hoped that Nazism would become more moderate if the grievances of Germany were redressed through a policy of appeasement. And most of the young generation were convinced that, if the worst came to the worst and Britain was called upon to fight another war with Germany, it must be fought for ideals that were very different from those that had inspired Kipling. His speech to the Royal Society of St George, a speech that was broadcast by the BBC., prompted a satirical rejoinder from Sassoon:

> And if indeed it was the astringent truth
> He told us with such incomparable concision –
> That we must now re-educate our youth
> With 'Arm or perish' as their ultimate vision –
> Let us at least be candid with the world
> And stitch across each Union Jack unfurled
> 'No bargain struck with Potsdam is put over
> Unless well-backed by bombers – and Jehovah!'

This was very far from being one of Sassoon's more inspired efforts, but it helps to explain why Kipling's reputation was at its nadir by the time of his death.

A few years later, with the outbreak of the Second World War, of course, his stock began to rise again. Eliot began the rehabilitation by his preface to a selection of Kipling's poetry in which he maintained that while Kipling could not exactly be described as a poet, he was much under-rated as a writer of verse. This was not an entirely satisfactory description – it failed to explain why the man who wrote 'Cities and Thrones and Powers' and 'Gethsemane' could not be regarded as a poet – but Eliot's work was an indication of a change in public mood, a change that was confirmed by Orwell's important essay which appeared soon afterwards.

Orwell's view of Kipling was obviously influenced by a situation in which Britain was fighting for her survival, and Orwell, being the man he was, could not resist the temptation to use Kipling as a stick to beat the pacifists and the left-wing intelligentsia. But at a deeper level it was perhaps the very ambiguity of Orwell's attitude to Kipling that made him so stimulating a commentator on him. Throughout Orwell's work there is a vigorous denunciation of the corrupting influence of the Empire on the imperialists, not least on Kipling himself, whom Orwell describes as often 'morally insensitive and aesthetically disgusting'.[31] At the same time there is in Orwell's writings an unmistakable undertone of nostalgia for the peace and security of the days of British power before 1914, a theme that was to emerge even more strongly in Orwell's work as Britain's role became subordinate to that of the United States and the Soviet Union in the course of the Second World War, a theme that was to reach its culmination in his depiction of the battered and down-at-heel Britain, a mere province of the totalitarian 'Oceania', that appears in *1984*.

Kipling himself did not live to see the rise in his reputation that has accompanied, and has possibly been facilitated by, the collapse of British power. Indeed, since the Second World War his rehabilitation has proceeded apace, and it has become fashionable to dismiss his imperialism as an accidental factor in his work, as a metaphor by means of which he explored the absurdity of life in an indifferent universe.[32] But this is to elevate him to the rank of a Conrad, and any attempt to divorce Kipling from the power structures of his day ignores the extent to which, to a far greater degree than a real expatriate like Conrad, he attempted to seek refuge from his terrors in the values and service of empire.

Despite the subtlety and the intricate craftsmanship of many of his short stories like the much-admired 'Mrs Bathurst' (1904) and 'Dayspring Mishandled' (1928), ultimately even the most sympathetic commentator on his career is likely to find Kipling's universe stifling and claustrophobic. W.W. Robson has argued that his style shows that his vision of life 'owes more to the will than to the imagination. His complexity lies on the surface. It is like an artificially made jewel rather than a flower.'[33] It may be felt that this comment underestimates the sensitivity and wide-ranging curiosity of Kipling's imagination, qualities which sometimes subvert his avowed intentions, but it is a comment which rightly emphasises the extent to which Kipling constantly fought to hold himself in check. In Kipling's writings one is constantly aware of the elemental, the mysterious and the intuitive, but for the majority of men, even in the later stories, this is a part of experience that must be controlled, sublimated in work, duty, love of dogs, comradeship and ritual, or, in the last analysis, repressed. No good will come of rebelling against this situation. There is the safety-valve of humour, of course, but Kipling's humour verges on the hysterical, as in 'The Village that Voted the Earth was Flat'. Men are continually at breaking-point, and are constantly under the gaze and judgement of other men. Only women, children and the occasional Brushwood Boy, savant or holy man, it seems, are allowed to possess a truly autonomous inner life. Politically, too, his work is subjected to the same kind of desolating self-mutilation. Everything is compartmentalised. Certain groups are good, other groups are bad, and the exceptions only prove the validity of the general rule. Moslems and Sikhs are loyal friends and formidable opponents. Hindus on the whole cannot be trusted. Jews must be closely watched, but it is foolish and self-defeating to attempt to persecute the Chosen Race. Arabs are admirable. Frenchmen are admirable. Germans, however, do not form part of civilised Europe. They are outside Heaven, too, if one is to trust the evidence of 'On the Gate'. As for the English, Chesterton once said of Kipling that he admired England because she was strong, not because she was English. Kipling was never a pessimist and a defeatist about his nation like Maurras, but perhaps the final limitation of Kipling is that, although Chesterton's remark is a gross exaggeration (despite the fact that Chesterton backed it up with quotation), it still contains an element of truth.

Perhaps it was fortunate for Kipling, then, that he should have been permitted to die when he did, at a time when the Empire was still intact, only two days before the death of George V, the monarch to whom he had given much unobtrusive aid and encouragement, the friend and fellow-Victorian who had worshipped the same gods of the copy-book headings, gods whose authority had been so deeply undermined by the First World War. Even to contemporaries it was clear that the passing of these two men marked the passing of an era. As the saying of the time had it, 'The King has gone and taken his trumpeter with him.'

— PART III —

The decline of the West

Paul Nash (1889–1946), *We Are Making a New World*

Sweet laughter charred in the flame
That clutched the cloud and earth
While Solomon's towers crashed between,
The gird of Babylon's mirth.

Isaac Rosenberg, 'The Destruction of Jerusalem
By the Babylonian Hordes',
Trench Poems 1916–18.

Romain Rolland: above the battle

A feeling that European civilisation was in the throes of disintegration was by no means uncommon in the years before the outbreak of the First World War. In Germany Spengler gave currency to the phrase 'The decline of the West' at the end of the conflict, but the inspiration for his thinking came before the war, at the time of the Second Moroccan Crisis. Behind the affirmations of the Nationalists in France and Kipling in England there was a haunting fear of decadence. Wells had expressed his gloom over the future of the world in his scientific romances of the 1890s, while from a totally different point of view, D.H. Lawrence was already prophesying the collapse of Western industrialised society in the era before 1914.

But if the theme of the decline of the West was one that had many variations, undoubtedly one of the most striking was that offered by the French writer Romain Rolland in the years preceding 1914. Unlike Jaurès, Rolland believed that war was sooner or later inevitable. Unlike Péguy, he derived no pleasure from recognising this fact, but warned instead that the only outcome of the coming war would be the undermining of European civilisation. Unlike Spengler, he was horrified by the imminent collapse of Western humanism and the advent of a new epoch of barbarism and war. When the conflict finally broke out Rolland attempted to salvage something from the wreck by appealing to the élite of Europe to hold themselves aloof from the hatreds of the epoch, but the course of events after 1914 convinced him that the world was in the throes of a crisis far more profound than he had previously imagined, and that salvation, if it existed at all, would only be found outside the West.

Romain Rolland was born in Burgundy in 1866. His father was of an extrovert and genial disposition, his mother a deeply religious

woman of Jansenist inclinations to whom conscience was all. Rolland
took after his mother. Ambitious for her son, she moved the whole
family to Paris in furtherance of his academic career, a career which
led him to the Ecole Normale in Paris, the French School in Rome, and
ultimately to a professorship in the history of music at the Sorbonne.
His first marriage to Clotilde Bréal, the daughter of a worldly and
sophisticated Jewish family, did not last, and, after the divorce, his
wife married the pianist Alfred Cortot. She obviously preferred the
fruits of immediate acclaim to the more arduous mission that Rolland
had assigned to himself as the analyst of European decadence and as
the prophet of a possible rebirth.

A sense of doom and decline was something to which he became
accustomed at an early age. In his childhood he was deeply affected
by the death of a sister, and he soon became aware that his own
health was precarious and that he would suffer for the rest of his life
from severe respiratory problems. Then there was the atmosphere of
the France in which he grew up, a France humiliated by her defeat in
the Franco-Prussian War and the terrible aftermath of the Commune.
In the *Mémoires* that he wrote many years later he confessed that
from the early 1880s he had been conscious that he was living in one
of the most tragic periods of history, and that from this time he had
been haunted by the idea of ruin, the ruin of a civilisation:

Je la reniflais autour de moi, dans l'art du temps comme une odeur de
lagune.[1]

(I sniffed at it all around me, in the art of the time, like the odour of a lagoon.)

Having lost his faith in Catholicism during his adolescence, and
repelled, like Barrès and Maurras, by the nihilism that he detected in
the French intellectual scene in the 1880s, he sought refuge in a kind
of heroic and humanitarian pantheism that recognised the primacy of
suffering:

Life is a tragic spectacle. In order to endure it one must be very heedless or
very strong. Heedless, we can no longer be; strong, we cannot always be.
And so we must suffer and help others to suffer.[2]

It was only through suffering that one could affirm the brotherhood
of mankind. It was only through suffering that one could ultimately

affirm – as music did, as Spinoza did – the coherence and rationality of the universe.

Intensely élitist by temperament, Rolland was still anxious to offer his message to mankind as a whole. This sense of himself as a man with a prophetic mission helps to explain the role that he was to assume as the conscience of Europe during the First World War. It was responsible, too, for the earlier attempts that he made to appeal to popular audiences through the medium of literature and the drama: the 'tragédies de la foi' of the 1890s; the plays on the insoluble moral dilemmas raised by the French Revolution that he wrote at the time of the Dreyfus Affair; the 'vies des hommes illustres' – biographies of men like Beethoven, Tolstoy and Michelangelo (which D.H. Lawrence particularly admired) – that he produced in the years before 1914 to underline his belief in the possibility of regeneration and redemption through suffering.

From the vantage point of the late twentieth century it is easy to mock the artless idealism that underlay these enterprises, but to do this would be to miss the essential innocence of the world before 1914. It was an era in which boundless hopes were still possible, an era in which in every department of life a whole variety of choices still remained on offer, an epoch in which the terrible simplifications of the twentieth century had not yet made themselves manifest. Rolland's introduction to his *Vie de Beethoven* (1903) conveys both the frustrations and the ultimate optimism that was so characteristic of the time:

L'air est lourd autour de nous. La vieille Europe s'engourdit dans une atmosphère pesante et viciée. Un matérialisme sans grandeur pèse sur la pensée, et entrave l'action des gouvernements et des individus. Le monde meurt d'asphyxie dans son égoisme prudent et vil. Le monde étouffe. – Rouvrons les fenêtres. Faisons rentrer l'air libre. Respirons le souffle des héros.[3]

(The air is heavy around us. The old Europe is sunk in torpor in an oppressive and corrupt atmosphere. A form of materialism without greatness weighs down thinking and prevents governments and individuals from action. The world is dying of asphyxia in a self-seeking and ignoble form of egoism. The world is choking. – Open the windows again. Let in the fresh air. Let us breathe the breath of heroes.)

These were noble sentiments, but they did not translate themselves easily into political options. During the Dreyfus Affair, for
example, he was far too disillusioned by the political activities of his
wife's family and acquaintances on behalf of Dreyfus to believe in
the immaculate nature of the Dreyfusard cause. His attitude then of
being above the battle, repelled by the sordid nature of the methods
employed by both sides in the Affair, foreshadowed to a certain
extent the position that he was to take in the wider conflict that was
to take place with the outbreak of the First World War. But this was
all in the future when, in the aftermath of the Affair, he began
writing his 'Jean-Christophe', the *roman-fleuve* in ten volumes that
he was to publish between 1904 and 1912, the novel that was to bring
him European fame.

The idea of writing a novel based on the life of a latter-day
Beethoven figure living in the Germany and France of the Belle
Epoque went back a long way, to Rolland's period in Rome in the
early 1890s. Like Edward Gibbon before him he was overwhelmed
by the splendour and transience of the Roman Empire, but in his case
the experience determined him to write a work of fiction that would
reflect the splendour and transience of his own era.

It would be impossible within the space available in this book to
give an adequate summary of the 'plot' of the novel that resulted
from this decision, for *Jean-Christophe* is a vast canvas that depicts
events in France, Germany and Italy, and deals with many of the
major political and cultural movements of the day. Basically,
however, it is a kind of *Bildungsroman*, telling the life story of Jean-
Christophe Krafft, a German musician and writer who is progressively disillusioned by the materialism and vulgarity of his native
land, and, after being forced to leave Germany, settles in France. At
first he is repelled by the corruption and cynicism that he encounters
in the artistic world of Paris, but in his friend Olivier and in Olivier's
sister he eventually discovers the 'real' France, the France of
provincial integrity and culture.

Together the three of them hope for peace and Franco-German
reconciliation. These hopes are not to be realised, however. During
the First Moroccan Crisis Jean-Christophe's reactions are those of a
patriotic German, and it is Olivier who, while protesting at

Germany's bullying tactics, warns of the disastrous consequences of war on the future of European civilisation:

L'Occident se brûle . . . Bientôt . . . Bientôt . . . Je vois d'autres lumières qui se lèvent du fond de L'Orient. – Laisse-moi tranquille avec ton Orient! dit Christophe. L'Occident n'a pas dit son dernier mot.[4]

(The West is destroying itself . . . Soon . . . Soon . . . I see other forms of enlightenment rising from the extremities of the East. – Don't bother me with that East of yours! said Christophe. The West has not had its final say.)

In the years that follow this conversation Jean-Christophe himself comes to realise that in an age of competing nationalism it is essential that men should stand above the hatreds of the epoch, but, by the time of the publication of the final volume of the novel, *La Nouvelle Journée*, in 1912, Rolland was increasingly pessimistic that catastrophe could be avoided. Towards the end of the book, the outbreak of a European war is clearly imminent:

L'incendie qui couvait dans la forêt d'Europe commencait à flamber. On avait beau l'éteindre, ici; plus loin, il se rallumait; avec des tourbillons de fumée et une pluie d'étincelles, il sautait d'un point à l'autre et brûlait les broussailles sèches. A l'Orient, déjà, des combats d'avant-garde préludaient à la Grande Guerre des Nations. L'Europe entière, l'Europe hier encore sceptique et apathique, comme un bois mort, était la proie du feu. Le désir du combat possédait toutes les âmes. A tout instant, la guerre était sur le point d'éclater. On l'étouffait, elle renaissait. Le prétexte le plus futile lui était un aliment. Le monde se sentait à la merci d'un hasard, qui déchaînerait la mêlée. Sur les plus pacifiques pesait le sentiment de la nécessité. Et les idéologues . . . célébraient dans la guerre le plus beau titre de noblesse de l'homme . . .[5]

(The fire that was smouldering in the forest of Europe began to break into flame. If it was extinguished in one place it broke out in another; billowing with smoke and with showers of sparks it spread from one place to another and consumed the dry undergrowth. In the East the early battles heralded the great war of Nations. The whole of Europe which had hitherto been apathetic and sceptical, like a dead wood, was now open to the fire. The desire for war dominated everyone. At every instant war was on the verge of breaking out. It was averted, but then it reasserted itself. The most trivial incident helped to increase it. The world was at the mercy of any accident that would unleash the struggle. The most pacific were weighed down by a sense of fatalism. And the ideologues . . . hailed the idea of war as the noblest form of human activity . . .)

Olivier has died some years previously, and now there is no friend to comfort Jean-Christophe as he is forced to witness the spectacle of European civilisation embarking on an act of suicide:

C'était donc à cela que devait aboutir la résurrection physique et morale des races de l'Occident! C'était à ces boucheries que les précipitaient les courants d'action et de foi passionnées! Seul, un génie napoléonien eût pu fixer à cette course aveugle un but prévu et choisi. Mais de génie d'action, il n'y en avait nulle part, en Europe. On eût dit que le monde eût, pour le gouverner, fait choix des plus médiocres.[6]

(So this is where the physical and moral resurrection of the races of the West was to end, then! It was to these butcheries that the movements of action and passionate faith had precipitated them! Only a Napoleonic genius could have given a definite aim to this blind stampede. But nowhere in Europe was there a genius of action to be found. One could say that people had chosen the most mediocre to rule over them.)

The ageing hero flees from the hate-filled atmosphere of Paris to Italy, only to find that Nationalism is rampant there, too. Eventually he makes his way to Germany, where he dies by the side of the Rhine, the river that marks the divisions of Europe, the river that is also the symbol of reconciliation and rebirth.

As one volume succeeded another, and as the scope and the significance of the novel became clear, *Jean-Christophe* was widely acclaimed. In England, for example, a country which Rolland did not know well, but the first country in which it was published outside France (in a translation by the novelist Gilbert Cannan), its diffuse idealism made a strong appeal. H.G. Wells, Arnold Bennett and John Galsworthy published a manifesto in 1911 opposing 'art for art's sake' and cited *Jean-Christophe* as the model of what a novel should be. This was a somewhat ironical development in view of Virginia Woolf's later claim in her *Mr Bennett and Mrs Brown* (1924) that human nature changed around December 1910 and that the Edwardian 'materialism' of men like Bennett was now doomed. But there can be no doubt of the appeal that *Jean-Christophe* possessed in the England of its time. Edward Marsh called it in one of his letters 'easily the best novel in the world',[7] while E.M. Forster was later to recall the excitement with which he and his contemporaries reacted to the publication of the early volumes:

We were full of hopes then, easily held hopes, we did not know the severity of the problems which Fate was reserving for us, and the volumes were both civilized and inspiring, and how few books are both! They were intensely human, they had integrity, they possessed the culture of the past, yet they proclaimed that culture is not time-bound or class-bound, it is a living spirit to be carried on.

'Have you read the latest John Christopher?' we were saying. 'Has he got to Paris yet?'[8]

In retrospect Forster himself considered that the best of the novel lay in the earlier parts, before the whole project became weighed down by a great mass of semi-documentary material on the political and cultural ideas of the day. And inevitably, it is these parts of the work that have worn least well. As a result of this *Jean-Christophe* is now either ignored in France, or is regarded at best as irredeemably old-fashioned, a historical curiosity that might have some residual appeal to adolescents. Whilst acknowledging that its use of leitmotifs and its symphonic structure distinguished it from the run-of-the-mill novel, aesthetes never liked it. Gide was prepared to admit that Rolland's good faith was so transparent as to be almost disarming, but he was repelled by its didacticism and considered the work to be essentially mediocre in its lack of the classical French virtues of clarity and economy.[9] In *Contre Sainte-Beuve*, (written before 1910, but not published until 1954) Proust was even more contemptuous:

Monsieur Romain Rolland continue à entasser banalités sur banalités . . . C'est une œuvre de recherche et non de trouvaille, et où il est inférieur à tout écrivain d'aujourd'hui.[10]

(Monsieur Romain Rolland continues to pile banalities on banalities . . . it is a work of research and not of invention, in which he is inferior to every other writer writing today.)

But if Proust's attack was the definitive coup de grace as far as the French literary world was concerned, there is in Rolland's work a humanity and a sensitivity to the natural world (a quality which he shared with his arch-enemy Barrès), and an overwhelming sense of impatience with French narrowness, which helps to remind the English reader that French literature has a richness and a variety that is often obscured by the tendency of successive mandarins, both literary and academic, to reduce it to a matter of systems and formulae. And even if it is conceded that Rolland's fiction is unlikely to survive as an artistic achievement, there can be no doubt that as a witness of his epoch he had few rivals. The writing of *Jean-Christophe*, in fact, represented only one part of his activity in the years before 1914, and, looked at as a whole, his work during this period constitutes an immense archive – made up of letters, novels, memoirs, biographies, and studies of French, German and Italian music – that bear eloquent testimony both to his Europeanism (a quality that distinguished him markedly from many of the French intellectuals of his time) and to his over-riding concern with the state of relations between France and Germany.

His knowledge of German culture, although far from exhaustive, was considerable. In his youth in Italy he had been a close friend of the much older Malwida von Meysenbug, who had known Nietzsche and Wagner as well as Alexander Herzen and Mazzini. Through Malwida and through his own wide reading in German literature and experience of German music he acquired a sound knowledge of German civilisation that was further reinforced by the extensive correspondence that he maintained with some of the leading figures on the central European cultural scene. Prominent amongst these was the Austrian Stefan Zweig, a lifelong admirer, who wrote a study of his work. Hermann Hesse was another correspondent. Richard Strauss was yet another, and an important one, despite the many reservations that Rolland entertained over his influence and work. Whilst recognising Strauss's genius, Rolland much preferred the purity and restraint of Debussy, and once called Strauss 'the decadent Attila of German music'.[11] Despite the fact that Strauss enlisted his aid in utilising Oscar Wilde's original French text for French performances of his opera, Rolland was revolted by Strauss's *Salomé*, the heroine of which he described as 'Isolde's daughter', and wondered what kind of daughter she would give birth to in turn.[12] And in a letter that he wrote to Strauss himself on the subject he was clearly concerned that the opera had wide and disturbing implications:

Vous avez triomphé de l'Europe de notre temps. Maintenant, sortez de notre Europe, élevez-vous au-dessus. Il y a dans le monde européen d'aujourd'hui une force effrénée de décadence, de suicide – (sous des formes variées, en Allemagne en France) – gardez-vous d'assimiler votre cause à la sienne.[13]

(You have vanquished the Europe of our time. Now you must leave this Europe behind and rise above it. In today's Europe there is a wild tendency towards decadence and suicide – (taking different forms in Germany and France) – take care not to identify yourself with it.)

To Rolland, in fact, the career of Richard Strauss exemplified the dangers that faced Wilhelminian Germany as a whole. The old idealistic German culture represented by Malwida von Meysenbug was in the process of being perverted into a ruthless quest for material power in the realms of politics and economics, and a restless search for the titanic and the *kolossal* in the arts – above all, in music. On the one hand there was Bismarck, who had encouraged the worship of Macht by his belief in blood and iron and his brutal amputation of Alsace–Lorraine from France, bequeathing to his successors a standard of behaviour that they were only too anxious to follow:

Quelle lumière l'Allemagne de Sedan a-t-elle apportée au monde? L'éclair des baïonnettes? Une pensée sans ailes, une action sans générosité, un réalisme brutal, qui n'a même pas l'excuse d'être sain; la force est l'intérèt: Mars commis-voyageur.[14]

(What form of enlightenment had the Germany of Sedan given to the world? The gleam of bayonets? A narrow way of thinking, action without generosity, a brutal realism that does not even have the excuse that it is sensible; ruthlessness pays dividends, Mars a commercial traveller.)

On the other hand there was Richard Wagner, seemingly the antithesis of Wilhelm II, but in reality a fellow-peddler of shoddy goods: 'faux idéalisme, faux christianisme, faux gothisme, faux légendaire, faux divin, faux humain'[15] ('false idealism, false Christianity, false Gothic, false myth, false divine, false human'). Rolland made these comments on Wilhelminian Germany and Wagner (comments with which admirers of Wagner may only partially agree) in *Jean-Christophe*, but already in his journal in January 1898 he had remarked upon the affinity between the art and the politics of the

new Germany; after a performance of Strauss's tone-poem *Also
sprach Zarathustra* he pondered on the phenomenon of Richard
Strauss, Nietzsche and Wilhelm II, and concluded that there was
'du Néronisme dans l'atmosphère'[16] ('an element of Neroism in the
atmosphere').

The situation in Germany might not have been so serious had there
not been the danger of a major European war, but on this subject
Rolland's anxieties had always been acute since the days of his
youth, a youth dominated by the after-effects of France's defeat in
1870. Already in 1888 at the age of twenty-two he had noted that his
was a generation dominated by a sense of the imminence of war:

On aura peine à comprendre plus tard la situation morale dans laquelle nous
aurons passé notre jeunesse, nous la génération née de 66 à 72. Ceux qui ont
vécu avant, ceux qui vivront après, ont eu, auront toujours, l'idée de la mort
qui peut venir, à tout instant. Mais c'est une mort indécise, indéterminée,
vague, générale. Pour nous, elle est toujours présente et précise: c'est la
guerre. Depuis 1875, le pays vit dans l'attente de guerre. Depuis 1880, la
guerre est certaine; elle est imminente . . .[17]

(Later generations will scarcely comprehend the conditions in which we
spent our youth, my generation, the generation of '66 to '72. Those who live
before us or after us have to face, and will always have to face, the possibility
of death occurring at any moment. But it is a vague, generalised and
indeterminate notion of death. To us the idea of death was always an
immediate and definite possibility: the threat of war. After 1880, the war
seemed certain and imminent . . .)

Admittedly the sabre-rattling associated with the Schnaebelé incident of 1887 and the rise of General Boulanger did not lead to a
conflict, and, in the course of the next decade, France and Germany
tended to clash with Britain rather than with each other, but, with
the conclusion of the Anglo-French entente and Germany's attempt
to break that entente at the time of the First Moroccan Crisis, the
danger of a Franco-German war was back on the agenda as an
inescapable factor in international politics.

In the biography of Péguy that he published towards the end of his
life Rolland claimed that, unlike Péguy, he had been little affected by
the crisis of 1905, since by that time he had become so accustomed to
the idea that war was sooner or later inevitable that the crisis did not

shock him.[18] But at the time he seems to have been more agitated than he remembered, for he was appalled by the aggressive nature of German tactics, and, while he was relieved that the crisis ended peacefully, his resentment at the successive humiliations that France had suffered at the hands of Germany flared up fiercely.

Over the next few years, however, his attitude, like that of Jean-Christophe, underwent a change. While welcoming some aspects of the Nationalist revival in France as part of a wider movement of revolt against the decadence that had characterised the fin-de-siècle, he deplored the Germanophobia, the burning desire for 'revanche', and the cult of action and violence that the revival encouraged, believing that this made war ever more likely. And he was now convinced that such a war would be not merely a tragedy for France and Germany but a catastrophe for Western civilisation as a whole. At the time of the Second Moroccan Crisis in 1911 he wrote in one of his letters:

Quel que soit le vainqueur, dans une guerre, le premier, l'irrémédiablement vaincu sera tout l'Occident. Sa pensée sera rejetée de Dieu sait combien d'années en arrière! C'est une grande douleur de ne pouvoir plus partager les passions de ses contemporains, et de voir leur folie injuste et cruelle, qui se retournera contre eux, et dont soi-même on sera victime, sans pouvoir rien pour l'empêcher.[19]

(Whoever is the victor in a war, the first inescapable victim will be the whole of the West. Its thinking will be set back for God knows how many years! It is a very sad thing for one to be unable any longer to share the passions of one's contemporaries and to be forced to observe the way in which their cruel and unjust folly will rebound on them, with oneself as a victim, without one being able to stop it.)

This was to be his attitude during the remaining years before the outbreak of the war. In July 1911, when he began writing the last volume of *Jean-Christophe*, the Second Moroccan Crisis had just started. Soon after he finished it, in June 1912, the First Balkan War broke out. Despite his predictions of imminent catastrophe in that final volume he still *hoped* that a major European war might be averted, but in December 1912 he wrote that he felt the danger of a general conflict was 'suspended in the air',[20] and, a little over a year later, in January 1914, he confessed that he was convinced of the 'imminence' of war.[21] On 22 May 1914, after the publication of *Colas Breugnon*, the light-hearted picaresque novel that he wrote as a form of relief after his labours on *Jean-Christophe*, he admitted to one of his friends that his mood while writing it had not been one of unrelieved gaiety:

Tout en riant avec Breugnon, j'ai une autre partie de moi-même, un veilleur sur le faîte de la Tour, qui regarde au loin à travers les ténèbres et voit les cavaliers de l'Apocalypse.[22]

(Whilst laughing with Breugnon there is another part of me who is looking out across the darkness from the top of the tower, and sees the horsemen of the Apocalypse.)

Ten weeks after he wrote this letter the First World War broke out.

In the later stages of his life Rolland could claim, with considerable justification, that he had foreseen the disaster of the First World War and the collapse of European civilisation that would take place as a result of it:

Je ne m'y suis pas trompé, dès le premier regard d'adoloscent: j'ai vu se renouveler la fin du monde antique, le cinquième acte qui vient de la grande tragédie d'Occident . . . Déclin d'Europe, contre lequel l'énergie de Christophe . . . réagit contre la vue de cristal sans défaut d'Olivier désabusé – Avec Christophe j'ai lutté contre le destin que je voyais venir. Et j'ai appelé à la lutte les jeunes générations. L'espoir a persisté jusqu'à l'année funèbre qui scella la destinée d'Occident, 1914, l'année de la mêlée, qui faucha mes jeunes frères, mes fils spirituels, l'Europe en fleur.[23]

(Since my adolescence I have not been mistaken. I saw the end of the ancient world being re-enacted, the fifth act which came from the great tragedy of the West . . . The decline of Europe, against which the energy of Christophe reacted . . . in spite of Olivier's crystal-clear disillusionment – With Christophe I fought against the fate that I saw coming. And I called the younger generation to the struggle. Hope remained until 1914, the fateful year that sealed the destiny of the West, the year of the conflict that mowed down my young brothers, my spiritual sons, the flower of Europe.)

But despite his prophetic intuitions, he could have had no idea then of the scale of the catastrophe that was about to overwhelm Europe. Nor could he have foreseen then the precise nature of the events that were to unfold in the summer of 1914.

Indeed, like all his contemporaries, he was taken by surprise by the war when it actually happened. Not long before the outbreak of the conflict he had embarked on an affair with a young American actress, Helena Van Brugh de Kay, and the crisis caught him off guard whilst he was on his annual holiday in Switzerland. It was not until the Austrian declaration of war against Serbia that he began to take matters seriously:

Les six mois précédents m'avaient enveloppé d'un rêve de bonheur . . . Je ne voyais plus le monde que dans les yeux de la bien-aimée. Je me souviens de l'indifférence heureuse que j'y lus et goûtai, ce jour où nous apprîmes, dans un hôtel de Spiez, le meutre de l'archiduc, qui allait déchaîner sur l'Europe les Erynnyes.[24]

(During the six months that preceded the war I was caught up in a happy dream . . . I only saw the world in the eyes of my beloved. I remember the carefree indifference with which I read and enjoyed myself, the day when we learnt in a hotel in Spiez of the death of the Archduke, which was to bring down the Furies on Europe.)

When the war became a reality, however, his reaction was one of horror. After the German ultimatum and the outbreak of the war between Germany and France he wrote in his journal:

Je suis accablé. Je voudrais être mort. Il est horrible de vivre au milieu de cette humanité démente, et d'assister, impuissant, à la faillite de la civilisation. Cette guerre européenne est la plus grande catastrophe de l'histoire, depuis les siècles, la ruine de nos espoirs les plus saints en la fraternité humaine.[25]

(I am overwhelmed. I wish I was dead. It is horrible to live in the midst of a humanity that has gone mad and to be a helpless witness to the collapse of civilisation. This European war is the greatest catastrophe for centuries, the ruin of our most sacred hopes for human brotherhood.)

Because of both his age and the state of his health he was exempt from the demands of military service, so he decided to stay in his beloved Switzerland. In any case he believed at this stage that the war would soon be over. In the meantime he worked for nearly a year for the International Agency for Prisoners of War at Geneva:

In Switzerland, and in Switzerland alone I was in a position to listen to the confidences of both camps. In Switzerland alone I could judge impartially, from there and there alone I could assemble all the documents for the inquest.[26]

After the initial horror, his first reaction to the war was one of profound hostility towards a Germany which, he believed, must bear the major responsibility for the conflict. He was particularly incensed by the notorious manifesto of ninety-three German intellectuals who supported the war and defended Germany's action in violating Belgian neutrality. This provoked his famous open letter to the dramatist Gerhart Hauptmann, one of the signatories to the manifesto, in which he protested at the German bombardment of the ancient university city of Louvain:

Etes-vous les petit-fils de Goethe ou ceux d'Attila? Est-ce aux armées que vous faites la guerre, ou bien à l'esprit humain?[27]

(Are you the grandchildren of Goethe or of Attila? Do you make war on armies or on the mind of man?)

This appeared on 2 September. Three weeks later, when he published his famous 'Au-dessus de la mêlée', however, he was already turning his attention to the implications of the disaster for Europe as a whole.

At the beginning of this article he made it clear that his sympathies lay with *all* those who had been called upon to fight:

O jeunesse heroïque du monde! Avec quelle joie prodigue elle verse son sang dans la terre affamée! Quelles moissons de sacrifices fauchées sous le soleil de ce splendide été! . . . Vous tous, jeunes hommes de toutes les nations, qu'un commun idéal met tragiquement aux prises, jeunes frères ennemis – Slaves qui courez à l'aide de votre race, Anglais qui combattez pour l'honneur et le droit, peuple belge intrépide, qui osas tenir tête au colosse germanique et défendis contre lui les Thermopyles de l'Occident, Allemands qui luttez pour défendre la pensée et la ville de Kant contre le torrent des cavaliers cosaques, et vous surtout, mes jeunes compagnons français, qui depuis des années me confiez vos rêves et qui m'avez envoyé, en partant pour le feu, vos sublimes adieux, vous en qui refleurit la lignée des héros de la Révolution – comme vous m'êtes chers, vous qui allez mourir! [28]

(Oh, heroic youth of the world! With what prodigal joy you pour your blood on to the greedy earth! What sacrificial harvests have been cut down under

the sun of this splendid summer! . . . All of you young men, from every
nation, that a common ideal has tragically set one against another, young
brother enemies – Slavs who rush to the defence of your race, Englishmen
who fight for honour and justice, intrepid Belgians who have dared to refuse
to give in to the German colossus and have defended the Thermopylaes of
the West against it, Germans who fight to defend the thought and the city of
Kant against the onrush of Cossack horsemen, and above all you, my young
French companions, you who have confided in me your dreams and have
sent me sublime adieux as you left for the fire, you who are in the line of
descent from the heroes of the Revolution – how dear to me you are, you
who are going to your death!)

The two great international movements of Socialism and Christianity
had failed to prevent the conflict and adherents of both faiths were
slaughtering one another in the war. Meanwhile the intellectuals had
entered the fray, all of them convinced that they were defending
liberty and justice: Eucken was battling with Bergson, Hauptmann
with Maeterlinck, Rolland with Hauptmann, Wells with Shaw.
Kipling, d'Annunzio, Dehmel and de Régnier composed hymns to
war, while Barrès and Maurras opened the floodgates of hatred.

What was to be done in this situation? Rolland still believed that
the most dangerous form of aggression in Europe was that of Prussia,
its obsession with war the expression of a military and feudal caste
that must be destroyed. But Prussia was not the only danger. Tsarism
represented another, even more reactionary force that was attempting to prolong its life by embarking on imperialism. In these
circumstances, circumstances in which neither of the alliance
systems had a monopoly of justice on their side, it was imperative
that the intellectuals should not abandon their independence of
thought:

Elite européenne, nous avons deux cités: notre patrie terrestre, et l'autre, la
cité de Dieu. De l'une nous sommes les hôtes; de l'autre, les bâtisseurs.
Donnons à la première nos corps et nos cœurs fidèles. Mais rien de ce que
nous aimons, famille, amis, patrie, rien n'a droit sur l'esprit. L'esprit est la
lumière. Le devoir est d'élever au-dessus des tempêtes et d'écarter les nuages
qui cherchent à l'obscurcir. Le devoir est de construire, et plus haute,
dominant l'injustice et les haines des nations, l'enceinte de la ville où
doivent s'assembler les âmes fraternelles et libres du monde entier.[29]

(Elite of Europe, we have two cities: our country on this earth, and the other, the city of God. We are inhabitants of one of them and builders of the other. Let us give to the first our bodies and our faithful hearts. But none of the things that we love, family, friends, country, have superiority over the mind. The mind is the light and we must rise above the tempests and disperse the clouds that hide it from view. Our duty is to build ever higher, dominating the injustice and hatred of nations, the walls of the city where all the free and fraternal souls of the world must be gathered together.)

As is the case with so many of Rolland's writings, the rhapsodic cadences of 'Au-dessus de la mêlée' strike the modern reader as being noble in intention but archaic, and irredeemably spoiled by rhetoric and cliché. Despite the fact that the article impressed public opinion in the neutral countries and was undoubtedly instrumental in his being awarded the Nobel Prize for literature in 1915, to many of his contemporaries there was a smugness about his stance that was utterly unacceptable. In Vienna, the satirist Karl Kraus refused to be impressed. When Rolland praised the Zürich performance in 1918 of Stefan Zweig's anti-war play *Jeremiah*, Kraus mocked at his claim that, by writing his work, Zweig had shown great courage: Rolland, he remarked, had certainly never heard of Kraus's magazine *Die Fackel*, which attacked the war from behind the lines of the enemy.[30] In England, individuals opposed to the war, such as Bertrand Russell, E.D. Morel and some of the contributors to the *Cambridge Magazine*, sympathised with Rolland's stance, but Wells characteristically found his position to be 'irritatingly self-important and irritatingly unhelpful'.[31] And even Shaw was to point out that, however much he hated the war, he had not followed Rolland's example and gone abroad to denounce it but had addressed his views directly to the British people. Rolland regarded Shaw as frivolous. Shaw regarded him as a sanctimonious and pretentious French intellectual. When, at the end of the war, Rolland tried for a time to establish an international organisation of intellectuals to maintain freedom of thought – something which he had dreamed of doing before the war started – Bertrand Russell was amongst those like Croce, Einstein, Tagore and Heinrich Mann, who signed Rolland's 'Declaration of Intellectual Independence', but Shaw's response was brusque:

The man of thought does not exist. I am not thought. I am Bernard Shaw.
You are Romain Rolland. We eat, and eight hours after, we forget our
philosophy, and only feel hungry . . . No man is above the battle.[32]

In France, predictably, apart from a few individuals like Roger
Martin du Gard, the response to Rolland's wartime activities was
even more hostile. Not only was Rolland unable to halt the torrent of
hate propaganda that was directed by French intellectuals against
Germany, he himself was now the subject of vitriolic attack. Some of
these onslaughts were simply scurrilous, like the accusations that he
had always been spiritually pro-German and was now in the pay of
Germany as well. But in view of Rolland's tendency to liken himself
to prophets like Isaiah, Barrès made a legitimate point when he
accused him of being guilty of the sin of spiritual pride,[33] while Henri
Massis (who had already attacked Rolland for his cosmopolitanism
and cultural eclecticism before the war) now found a perfect target
for his polemic.[34] Perhaps it was Rolland's old friend, the writer
Louis Gillet, however, who made the most telling criticism of the
former's position during the war. Relations between the two men
began to deteriorate after Gillet was called up in 1914, but it was in
1915 that their friendship was broken after Gillet became increasingly irritated by Rolland's admonitions and exhortations from
Switzerland:

L'horizon des tranchées est tout à fait borné. Le vôtre est peut-être trop
vaste. Je n'entends du matin au soir que la bruit du canon. Vous entendez
toutes les cloches, peut-être trop de cloches et le tout peut-être de trop
loin.[35]

(The view one has from the trenches is totally limited. Yours perhaps is too
vast. From morning until night I hear nothing but the sound of guns. You
hear all the bells, perhaps, too many bells, and everything from perhaps too
great a distance.)

By the early months of 1915 Rolland was in deep despair over the
attacks that had been made on him:

Je sens la haine qui monte en France contre moi . . . Je suis seul. Je passe les
journées les plus tristes de ma vie, dans un sentiment de solitude morale, de
détresse de coeur et d'esprit . . . A certaines heures, je n'y tiens plus. Je me

jette sur ma chaise longue, je me couvre le visage, et je cherche à goûter la saveur de la mort.[36]

(I sense the hatred that is rising against me in France . . . I am alone. I am spending the most unhappy days of my life in an atmosphere of moral isolation, of sadness of heart and mind . . . At certain moments I can bear it no longer. I throw myself on my chaise longue, cover my face, and try to acquire a taste for death.)

There was no possibility of any reconciliation with his critics in France, for by now he felt alienated from the passions that animated all the combatant powers. After reading the British *Blue Book* and the French *Livre jaune* he reacted with distaste to the evidence of the role played by secret diplomacy in causing the conflict, and, like Bernard Shaw, began to suspect that the lack of clarity in British policy had been a factor that tempted Germany to take the path of war. Whilst still holding that Germany must bear the major responsibility for provoking the conflict – 'Je n'en ai jamais douté. Elle porte tout à l'excès. Sa caractérisque constant est le déséquilibre, dans le mal comme dans le bien'[37] ('I have never doubted it. She carries everything to excess. Imbalance is her constant characteristic, in bad as well as good') – a position that he maintained until the end of the war, he now considered that guilt for the war should be assigned on a collective basis.

For a few months in the first half of 1915 he was hopeful that after the stalemate on the Western Front Germany might be interested in the possibility of a negotiated peace. After all, there *were* a number of writers in Germany who were against a continuation of the war. There was the group round the magazine *Die weissen Blätter* in Munich. There were pacifists like Albert Einstein and Friedrich Wilhelm Förster. And if Thomas Mann proclaimed that it was the mission of the Central Powers to defend European *Kultur* against the decadence of the West and the barbarism of the East, his Francophile brother, Heinrich, took a very different view. But all these opponents of the war were in a tiny and impotent minority, and the chances of an early end to the conflict were never very high. Throughout the war Rolland himself, as a French patriot, rejected the Leninist policy of revolutionary defeatism and was insistent that any peace was dependent on a German withdrawal from occupied French and Belgian territory. Against this background, and the obvious determination of Germany – a Germany ruled after 1917 by a ruthless military dictatorship – to make annexations in the course of the war, the belief that Rolland affirmed on several occasions that peace was possible if the western allies moderated their own demands can only be described as being the product of wishful thinking.

But by the summer of 1915 he had basically come to the conclusion that no amount of argument or debate could prevent Europe's determination to destroy itself. By that time he had lost all trust in the ability and willingness of the press in either France or Germany to print what he had to say without distortion, and for nearly eighteen months after July 1915 he kept up with his journal and his vast correspondence, but published very little. At length, after a long period of silence and rumination, he proclaimed that he had now passed beyond the stage of being primarily concerned with the problem of Franco-German hostility. It was the decline of Europe as a whole that now dominated his thoughts.

'Aux peuples assassinés', the article in which he made his new thinking public at the end of 1916, was profoundly influenced by, and contained extensive quotations from, a speech given by the Indian writer Rabindranath Tagore at the Imperial University of Tokyo in the summer of 1916, a speech in which Europe's claim to the moral leadership of the world, at a time when it was tearing itself apart in a brutal war, was held up to scorn:

The political civilisation which has sprung up from the soil of Europe and is over-running the whole world, like some prolific weed, is based on exclusiveness . . . It is carnivorous and cannibalistic in its tendencies, it feeds upon the resources of other peoples and tries to swallow their whole future . . . Before this political civilisation came to its power and opened its hungry jaws wide enough to gulp down great continents of the earth, we had wars, pillages, changes of monarchy and consequent miseries, but never such a sight of fearful and hopeless voracity, such wholesale feeding of nation upon nation, such huge machines for turning great portions of the earth into mincemeat, never such terrible jealousies with all their ugly teeth and claws ready for tearing open each other's vitals. This political civilisation is scientific, not human . . . It betrays trust, it weaves its meshes of lies without shame, it enshrines gigantic idols of greed in its temples, taking great pride in the costly ceremonies of its worship, calling this patriotism. And it can be safely prophesied that this cannot go on.[38]

Looked at with the benefit of hindsight it is clear that Tagore's hopes that Japan and Asia would be able not only to throw off European political domination but also to avoid the errors of Western imperialism were not to be fulfilled. Nevertheless his indictment of the greed and violence of the West is not unimpressive, and in endorsing this indictment Rolland called upon Europe to repent of its sins and to search for a new form of unity based on new moral principles.

The possibility of this being achieved during the second half of the First World War was not very high, however. In 1916–17 the conflict intensified as Lloyd George replaced Asquith in England (where E.D. Morel was sentenced to six months hard labour in 1917 – a sentence that undermined his health on a trumped-up charge of attempting to send an anti-war pamphlet to Rolland), as America entered the war (a development that Rolland at first deplored, seeing it as a further obstacle to a compromise peace),[39] as the army took over power in Germany, and as Clemenceau was finally summoned to be Prime Minister of France. Admittedly in Russia the Tsarist system collapsed in 1917, and for a time there was a widespread hope in Europe (which Rolland shared) that, by removing the main justification for the involvement of the Central Powers in the conflict, the Russian Revolution might lead to a general peace. But the advent to power of Lenin later in 1917 and the conclusion of the Treaty of Brest-Litovsk early in the following year enabled Germany to dream of a final victory in the west, a dream that was only shattered by the superior strength of the western allies in the course of 1918.

Despite all Rolland's hopes, therefore, all the changes that had been effected in Europe by the end of the war had been achieved by brute force. In the Soviet Union Lenin was appealing for a world revolution against imperialism, but this revolution was to be achieved by violence, while the reports that Rolland was to receive from correspondents like Maxim Gorki over Lenin's use of terror against his opponents at home were to alienate him even further from the Bolshevik experiment. In the West Rolland hoped for a time that Wilson might triumph over Clemenceau and Lloyd George in the peace negotiations at the end of the war, but the terms of the Treaty of Versailles were a bitter disappointment to him. 'Triste paix!' he commented on the day that the treaty was signed, adding that it was a peace that would only turn out to be an 'entr'acte dérisoire entre deux massacres des peuples!'[40] ('A sad peace! A derisory intermission between two massacres of the peoples!')

Alienated as Rolland was from the brutality of the Bolsheviks and the hypocrisy of the liberal democracies by the early 1920s, he was now increasingly inclined to abandon his hopes for Europe altogether and to place his faith in India, believing that it was there, perhaps, that the true heirs of Tolstoy might be found. Already in the course of the war he had become increasingly interested in Indian philosophy and religion, alerted by his correspondence with Hesse, and with Ananda Coomaraswamy (who exercised a considerable if largely hidden influence on the English cultural scene) discovering in the Indian tradition an emphasis on redemption through suffering, a sense of the importance of the natural and the animal creations, and an acceptance of the possibility of many redeemers, that he found intensely sympathetic. At the same time he had been alerted to the Indian revolt against Western imperialism by his reading of Tagore. Now in Gandhi and the idea of non-violence it seemed that he had discovered a form of revolutionary action of which he could approve.

It is no accident, therefore, that in the decade after the end of the First World War Rolland devoted a great deal of attention to Indian affairs. In August 1919 he published a laudatory article on Gandhi in the magazine *Europe* (a publication with which Rolland was to be closely associated for many years). Towards the end of the 1920s he wrote biographies of Ramakrishna and Vivekananda, and in 1931 there took place a famous encounter between Rolland and Gandhi at Rolland's home in Switzerland.

Gandhi had just attended the abortive Round Table Conference in London, where the British government had in effect committed itself to the creation in due course of an all-Indian self-governing federation, but had failed to overcome the fears of the Congress movement that this federation would be dominated by the princes and the Moslems. After leaving London Gandhi was on his way back to India where, on his return, the British felt obliged to resort to imprisoning Congress leaders.

For a few days in Switzerland, however, he and Rolland were able to discuss the problems of a world bedevilled by European imperialism, the onset of the Great Depression, and the rise of Fascism. In many ways this meeting represented the climax of Rolland's career as the voice of the European conscience. The paradox of the situation was that by this time he was moving away from Gandhian ideals towards a growing rapprochement with Communism and the Soviet Union.[41]

At first sight this seems to be an incomprehensible volte-face. During the Tsarist era Rolland had not been noticeably susceptible to 'le charme Slave', apart from his veneration of Tolstoy. After welcoming some features of the Bolshevik Revolution he had made clear his differences with Lenin and the Bolsheviks on many occasions, and in the early 1920s there had taken place one of those controversies that are the life-blood of the French intellectual world – a quarrel between Rolland and the novelist Henri Barbusse on the question of Bolshevik violence. The full details of this controversy may be found elsewhere,[42] but in essence Barbusse, who had had bitter first-hand experience of the war as a combatant, claimed that, however great his contribution towards discrediting the old order that had brought the war, Rolland was shirking the next and most necessary stage of development that was needed if another war was to be avoided – the creation of a Socialist society. This was a society that could only be constructed if *all* means, including violence, were considered.

Rolland's response to this was predictable. He reaffirmed the horror that he felt at the cruelties of the Bolshevik régime in Russia and expressed his fear that the terror being employed by the Bolsheviks would turn out to be, not simply a temporary expedient, as Barbusse had claimed, but a permanent feature of their rule; after all, he argued, this outcome seemed to be all the more likely since the rigours of the Bolshevik dictatorship had in no way been relaxed even with the ending of the Russian Civil War. Whilst reiterating the sympathy that he felt for many of the aims of the Russian Revolution, Rolland ended his statement of position by saying that the attitude he had adopted towards violence since the outbreak of the First World War had been a consistent one, and that the guiding principle behind all his actions could be summed up in the words of Schiller's motto, 'In tyrannos'.

But if he adopted this attitude in the early 1920s, why then did his views change so radically in the second half of that decade? Undoubtedly it was his fear of a renewed capitalist intervention against Russia, his horror at the rise of Fascism, and his growing doubts that Gandhian non-violence could meet these threats, that were the main reasons behind this transformation. Even during the most ardent phase of his love affair with India he had been disconcerted by the vagueness and fluidity of certain aspects of the Hindu tradition, contrasting it unfavourably with the harder, more precise, nature of the Christian inheritance of the West. He was also repelled by the way in which so many of the Indians with whom he came into contact seemed to be infected with the European disease of nationalism, and was particularly shocked by Tagore's inexplicable admiration for Mussolini. Faced by this, and faced, too, with the rise of Hitler in Germany, Rolland came to the conclusion that, whilst non-violence might remain a viable policy in fighting the British in India, Communism alone was capable of halting the march of the reactionary forces in Europe.

And so, from 1930 onwards, Rolland emerged as one of the most prestigious of the many fellow-travellers that Moscow was able to attract into its orbit in the course of the new decade. In 1931 he attempted to convince the sceptical Gandhi of the virtues of the Soviet system during the latter's visit to Switzerland. In 1932 he was a sponsor, together with Barbusse, of the Communist-dominated World Committee against Fascism and War, which solicited the support of the unpredictable duo of Wells and Shaw amongst many other prominent intellectuals from all over the world such as Gorki, Russell, Einstein, Heinrich Mann, Dreiser and E.M. Forster, and which held two great congresses, in Amsterdam in 1932, and in the Salle Pleyel in Paris the following year.[43] In 1933, too, Rolland finished the final volume of another *roman-fleuve*, *L'Ame enchantée* (a heavily didactic work, resolutely hostile to the literary and artistic avant-garde that Rolland had on occasion supported in the years before 1914, and lacking the freshness and spontaneity of *Jean-Christophe*), which tells the life story of Annette Rivière and some of her contemporaries, members of the generation that experienced the First World War and its aftermath and were now to find their salvation in Communism. Finally, in the summer of 1935 after a long and slow journey (with several halts made necessary by the state of his health) Rolland arrived in Moscow itself, where he had two interviews with Stalin, witnessed a parade in Red Square, attended a gala performance of his works in the theatre, and was everywhere received with the adulation that the régime was careful to make available for honoured guests.

On the surface Rolland's flirtation with Bolshevism was going extremely well. In the preface that he wrote to his *Quinze ans de combat* which also appeared in 1935 he made it plain that he had now abandoned many of the reservations that he had formerly held on the use of revolutionary violence. In the early 1920s, he explained, he had been a victim of that kind of bourgeois ideology which maintains that intellectuals can retreat into their ivory towers and isolate themselves from the common struggles of mankind. Now he had come to realise that it was only in the Soviet Union that real liberty had been achieved. The violence that had appalled him in the early years of the Bolshevik régime had now diminished and under the 'firm but gentle' leadership of Stalin the moderate forces within the Soviet Union had reasserted themselves.[44]

This is what Rolland proclaimed for public consumption. Privately he was not so sure. He was not unaware of the sinister aspects of Soviet society: his conversion to Communism had not taken place without prolonged inner turmoil, and already in the early 1930s he had deplored the brutality of the régime towards the kulaks. On the other hand there were things that a person of his eminence could do to improve the situation of certain individuals under Soviet rule. On his visit to Moscow in 1935 he intervened with Stalin to secure the release of Victor Serge from the Soviet Union where he had been condemned to internal exile for Trotskyist activities. On the same visit he was successful in helping to ameliorate the living conditions of the parents of his own second wife, Maria Koudacheva, the widow of a Russian officer who had fought with the Whites during the Civil War.

But he was deeply disturbed by his meetings with Gorki in the course of that visit, meetings to which he had been looking forward with great eagerness. It was Gorki, after all, who had been his most important informant on Russian affairs in the early 1920s, alerting him to the activities of the Cheka and the cruelties of the régime towards the intelligentsia. It was Gorki, too, who, after his return to the Soviet Union from exile in Capri, had encouraged Rolland to take a more positive view of the Soviet achievement towards the end of the decade. What he discovered when he visited Gorki in Moscow, however, was that the latter seemed to be virtually a prisoner in his own house, living in fear and under the constant surveillance of his secretary. This was bad enough, but far worse was to follow. In 1936 Gorki died in mysterious circumstances and his death was made one of the pretexts for the arrest and execution in 1938 of Yagoda, the head of the NKVD, who was charged with having instructed Gorki's secretary, a police agent, to poison him. By this time the purges were in full swing in the Soviet Union, and the world looked on in astonishment as millions of Soviet citizens were imprisoned, shot, deported to labour camps, or simply disappeared.

How did Rolland react to all this? In 1935 he defended the Soviet Union fiercely, claiming that the exile of Kamenev and Zinoviev had been a much milder form of punishment than the measures which had been taken during the French Revolution.[45] At the time of the trials of the old Bolsheviks in 1936 he declared publicly that he believed completely in the guilt of the accused and saw no reason to doubt the impartiality of the judicial system that condemned them.[46] In the privacy of his journal, however, he recorded his stupefaction when he heard of the execution of Kamenev, Zinoviev and the others, recalled the fratricidal hatreds that had broken out amongst the leaders of the French Revolution, and was appalled by the vilification of the dead men by Radio Moscow, contrasting this with the same station's eulogies of Stalin, whom it described as 'The sun' of the people of the USSR.[47] The whole incident left him wondering whether Stalin and his entourage, like Louis XIV and his courtiers, had taken leave of their senses. A few months later he involved himself in further contradictions by attempting to reassure the doubting Stefan Zweig that matters were not too bad. One must remember that the Nazis were plotting against the Soviet Union, that the Russian leaders lived in constant fear of assassination. After all, he himself had to be guarded whilst he was in Moscow:

Je *crois* que plusieurs des condamnés du procès de Moscou étaient tombés, sans le savoir, dans les filets de la Gestapo. Mais je *suis certain* que, ces filets, la Gestapo les avait tendus . . . J'estime hautement Staline. Je n'aime pas ses effigies et les nuages d'encens dont on l'enveloppe. Mais lui-même est simple . . . il n'a point de goût pour les compliments.[48]

(I *believe* that several of those condemned at the Moscow trial had fallen into the trap of the Gestapo without their being aware of it. But I *am certain* that the Gestapo had laid this trap . . . I have a high regard for Stalin. I do not like the effigies and the clouds of incense that surround him. But he himself is simple . . . he has no taste for compliments.)

The spectacle of two such eminent representatives of the European humanist tradition as Rolland and Zweig attempting to come to terms with the new world that had been created by the First World War and the Russian Revolution is not an edifying one. Slowly, however, the truth of the situation began to dawn on him. When Gide's famous *Retour de l'URSS* was published in 1936 (which, in however idiosyncratic a manner, made many of the same criticisms of the system that Rolland was making in private) he felt able to denounce it publicly as mediocre, superficial, childish and contradictory.[49] When the purges intensified in their ferocity, however, he could no longer ignore the situation. Appeals that he sent to Moscow on behalf of some of the victims were ignored. In 1938, he was distressed to discover that Dr Levine, one of the doctors who had looked after him during his stay in the Soviet Union, was now under arrest. Rolland sent a telegram to Stalin on the latter's birthday pleading for clemency. This, too, was ignored, but by now the disillusionment recorded in his journal was complete:

C'est le régime de l'arbitraire incontrôlé le plus absolu . . . J'entends en moi gronder la douleur et la révolte.[50]

(It is a régime of totally unrestricted arbitrariness . . . I feel stirring within me feelings of anguish and of revolt.)

It seems likely that it was only his horror of Nazism, his belief that by denouncing the Soviet system he would be giving aid and comfort to the Fascists, and his concern to avoid reprisals against his wife's parents and children in the Soviet Union, that prevented him from an open break.

In August 1939, however, some of the reasons for his remaining silent were removed. The conclusion of the Nazi–Soviet pact meant that the Soviet Union had now withdrawn from the struggle against Fascism and that France was left open to the German aggressor. And now that Rolland was living in France again – he had returned in 1937, partly for financial reasons, partly because he felt his freedom to engage in the battle against Fascism was restricted in Switzerland – his duty was abundantly clear. Although he did not publicly denounce the pact, he resolved to ignore it and advised his friends to do the same. He also resigned from the Franco–Soviet Friendship Society. When the war broke out a few days later he addressed an open letter to Daladier, the French Prime Minister, in which he assured him of his full support in the coming struggle. Rolland was to find himself approaching the Second World War with feelings very different from those of 1914.

Although he was absolutely convinced that France was fighting a just war in 1939, Rolland could hardly fail to note the lack of enthusiasm which characterised the French war effort. Whilst many Communists and fellow-travellers reacted as he did and took no notice of the Pact, others followed the party line and denounced the war as a conflict between competing imperialisms, a path that was made easier to take because of the action taken by the French government in proscribing the party. On the Right there were many who felt that France and Britain should be fighting Communism and not Nazi Germany. Throughout the rest of French society there was a widespread revulsion against the idea of war, a determination that there should be no repetition of the holocaust of 1914–18, and the hope that the defences of the Maginot Line would be sufficient to deter the aggressor.

In May and June of 1940, however, this hope was shown to be illusory. Germany conquered Holland and Belgium, and France itself collapsed under the shock of the German onslaught. After many hesitations Rolland and his wife decided to leave their house at Vézelay, not far from Nevers, and head for the South, but they were prevented from doing so by the very speed of the German advance. Trapped as he was in the Occupation zone, therefore, Rolland as a prominent anti-Nazi expected to suffer considerably at the hands of the Germans, but, apart from a few incidents of petty persecution on the part of the Vichy authorities (who disliked him far more than did

those members of the German officer corps who remembered his
stance during the First World War and his denunciation of the
Versailles Settlement at the end of it) he was left largely undisturbed.

Indeed, while the years of the Occupation were to be years of
humiliation and suffering for France, and while Rolland identified
himself completely with his country's agony, they were also to be
years in which he himself enjoyed a kind of Indian summer. Freed
from all the political quarrels of the past, he now experienced the joy
of resuming old friendships with Louis Gillet and Paul Claudel. He
also experienced a remarkable sense of creative renewal that enabled
him not only to do further work on his memoirs, and finish the final
volume of the major biography of Beethoven that he had started in
the 1920s, but also to embark upon and complete a biography of his
long-dead friend and collaborator Charles Péguy.

Perhaps the use of the word 'friend' is misleading, since the
relationship between Rolland and Péguy was very much a one-sided
affair. Péguy had been happy to publish much of Rolland's work in
the *Cahiers de la quinzaine* – the early life of Beethoven, the
biography of Tolstoy and *Jean-Christophe*, for example – because it
had broadened the appeal of his magazine and was sufficiently
popular to increase its financial viability. But there was little really in
common between the two men. Rolland deeply admired Péguy as a
spokesman for 'l'ancienne France' – a France to which in so many
ways he himself belonged – and as a puritan and idealist who, like
himself, was engaged in a crusade to save France from the decadence
of the fin-de-siècle. On the other hand, Péguy for his part could not
admire the vague internationalism that animated Rolland's work
and, in writings that were not published until years after both men
were dead, cruelly mocked the latter's bloodless idealism and
constant valetudinarianism.

It is true that Péguy talked to Rolland about many of the
difficulties in his private life, but after his death it was apparent that
he had 'confided' in many people. Like many of those who had
known him, however, Rolland continued to believe that he had some
kind of special relationship with Péguy even after it became clear
that the latter was jealous of his financial and critical success.
Evidence of this jealousy is not difficult to find. Despite the fact that
Rolland received no royalties from the work he allowed Péguy to

publish, the latter attempted to assert that all the rights pertaining to this work belonged to the *Cahiers*. And, many years later, after the death of the two men, René Johannet revealed that in writing his polemical article on Rolland, 'Ainsi parlait Romain Rolland', which appeared in June 1914, he had done so at the instigation of Péguy and with the latter's constant encouragement.[51]

Rolland quarrelled with Péguy over the question of copyright, and perhaps suspected that Péguy was behind Johannet's attack, but it is a tribute to his essential magnaminity that, once Péguy was killed, he put these incidents out of his mind and concentrated his attention on attempting to convey to posterity some idea of the nature of the latter's gifts, both as a writer and as a prophet. Throughout the years laudatory references to Péguy can be found in Rolland's writings: even in 'Au-dessus de la mêlée', a manifesto that Péguy would surely have hated, there is in a footnote a tribute to his valour in dying for France. It was only fitting then that, during the years of the Occupation, when both Vichy and even the Collaboration attempted to capitalise on Péguy's message for their own ends, Rolland should have devoted himself to writing this magnificent biography, in which the intellectual atmosphere of the years before 1914 is captured just as surely as is the personality of Péguy himself.

It is not hagiography. Péguy's many faults are not glossed over; neither are the unforgivable words which he had employed in his attacks on Jaurès, whose demagogic gifts had alienated Rolland during his lifetime, but whose death had transformed him into a heroic figure. On the other hand, Péguy's idealism, his passion for liberty and the richness of his poetic achievement are all fully recognised. Early in 1912, after reading the latter's 'Le Porche du mystère de la deuxième vertu', Rolland had written in his journal:

Je ne puis plus rien lire après Péguy. Tout le reste est littérature. Comme les plus grands sonnent creux, auprès de lui!

(I can no longer read anybody after Péguy. Tout le reste est littérature. How hollow the greatest writers sound next to him!)

Rolland quoted these words in his biography thirty years later and added, 'Je pense encore de même, aujourd'hui'[52] ('I still think so today'). The two volumes of the biography form a worthy monument to both men.

And yet, if this biography is without any doubt Rolland's masterpiece, its very excellence raises in an acute form the problem of formulating any kind of satisfactory verdict on its author, for the contrasts between Rolland and Péguy are striking. In the course of his career Péguy was guilty of much violence and many injustices, but the integrity of his commitment was never in doubt, and his determination to sacrifice everything, including his own life, to the cause of liberty was total. It is doubtful whether the same can be said of the Olympian Rolland, especially during his period as a fellow-traveller in the 1930s.

Understandably enough, for some victims of Stalin's rule within the Soviet Union, Rolland's behaviour during this period of his career was unforgivable. In her autobiography *Hope against Hope* Ossip Mandelstam's widow, Nadezdha, found it incomprehensible that Rolland should have known of some of the conditions within the Soviet Union and should have confined himself in public to unstinted paeans of praise.[53] And in his autobiographical *Testimony*, Shostakovitch, whose opera *Lady Macbeth of Mtsensk* had led to his being attacked as a morbid and decadent 'enemy of the people' by the Soviet authorities in the 1930s, reacted with indignation to the lack of support that he and other victims of Stalin received from the fellow-travellers:

And what about Romain Rolland? It makes me sick to think about him. I am particularly disgusted because some of these famous humanists praised my music. Shaw, for one, and Romain Rolland. He really liked 'Lady Macbeth'. I was supposed to meet this famous humanist from the glorious pleiad of lovers of truthful literature and just as truthful music. But I didn't go. I said I was ill. Once I was tormented by the question: Why? Why? Why were these people lying to the whole world? Why did these famous humanists not give a damn about us, our lives, honour and dignity? And then I suddenly calmed down. If they don't give a damn, then they don't. And to hell with them. Their way of life as famous humanists is what they hold dear. They became like children for me. Nasty children – a hell of a difference, as Pushkin used to say.[54]

These are serious charges, and it is not surprising that Rolland's reputation has slumped catastrophically in the half-century that has elapsed since his death. Still, even his most implacable opponent could hardly deny that he performed an essential service as a witness to the events that took place in Europe in the period before and during the First World War. Nor could it be denied that his career as a whole has an enduring, if a somewhat eerie, fascination. Despite the naïvetés and sophistries of which Rolland was guilty, the observer of his career can hardly fail to marvel at the good fortune that enabled this last of the Romantics to survive the perils of the twentieth century, and to retain to the end the elusiveness of an enchanted soul.

The story of the last few months of his life is briefly told. He finished writing the biography of Péguy in the early months of 1944, at a time when the countryside around Vézelay was already alive with the actitivies of the Maquis. Soon after completing the book his health began to deteriorate, but he lived to see the liberation of France in the summer of 1944. He died on 30 December of the same year.

In the years since 1939 he had been strongly attracted by the idea of returning to Catholicism – the conversion of Madame Rolland and the urgings of Claudel were obviously important factors in this development – but he finally decided that, whilst venerating many aspects of the Christian faith, he could not find a lasting home within the confines of any dogma. Despite all this, in deference to the wishes of his wife and family, he consented to a religious funeral. The situation was further complicated by the fact that he had taken the opportunity offered by the Liberation to reconcile himself with his Communist friends. This was in no way an unexpected development, for, like many Frenchmen in 1944 and 1945, he was deeply impressed by the role that the Communists had played in the Resistance and was looking forward to the burying of old quarrels and the creation of a new France.

When the congregation gathered in the cathedral of Vézelay a few days after his death, therefore, a situation of considerable ambiguity was created, as befitted Rolland's role as a French intellectual. Both Catholics and Communists turned out in strength to salute the memory of a man whom both groups could regard as a 'compagnon de route'. The Resistance-inspired, and Communist-dominated, Comité National des Ecrivains had urged that the ceremony should be accorded state recognition.[55] At a time when the attention of many people was focussed on the outcome of the Ardennes offensive,

Hitler's last desperate effort to reverse the tide of German defeat, this decision posed a number of problems, but in the end even these difficulties were overcome.

And so the scene was set for the last paradox of Rolland's career, a final ironical commentary on all the hatreds that he had inspired by the stand he had taken in 1914. After the funeral service was over the congregation left the cathedral and assembled in the snow and slush outside. The tricolour and the Soviet flag fluttered in the breeze. 'Mein Reich ist in der Luft', Beethoven once proclaimed, a phrase that Rolland treasured, and one that could have served as his epitaph. But, at the end, the twentieth century had its own kind of tribute to offer, and it was to the accompaniment of military honours from a detachment of the French Forces of the Interior that the author of 'Au-dessus de la mêlée' was finally laid to rest.

— 8 —

D.H. Lawrence: nightmare and escape

It could be argued that in many ways the First World War was not of crucial importance for the career of D.H. Lawrence. Many of the themes that were to dominate his work were already in place before 1914. Already in *The White Peacock*, the novel that he started in 1906, the gamekeeper Annable is described as

a man of an idea – that all civilisation was the painted fungus of rottenness. He hated any sign of culture . . . When he thought, he reflected on the decay of mankind – the decline of the human race with folly and weakness and rottenness. 'Be a good animal, true to your animal instinct', was his motto.[1]

And already in 1912 Lawrence had taken the decisive step of uprooting himself from England by eloping with Frieda Weekley. For the next two years the couple lived in Germany and Italy, and their return to England in 1914 was largely prompted by Frieda's desire to see her children. In a very real sense, therefore, the fact that Lawrence was present in England for the duration of the war was only an accidental and incidental detail in a career that had already settled into a pattern of *dépaysement* and flight.

And yet, once all this has been taken into account, the significance of the war for Lawrence's future development can hardly be exaggerated. The fact is that, in the years after the death of his mother and his departure for Europe with Frieda, the two years immediately before the outbreak of the war, he experienced an immense sense of liberation and of hope. In his famous letter to Ernest Collings, written in January 1913, he proclaimed that his great religion was now

in the blood, in the flesh, as being wiser than the intellect. We can go wrong in our minds. But what our blood feels and believes and says is always true.[2]

And he now felt that England was capable of liberating herself from all those mechanical and industrial forces that were stifling her creativity:

I write because I want folk – English folk – to alter, and have more sense.[3]

In March 1913 he started work on the first draft of *The Sisters*, the text that was to form the basis both of the present *The Rainbow* and parts of the sequel that is now known as *Women in Love*. It was a novel that was to trace the story of the regeneration of England, and to affirm his own emancipation from that debased relationship between the sexes, that domination of the mother, that he had depicted in *Sons and Lovers*.

It was in March 1913, too, that there appeared his remarkable article 'The Georgian Renaissance', written for Middleton Murry's short-lived magazine *Rhythm*, an article in which, in the course of reviewing the first volume of Marsh's *Georgian Poetry*, a volume in which some of his own work appeared, Lawrence made his most ecstatic affirmation of hope in the rebirth of England. It is written with an ardour that makes the other Georgians appear tepid and suburban:

We are waking up after a night of oppressive dreams. The nihilists, the intellectuals, hopeless people – Ibsen, Flaubert, Thomas Hardy – represent the dream we are waking from. It was a dream of demolition. Nothing was, but was nothing. Everything was taken from us. And now our lungs are full of new air and our eyes see it is morning . . . In almost every poem in the book comes this note of exultation after fear, the exultation in the vast freedom . . . This great liberation gives us an overwhelming sense of joy, joie d'être, joie de vivre . . . The joy is sure and fast . . . We have faith in the vastness of life's wealth . . . There is no winter that we fear.[4]

Such euphoria was bound to be dissipated sooner or later, and even if the war had not broken out, it was inevitable in the long run that Lawrence should have experienced bitter disillusionment at England's inability to respond to the opportunities that were now open to her. Having said all this, however, the contrast between the optimism of 1913 and the traumas that he was to experience during the war could not be more striking. Trapped in England for the duration of the conflict, this fierce and disconcerting but intensely

English writer was forced to witness the shattering of all his hopes for his native land and was doomed thereafter to wander the world in a vain search for an alternative Utopia.

Lawrence heard the news of the outbreak of the war when he was on a walking tour of the Lake District. On his return to London he suffered a second blow, when he was informed that *The Sisters* (or *The Rainbow* as he now called it) which he had finished in May 1914 had now been rejected by Methuen as unpublishable because of the sexual explicitness of certain passages. Lawrence put the manuscript aside and did not work on it for several months. For a time he seemed to be in despair. The war represented the triumph of all those forces that were undermining modern civilisation and all his hopes lay in ruins.

He was never a pacifist, of course. A certain element of savagery was always implicit in his exaltation of the primitive and elemental, an element that has always repelled many readers of his work, especially in France, where neither his passionate attacks on the soulless nature of contemporary industrial society nor his puritanical obsession with sex as a form of Revelation aroused any particular interest until Malraux and Drieu la Rochelle drew attention to his work in the 1930s. 'EXECRABLE!' was the inevitable response of a man of Gide's generation to what he considered to be the brutality, irrationality and shapelessness of Lawrence's achievement.[5] But Lawrence owed little to French aestheticism and humanism. He had a horror of the 'cher maître' approach to literature, and he was at one with Rolland in destesting Paris – 'that city of dreadful night', as he described it. Unlike Rolland, however, he had no pity for humanity in its present plight in 1914:

The war makes me depressed, the talk about the war makes me sick, and I have never come so near to hating mankind as I do now. They are fools, and vulgar fools, and cowards who will always make a noise because they are afraid of silence. I don't even mind if they're killed. But I do mind those who, being sensitive, will receive such a blow from the ghastliness and mechanical, obsolete, hideous stupidity of war, that they will be crippled beings, further burdening our sick society. Those that die, let them die. But those that live afterwards – the thought of them makes me sick.[6]

The situation was all the more senseless because, as he explained in a remarkably prophetic article, 'With the Guns', published in *The Manchester Guardian* on 18 August 1914, his own experiences observing the Bavarian army on manoeuvres in 1913 had convinced him that in the impersonality and paralysing din of modern warfare there was no place for the heroism of the past:

Why must I fire off my gun in the darkness towards a noise? Why must a bullet come out of the darkness pecking a hole in me? But better a bullet than the laceration of a shell, if it came to dying. But what is it all about? I cannot understand; I am not to understand. My God, why am I a man at all, when this is all, this machinery piercing and tearing?

It is a war of artillery, a war of machines, and men no more than the subjective material of the machine. It is so unnatural as to be unthinkable. Yet we must think of it.[7]

The more Lawrence thought of it, however, the greater was his misery. In January 1915 he wrote to Lady Cynthia Asquith, the daughter-in-law of the Prime Minister, that the war had finished him, that the outbreak of the hostilities had been 'a spear through the side of all my sorrows and hopes':

I had been walking in Westmorland, rather happy with water-lilies twisted round my hair . . . It seems like another life – we *were* happy – four men. Then we came down to Barrow-in-Furness, and saw that war was declared. And we all went mad. I can remember soldiers kissing on Barrow station, and a woman shouting defiantly to her sweetheart 'When you get 'em, Clem, let 'em have it', as the train drew off – and in all the tram-cars 'War'. Messrs. Vickers Maxim call in their workmen – and the great notices on Vickers' gateways – and the thousands of men streaming over the bridge. Then I went down the coast a few miles. And I think of the amazing sunsets over flat sands and the smoky sea – then of sailing in a fisherman's boat, running in the wind against a heavy sea – and a French onion boat coming in with her sails set splendidly, in the morning sunshine – and electric suspense everywhere – and the amazing, vivid, visionary beauty of everything, heightened up by immense pain everywhere.[8]

On the other hand the strength of the life-force within him can never be under-estimated, and the very exuberance of his language betrays a certain relishing of the experience on Lawrence's part. The fact is that by the time this letter was written, at the beginning of 1915, he was emerging from his despair. Indeed, there had already been signs of convalescence in the autumn of 1914 when he had immersed himself in writing an essay on Thomas Hardy, an enterprise that he had been thinking about for some time.

As was the case so often with Lawrence, once embarked on this essay he tended to relegate Hardy himself to the sidelines as he warmed to his real theme, the idea that war was due to the sickness of modern society, to the decadence of a civilisation that in a final act of desperation was attempting to find some kind of renewal. The form of therapy it had chosen might be a terrible one, but was the death of Western civilisation, as it was at present constituted, to be regretted? And did not the outbreak of the war demonstrate that mankind was tired of the real death-wish of modern culture, the principle of self-preservation at all costs? Western culture before the war had been like 'the hide-bound cabbage' going rotten at the heart:

Let there be an end, then, to all this welter of pity, which is only self-pity reflected on to some obvious surface. And let there be an end of this German hatred. We ought to be grateful to Germany that she still has the power to burst the bound hide of the cabbage . . . Where do I meet a man or a woman who does not draw deep and thorough satisfaction from this war? . . . After the war we must fight the renewed activity for self-preservation . . . If we are left maimed and halt, if you die, it will not matter so long as life shall sprout up again after this winter of cowardice and well-being.[9]

It was in a renewed state of optimism, then, that Lawrence began work on another draft of The Rainbow in the last six weeks of 1914, a draft which he finished in March 1915. By this time he had convinced himself that the war would end in 1915, and that his novel (the title of which was now charged with an extra significance) would help to usher in a new era, in which the epoch of law and the epoch of love would be succeeded by the new synthesis of the two, the epoch of the Holy Ghost, an epoch in which England – like Ursula in his novel – would move beyond the sterility of false relationships towards a new kind of society which repudiated materialism and greed.

Meanwhile he dreamed of leading a band of friends to found an ideal community, Rananim, from which the redemption of England could be begun. He was further encouraged in these hopes in the early months of 1915 by the beginnings of his friendship with two other opponents of war, Lady Ottoline Morrell and Bertrand Russell.

The story of this friendship has been told so often that only a bare outline need be given here. Looked at in retrospect it seems unlikely that there could ever have been any real meeting of minds between Russell and Lawrence, between the Whig patrician and the son of a Calvinist mother and a Nottinghamshire coal-miner, between the rationalist sceptic and the prophet of 'blood-consciousness'. On the other hand, they were both men animated by moral passion – the formative influence on Russell's childhood had been that of his intensely puritanical grandmother – and they were both believers in action through an élite of enlightened individuals to better the lot of mankind. At first it looked as if the enterprise might succeed. For his part, Russell was completely overwhelmed by Lawrence's fire:

He is amazing; he sees through and through one. He is infallible. He is like Ezekiel or some other Old Testament prophet, prophesying. Of course the blood of his nonconformist ancestors is strong in him, but he sees everything and is always right.[10]

Their ambition to give a joint series of lectures directed against the war and indicating the kind of social reconstruction they would like to see after it did not materialise, however. After a visit to Cambridge to meet possible sympathisers like Keynes Lawrence concluded that the Bloomsbury ethos was shallow, effete and corrupt, and, after briefly conceding to Russell that Socialism might form the basis of the campaign against war, all Lawrence's authoritarianism and hatred of democracy suddenly burst forth:

Can't you see the whole state is collapsing, Look at the Welsh Strike. This war is going to develop into the last great war between Labour and Capital. It will be a ghastly chaos of destruction, if it is left to Labour to be constructive. The fight must immediately be given a higher aim than the triumph of Labour, or we shall have another French Revolution. The deadly Hydra now is the hydra of Equality. Liberty, Equality and Fraternity is the three-fanged serpent. You must have a government based upon good, better and best. You must get this into your lectures at once. You are too old-fashioned. The back of the serpent is already broken.[11]

The Labour party must not be helped into power. Instead, in a future society authority should be vested in an absolute dictator and an equivalent dictatrix.

By September 1915 the temperamental incompatibility between

Lawrence and Russell had come right out into the open. When the latter proposed to call for an end to the war by appealing to mankind to restrain its hatred, Lawrence reacted violently. It was precisely modern civilisation's attempt to kill the instincts and the passions that had led mankind to vent its frustrations in war. It was the hatred of the emotions displayed by men like Russell that was the really destructive force in the modern world:

Your basic desire is the maximum of desire for war, you are really the super-war spirit. What you want is to jab and strike, like the soldier with the bayonet, only you are sublimated into words . . . to come as the angel of peace – no, I prefer Tirpitz a thousand times in that role. The enemy of all mankind you are, full of the lust of enmity. It is not hatred of falsehood which inspires you, it is the hatred of people of flesh and blood, it is a perverted mental blood-lust. Why don't you own it? Let us become strangers again. I think it is better.[12]

Russell claimed afterwards that he was so shocked by this letter that for twenty-four hours he contemplated suicide. However, he soon reassured himself that he was right and that Lawrence was wrong. After further attacks from Lawrence – 'Even your mathematics are only *dead* truth: and no matter how fine you grind the dead meat you'll not bring it to life again'[13] – communication between the two men ceased after the spring of 1916. In later years Russell was to be prominent amongst those who saw Lawrence as a precursor of Fascism.

In fairness to Lawrence the hysterical nature of his attack on Russell can partly be explained by the more general distress that he was experiencing by the summer of 1915, for by now he had come to realise that there would be no speedy conclusion to the war. On the continent the battles intensified. At home the strange death of Liberal England proceeded apace. Horatio Bottomley's influence increased through his bellicose articles in *John Bull* and in his highly-paid recruiting campaigns which enabled him to maintain himself in mistresses and champagne. Meanwhile there were growing demands for conscription. At the end of April 1915 Lawrence had written to Ottoline Morrell:

The death of Rupert Brooke fills me more and more with the sense of the fatuity of it all. He was slain by bright Phoebus' shaft – it was in keeping

with his general sunniness – it was the real climax of his pose . . . O God, O
God, it is all too much of a piece: it is like madness.[14]

But worse was to follow. The Dardanelles expedition was a failure. In
May Asquith gave way to the pressure of events and formed a
coalition government with the Conservatives. In September the
attempt to push the Germans back on the Western Front ground to a
halt in the bloody battle of Loos. At the end of that month, when his
new novel was coming out, Lawrence confessed sadly that he had set
his rainbow in the sky too soon before, instead of after, the deluge.
And on 21 October, commiserating with Cynthia Asquith on the
death of her brother at the Front, he revealed that he was now
attempting to leave England for America:

In the war, in the whole spirit in which we now maintain, I do *not* believe, I
believe it is *wrong*, so awfully wrong, that it is like a great and consuming fire
that draws up all our souls in its draught. So if they will let me I shall go away
soon, to America. Perhaps you will say it is cowardice: but how shall one
submit to such ultimate wrong as this which we commit, now, in England
and the other nations? If thine eye offend thee, pluck it out. And I am
English, and my Englishness is my very vision. But now I must go away, if
my soul is sightless for ever. Let it then be blind rather than commit the vast
wickedness of acquiescence.[15]

To the objection that his was the kind of reaction that would enable
Germany to triumph, his reply was predictable:

The Prussian rule would be an external evil. The disintegrating process of
the war has become an internal evil, so vast as to be almost unthinkable, so
nearly overwhelming us, that we stand on the very brink of oblivion.[16]

That he had reached a major turning point in his life was confirmed
on 2 November 1915 when the magistrates at Bow Street condemned
The Rainbow as obscene and ordered that copies of the novel should
be destroyed. The full truth about this trial has never been told. The
prosecuting solicitor was the same man who, two years later, was to
secure the conviction of E.D. Morel for sending a copy of his *Truth
and the War* to Romain Rolland in Switzerland, thus raising the
suspicion that Lawrence was already under surveillance by the
intelligence services. However that may be, Lawrence delayed his
departure for America in the hope that with the help of prominent

literary personalities like Arnold Bennett he might be able to get the ban lifted. But by the time that these attempts were demonstrated to be fruitless, his desire to leave England was blocked by the introduction by the government of the Derby scheme, in which, in a last effort to avoid the compulsory principle, men of military age were invited to register for military service. Guarantees were given that married men would not be called up until single men had been absorbed into the armies, but even these regulations were not sufficient to meet the army's demands and in January 1916 the government committed itself to the principle of universal conscription. On two occasions in the course of the war Lawrence was adjudged to be unfit for military service because of the state of his lungs, but the maze of bureaucracy in which he was now involved (a situation that was made even more complicated by the condemnation of *The Rainbow* and the fact that Frieda was of German birth) meant that he was refused passports to leave the country until after the war.

From now on Lawrence was like a caged animal. Far more than the shock of August 1914, it was this enforced captivity that he endured from the autumn of 1915 onwards that alienated him from England for ever. Several years after the end of the war he wrote that it was in 1915 that the old world ended:

In the winter of 1915–1916 the spirit of the old London collapsed; the city, in some way, perished, perished from being a heart of the world, and became a vortex of broken passions, lusts, hopes, fears, and horrors. The integrity of London collapsed, and the genuine debasement began, the unspeakable baseness of the press and the public voice, the reign of that bloated ignominy, *John Bull*.[17]

By the end of 1915 he and Frieda were living in Cornwall, where they were joined in 1916 by Middleton Murry and Katharine Mansfield.

This was not a satisfactory state of affairs, however. The Lawrences quarrelled incessantly. Murry failed to respond to Lawrence's offer of *Blutbrüderschaft*. The Murrys quarrelled with Lawrence and Frieda, and then departed. Meanwhile England's situation went from bad to worse. The Easter rebellion in Ireland, Lawrence told E.M. Forster, was 'another rent in the old ship's bottom'.[18] At sea there was the failure to secure a decisive victory at Jutland. On the land there was the disaster of the Somme offensive. In

December 1916 Asquith fell from power and was replaced by Lloyd George, whom Lawrence considered to be 'a clever little Welsh rat'.[19] In October 1917, victims of war hysteria, Lawrence and Frieda were expelled from Cornwall on suspicion of engaging in espionage.

But still he fought back. Unlike Rolland he did not believe that salvation would come from the East. As he told Ottoline, 'this wretched worship of Tagore is disgusting'.[20] But the West was undoubtedly doomed. To meet the situation he produced a series of essays (not all of which were published at the time) in which his Evangelical Calvinist background together with the influences of such diverse personalities as Joachim of Fiore, Blake, Ruskin, Carlyle, Nietzsche, Houston Stewart Chamberlain and Edward Carpenter resulted in a collection of apocalyptic commentaries on the times.

In the series of articles entitled 'The Reality of Peace' that he wrote in 1917, for example, Lawrence made it clear that he had no sympathy for those slaughtered at the Front. The war had been due to the subconscious desire of the masses for death, and they had willingly enlisted in the ranks of death. The war would not end until a civil war resulted in the birth of a new consciousness that repudiated mass industrialised civilisation. While Frieda claimed that Lawrence should have been awarded the Nobel Peace Prize for these articles, and Lawrence himself thought that they were a worthy successor to Norman Angell's 'The Great Illusion', the editor of *The English Review*, Austin Harrison, took a different view. At a time when the British army was enduring the horrors of Passchendaele the series was abruptly suspended.

Lawrence was unrepentant, however. For a time he hoped that the Russian Revolution might be the herald of the new consciousness that he desired, but by the end of 1917 his hopes had dwindled. After a series of aimless wanderings in London and Derbyshire in the course of the next twelve months he and Frieda ended up on Armistice Day at a party in London attended by Lytton Strachey, David Garnett and other leading lights of Bloomsbury. Whilst the intellectuals were celebrating the end of hostilities it was typical of Lawrence that he should have introduced a jarring note into the festivities by pointing out that the war was not over:

The hate and evil is greater than ever. Very soon war will break out again and overwhelm you . . . The Germans will soon rise again. Europe is done for; England most of all countries . . . Even if the fighting should stop, the evil will be worse because the hate will be dammed up in men's hearts and will show itself in all sorts of ways which will be worse than the war. Whatever happens there will be no Peace on Earth.[21]

In 1919 the Lawrences left England for the continent, Frieda to see her mother and sister in Germany, he for Italy where he would await her:

Then, finding the meaninglessness too much, he gathered his few pounds together and in November left for Italy. Left England, England which he had loved so bitterly, bitterly – and now was leaving, alone, and with a feeling of expressionlessness in his soul. It was a cold day. There was snow on the Downs like a shroud. And as he looked back from the boat, when they had left Folkestone behind and only England was there, England looked like a grey dreary-grey coffin sinking in the sea behind, with her dead grey cliffs and the white, worn-out cloth of snow above.[22]

This description comes from the famous 'The Nightmare' chapter of the novel *Kangaroo*, in which Lawrence bitterly recapitulated his war experiences some years later. The most significant work that he produced during the war itself, however, was undoubtedly *Women in Love*, which he wrote in 1916, utilising, changing and expanding material left over from the earlier drafts of *The Sisters* and *The Rainbow*. Although it is set in the period before the outbreak of the war the novel is charged with the apocalyptic violence of the war years. Ursula's lover, the school-teacher Birkin, who is very much a spokesman for Lawrence himself, repeatedly proclaims the imminent collapse of Western civilisation. The café Pompadour where the London intellectual and artistic world congregates is described as 'the centre and whirlpool of disintegration and dissolution'. Ursula's sister Gudrun is trapped in a loveless relationship with the industrialist Gerald Crich, who believes only in money and power. Birkin desires *Blutbrüderschaft* with Gerald – the homoerotic elements in the novel were only fully revealed when Lawrence's prologue was first published in 1963 – but Gerald does not reciprocate this desire. In any case he is doomed after Gudrun's liaison with the Jewish artist Loerke, and perishes in the Alps.

 Women in Love – Dies Irae was one title that Lawrence considered for it – is now recognised not only as one of Lawrence's most

powerful novels but also as one of the most remarkable realisations in
fiction of the passions and turmoils, the geological shifts in
perception, of the war years. Lawrence himself said of it that it
'actually does contain the results in one's soul of the war: it is purely
destructive, not like *The Rainbow*, destructive, consummating',[23]
Like Eliot's *The Waste Land* the novel may have its origins in private
trauma and a personal sense of desolation, but, again like *The Waste
Land*, it transcends its subjective components, and the intensity with
which Lawrence depicts the fragmentation of personality that takes
place in a civilisation shorn of traditional religious belief and in the
process of disintegration gives to *Women in Love* a far wider
significance that it would possess if it were merely a portrait of
Lawrence and Frieda, and various of their friends and enemies,
during the war years. Like all Lawrence's novels it is open to the
criticism that, while its diagnosis of the ills of mankind is often
profound and is successfully rendered in artistic terms, the remedies
it proposes are often too stridently, and, at the same time too
obscurely, conveyed to be convincing. Indeed, it may be felt that
throughout his career Lawrence, despite his advocacy of the
instinctive and the spontaneous, placed so great and so awesome a
burden of metaphysical and sexual responsibility on personal
relationships that humankind, bereft of traditional forms of social
and religious support, was incapable of living up to his ideals.

   And yet if he was perhaps bound to be less than totally successful
in trying to depict the human while at the same time attempting like
Emily Brontë to go beyond 'the old-fashioned human element', into
'that which is physic – non-human in humanity', as he described it in
a famous letter to Edward Garnett in April 1914, his achievement in
coming so close to his vision in *Women in Love* remains remarkable.
Not surprisingly, however, the novel made little impact when it was
first published in 1920. Like *Heartbreak House* its symbolism was too
rich, its proximity to the war was too great, for it to be properly
appreciated. It was years ahead of its time.

Convinced as he was that Western civilisation had destroyed itself in
the course of the war, Lawrence travelled widely outside Europe in
the early 1920s. From Italy he journeyed to Ceylon, Australia, the
United States and Mexico. In 1924 he paid a visit to Europe but then

returned to Taos, New Mexico, where he hoped for a time to establish his ideal community. In 1921 he finished the final version of *Aaron's Rod*. In 1923 he finished *Kangaroo*, and by 1925 he had completed the final version of *The Plumed Serpent*. It is the content of these so-called 'leadership' novels and some of his other writings in the early 1920s that has provided the main evidence for those critics who have accused Lawrence of holding views akin to those of Fascism.

It is an accusation that has a certain credibility. Lawrence's authoritarianism and hatred of democracy have already been noted. In *The Plumed Serpent*, Ramon and Cipriano are held up as models of supremacy to whom the masses, and the woman Kate, must submit. In the essay 'Education of the People', which he wrote between 1918 and 1920 (but which was not published in his lifetime), he laid stress on the inequality of ability that existed amongst children, and maintained that the majority, who were not suited for an academic education, should be taught simple utilitarian skills and should be content to be ruled by a superior caste. In the textbook *Movements of European History*, which he wrote for the Oxford University Press in the early 1920s, 'strong' leaders like Bismarck are constantly held up for praise. From an examination of Lawrence's writing and correspondence during this period it is quite clear that he believed that races should be kept separate from one another, that negroes were inferior, and that Jews were gifted but were often agents of decadence and disintegration. From all this, a whole dossier of quotations can be produced to substantiate the charge that his position was close to the Fascist ideologies of the inter-war years.

And yet there is equally ample evidence to refute this proposition. Many of Lawrence's views may be deeply repellent, but their force is continually undercut by his individualism and his distrust of power (especially in the hands of other people). Already in his writings during the First World War he had shown his dislike of the egoism of dictators like Caesar and Napoleon, and in 'Education of the People' he stressed that the individuality of all children must be respected. The references to Italian Fascism in his letters are almost uniformly critical or satirical, and in an epilogue to a new edition of *Movements in European History*, an epilogue which he wrote in 1925 (but which remained unpublished until 1972), he attacked Socialism, but went on to describe Fascism as 'only another kind of bullying'.[24] In the remarkably prophetic 'Letter from Germany' which he wrote for the *New Statesman* in March 1924 (an article which had even greater impact when it was first published ten years later), he pointed out that Germany was in the process of repudiating the West and was reverting to the spirit of Tartary and Attila, but, however much he may on occasion sound like Spengler, he did not derive any pleasure from this Spenglerian scenario in real life, attributing the present mood of Germany to the French occupation of the Ruhr, English 'nullity' and German 'false will', and quoting the tag 'Quos vult perdere Deus, dementat prius.'[25]

It is likely then, that Hitler, with his ruthless pursuit of material power and his glorification of modern technological warfare, would have held no attractions for Lawrence had he lived. In June 1914, long before the advent of the Fascist dictators, he had attacked Marinetti and the Futurists for their worship of industrialisation and the machine:

They will progress down the purely male or intellectual or scientific line . . . 'Italy is like a great Dreadnought surrounded by her torpedo boats'. That is it exactly – a great mechanism.[26]

Fascism might claim to repudiate the dehumanisation of modern scientific and mechanical civilisation, but in practice all that it offered was a demonic intensification of the destructive influences at work within this civilisation. Some writers, like Drieu la Rochelle, who admired Lawrence's work may have embraced Fascism, but Lawrence, ultimately like Spengler himself, is unlikely to have been deceived.

In any case his whole attitude towards the principle of authority underwent a profound change in the middle of the 1920s. The violence and the dark gods of *The Plumed Serpent* are intensely distasteful – here certainly Lawrence moves from the non-human to the inhuman – but perhaps the best way of looking at this novel is to see it as a work of fantasy and wish-fulfilment, a form of psychological over-compensation made necessary by the worsening state of Lawrence's health and by the continual battles of will between himself and Frieda, battles which he almost always lost. After his serious illness in Mexico City in 1925 and his return to Europe, however, there was a softening in his asperities. 'The hero is obsolete and the leader of men is a back number', he wrote to E.H. Brewster in March 1928:

We're sort of sick of all forms of militarism. The leader-cum-follower relationship is a bore. And the new relationship will be some form of tenderness, sensitive, between men and men and men and women.[27]

He was deeply moved by his last visit to Nottinghamshire in the aftermath of the General Strike when the miners were driven back to work in great bitterness and disunity:

Curiously I like England again, now I am up in my own regions . . . and there seems a queer, odd sort of potentiality in the people, especially the common people . . . They are not finished.[28]

This new 'tenderness' and this desire to return to his roots are clearly the inspiration behind the strange but touching *Autobiographical Fragment*, in which the author as a boy enters a crevice in the rocks in the Blue John area near Matlock, falls asleep and dreams that a thousand years later he wakens to a world in which all the evils of industrialism have been banished. But the most famous manifestation of the new spirit within Lawrence is, of course, *Lady Chatterley's Lover*.

By common consent this is not an unflawed novel. Nor is it by any means a work of universal 'tenderness' and love. On the contrary, the society that Lawrence depicts in schematic terms is characterised by extreme fragmentation and polarisation. Despite Lawrence's professions of optimism in the *Autobiographical Fragment*, and the essay 'Nottinghamshire and the Mining District', which he wrote towards the end of his life, the mass of the ordinary people of the mining villages are portrayed as corrupted by greed, while their leisure pursuits are characterised as vulgar, cheap and commercialised. There is little hope for them in the future:

There's a bad time coming. There's a bad time coming boys, there's a bad time coming! If things go on as they are there's nothing lies in the future but death and destruction for these industrial masses.[29]

At the other end of the scale there is the crippled Sir Clifford Chatterley, rendered in terms almost of caricature, a mixture of capitalist ruthlessness and baby-like dependence on Mrs Bolton.

In the middle of this divided community there is, it is true, the game-keeper Mellors, who has the intellectual ability to cross the class barriers and has plenty of ideas on the future of society. But Connie herself realises that 'even in him there was no fellowship left. It was dead.'[30] One might perhaps have expected some residual sense of comradeship and respect between Mellors and Sir Clifford, based on their common experience in the First World War, but, while Lawrence called repeatedly in his work for *Blutbrüderschaft*, he always had a great capacity for seeing what he wanted to see and for ignoring the rest, and clearly he found it convenient to deny the kind of blood-brotherhood that became a reality in the trenches. Perhaps an element of envy was at work here. In a famous passage in *Aaron's Rod* Rawdon Lilly denies that the war was a meaningful reality: 'It took place in the automatic sphere, like dreams do. But the *actual man* in every man was absent.'[31] And in *Lady Chatterley's Lover*, too, it is made clear that there was nothing in the war itself that might have brought Mellors and Sir Clifford closer together. The latter is described as being sexually and spiritually inadequate even before he was wounded in France, while Mellors appears to have spent the war, not on the Western Front, but in India and Egypt. Any bond between the two men, then, is firmly ruled out.

To Lawrence, of course, the loveless, disintegrating society depicted in the novel is redeemed by the relationship that develops between Mellors and Connie, a relationship that is obviously intended to indicate the way in which a society that is in danger of atomisation and collapse can achieve regeneration. But now that the element of excitement and shock occasioned by the author's sexual explicitness has long since ceased to influence readers, the love affair between Mellors and Lady Chatterley seems far less moving than Lawrence intended it to be. Despite his pleas for tenderness, the relationship between the two seems to have a somewhat forced and strained quality, a sense of the 'voulu', about it. Mellors may treat Connie with gentleness, but it is not only feminists who can react with distaste to the spectacle of a woman being initiated into the meaning of life by a man Lawrence clearly regarded as her natural lord and master. The attempt to resurrect the Anglo-Saxon vocabulary of sex, and the mirthless way in which Mellor's speech moves into dialect during the sexual encounters, are further factors which undermine the credibility of the central relationship.

And yet, if the human dimensions of the novel are not entirely satisfactory, Lawrence's fiercest critics have never denied the genius with which he responded to the natural world, and even the reader who wearies of Mellors is likely to be moved by Lawrence's elegiac descriptions of a countryside that is in the process of being despoiled and devastated by materialism and greed, a countryside that still offers to mankind the possibility of renewal and the discovery of a different system of values.

No human being in the novel, for example, is treated with quite the love and respect that Lawrence lavishes on the ancient wood of oak trees near Mellors's cottage, the wood which harbours the game-birds, the wood to which Connie flees for solace in her distress. The trees, we are told, are the remnant of a much larger forest that had once covered the land. Over the years more and more of this forest had been cut down – the most recent attack on it had taken place during the First World War, when Sir Clifford's father had felled many of the trees for trench timber. But Clifford himself loves the trees – it is perhaps the only redeeming trait that Lawrence allows him – and is determined to protect them. It is their vulnerability, as well as their living presence as a kind of mute chorus to the drama, that is a constant theme of the novel:

They, too, were waiting: obstinately, stoically waiting and giving off a potency of silence. Perhaps they were only waiting for the end; to be cut down, cleared away, the end of the forest, for them the end of all things. But perhaps their strong and aristocratic silence, the silence of strong trees, meant something else.[32]

Whether this indicates that there is some hope left for their survival is deliberately left unclear, however. Lawrence by now believed that the only way in which mankind could save itself from disaster was for it to rediscover the sacred significance of the sexual act, and that 'the bridge to the future is the phallus'.[33] But that did not mean that the English were ready for his message. When Horatio Bottomley's minions heard of the limited edition of *Lady Chatterley's Lover* that had been printed in Italy they described it as 'the most evil outpouring that has ever besmirched the literature of our country'. In 1929 there was the notorious incident when the police seized Lawrence's paintings that were on exhibition in London.

For Lawrence himself the only remedy for this situation was for

him to remain in exile in Italy until his death at Vence on the French
Riviera in 1930. For Mellors and Connie, too, the main hope seems to
be the possibility of escape from England – there is talk of Mellors
finding work on a farm in British Columbia. But whether either
Lawrence or his characters could ever really find a permanent refuge
from the ravages of the modern world is open to some question. The
present-day reader of Lawrence's work can hardly fail to reflect that
only fifteen years after his death it was in his beloved New Mexico, of
all places, that the atomic weapons were tested that were to be
employed with such devastating effect at the end of the Second
World War.

Do considerations like this mean that Lawrence's career as a
prophet and teacher must be considered a failure? Frank Kermode
has argued that they do not:

All Lawrence's temporal projections – his Third Age – are therefore, in the
last analysis, allegories of personal regeneration, rather than historical
prophecies. That is why he is not disconfirmed by the obstinate continuance
of the last days, the accelerated ruin of his countryside, the stubborn non-
appearance of his Holy Ghost. The 'bad time' prophesied by Mellors came
and stayed. Lawrence's remedy that men should die into a new life – is no
easier now than in his own day, and it is evident that he did not really expect
it to be. And at this level alone he is a failed prophet: the lesson, even if it is
right, is too hard.[34]

This is cogently stated, but perhaps it underestimates the essential
irony of Lawrence's career. For if, in the later years of his life,
repeated disappointments and the progressive collapse of his health
led to a dying down of the fires within him, there *had* been a time
when he believed that the kind of England he wanted could be
created, there *had* been an epoch when every kind of hope, however
extravagant, seemed capable of fulfilment.[35] 'The joy is sure and
fast', he had written in 1913; 'We have faith in the vastness of life's
wealth . . . There is no winter that we fear.' Less than eighteen
months later the guns started firing and he was doomed to perpetual
flight.

9

Isaac Rosenberg, Wilfred Owen: anthems for doomed youth

A sense that Western civilisation was collapsing as a result of the First World War was not confined to those like Romain Rolland and D.H. Lawrence who looked on the conflict from afar. Whilst the vast majority of combatants concerned themselves with the matter of daily survival, the more articulate of them could hardly fail to express their concern about the long-term implications of the slaughter. In France Barbusse, after writing *Le Feu*, was eventually to find salvation in Communism, while Céline was to embrace a form of anarchic, anti-semitic and intensely pessimistic pacifism which ultimately led him into the ranks of the Collaboration during the Second World War. In England the potential scandal arising from Sassoon's declaration in June 1917 that British aims in the war had now become those of 'aggression and conquest' may have been defused by the prompt intervention of Robert Graves and the decision of the military authorities to treat Sassoon as a victim of shell-shock, but he was not alone in expressing a sense of foreboding over the future. Already in the summer of 1916, for example, a few weeks after the-Easter Rising in Dublin and the battle of Jutland, a few days after the beginning of the battle of the Somme, Isaac Rosenberg sent some lines to Edward Marsh that raised the possibility that the British Empire itself might be a casualty of the conflict:

> A worm fed on the heart of Corinth,
> Babylon and Rome:
> Not Paris raped tall Helen,
> But this incestuous worm,
> Who lured her vivid beauty
> To his amorphous sleep.

> England! famous as Helen
> Is thy betrothal sung
> To him the shadowless,
> More amorous than Solomon.

While later on in the war Wilfred Owen, in 'Strange Meeting', warned of the hatreds that were being created for the future:

> Now men will go content with what we spoiled,
> Or, discontent, boil bloody, and be spilled.
> They will be swift with swiftness of the tigress.
> None will break ranks, though nations trek from progress.
> Courage was mine, and I had mystery,
> Wisdom was mine, and I had mastery:
> To miss the march of this retreating world
> Into vain citadels that are not walled.
> Then, when much blood had clogged their chariot-wheels
> I would go up and wash them from sweet wells,
> Even with truths that lie too deep for taint.
> I would have poured my spirit without stint
> But not through wounds; not on the cess of war.
> Foreheads of men have bled where no wounds were.

The rise of the totalitarian systems of the inter-war years is implicitly prophesied in this passage, and neither the dead English soldier, who is the narrator of Owen's poem, nor the German soldier whose words he quotes (and whom he has recently killed) can do anything to prevent this development.

Already in 1914 Rosenberg and Owen had reacted in apocalyptic terms to the outbreak of the war, but they had little idea then of the full extent of the disaster. Nor were they aware then that this was a conflict in which they themselves would be destroyed. For them, unlike Rolland and Lawrence, there was to be no escape.

Rosenberg and Owen were, of course, very different personalities with very different backgrounds. The former was born in Bristol in 1890, the son of Jewish refugees from Russia who eventually settled in the East End of London, where they lived in considerable poverty. After many struggles Rosenberg managed to attend the Slade School of Art where he came into contact with an extraordinary number of gifted personalities who were there at the same period – Bomberg,

Stanley Spencer, Gertler, Paul Nash, Edward Wadsworth, Dorothy Brett and Dora Carrington. For some years he hesitated between poetry and painting as his destined career. In 1912 he published at his own expense a small pamphlet of poems entitled *Night and Day*. In 1914 he was recuperating from illness at the home of his sister and brother-in-law in South Africa when he received news of the outbreak of war in Europe.

Owen, too, was outside England in 1914. Born in 1893, he spent his formative years in Shrewsbury in a family in which his mother was the dominant influence. From an early age he felt it was his destiny to be a poet, and, although his father, a poorly-paid railway official, could not afford to send him to university, he was determined to avoid a routine career as a school-teacher in England. After a period as a lay assistant to an Anglican vicar in a village near Reading – an experience that seems to have disillusioned him with the Evangelical Christianity in which he had been reared – he moved to France to teach English at the Berlitz School of Languages at Bordeaux. When the war broke out he was employed as a private tutor of English to a wealthy family living in the Pyrenees. He was also enjoying his contact with the veteran French Decadent poet Laurent Tailhade, whose work was much admired by Pound and the Imagists. It is difficult at this distance in time to estimate how deep was the influence that Tailhade exerted on Owen, although the former's pacifism and anarchism may have had some bearing on Owen's later development. What is certain, however, is the extent to which Tailhade reinforced Owen's own sense of the exalted nature of the poet's calling. As Dominic Hibberd has pointed out, it is also clear that it was from his reading in French poetry during the period that Owen picked up the ideas on para-rhyme that he was to employ in his 'From my Diary, July 1914' and that he was to use so effectively in later years.[1]

Both Owen and Rosenberg responded to the outbreak of the war with poems. The influence of Keats, Swinburne and the Decadents of the late nineteenth century on Owen's '1914' is patent:

> For after Spring had bloomed in early Greece,
> And Summer blazed her glory out with Rome,
> An Autumn softly fell, a harvest home,
> A slow grand age, and rich with all increase.

> But now, for us, wild Winter, and the need
> Of sowings for new Spring, and blood for seed.

In his 'On receiving News of the War' Rosenberg's debts to the Old Testament, William Blake and the Pre-Raphaelites are equally clear:

> O! ancient crimson curse!
> Corrode, consume.
> Give back this universe
> Its pristine bloom.

But these were largely academic exercises, and neither of them was particularly affected by the war at this stage. In the letters he sent home from France Owen's main concern was that, while 'the guns will do some useful weeding', he was furious with chagrin to think that the 'Minds which were to have excelled the civilisation of ten thousand years' were being annihilated.[2] While his friend Tailhade, despite his age and his pacifism, was anxious to enlist in the French army, Owen contented himself with instructing his family in the details of the injuries sustained by the French war-wounded.[3] As a citizen of a country where conscription did not apply, he certainly showed no desire to return home to volunteer. From the vantage point of South Africa, Rosenberg, too, was not disposed at first to regard the war with undue seriousness, and clearly thought that it would be over by the time he returned to England in the following year. On 8 August 1914 he wrote to Edward Marsh:

I despise and hate wars, and hope that the Kaiser Wilhelm will have his bottom smacked – a naughty aggressive boy who will have *all* the plum pudding . . . I really hope to have a nice lot of pictures and poems by the time all is settled again, and Europe is repenting of her savageries.[4]

By October of the next year, however, both men were in the army. Owen's employment in France came to an end in 1915, and, although the patriotic tone in his correspondence became stronger, and although he talked more and more of enlisting, he toyed with other alternatives to the very last minute – including the possibility of becoming the representative of a French perfume company in the Far East. Pressures on single men to enlist were rapidly growing, however, and the opportunity of a commission at the end of a period of training in the Artists' Rifles was too good to be missed. Rosenberg returned to England in the spring of 1915, and, after spending several months in an unsuccessful search for suitable work, enlisted as a private in a Bantam battalion – he was undersized – so that he could make a contribution to the finances of his family.

From the time that they joined up the careers of Rosenberg and Owen were to diverge sharply. For Rosenberg the main problem was to find congenial conditions to enable him to concentrate on his poetry. In 1915 he published a second pamphlet of poems, *Youth*, and in 1916 appeared a verse play, *Moses*, on which he had been working for some time. He was determined that he must use his war experience to fertilise his art, but the opportunities open to him were extremely limited. His painting activities were hampered by the lack of materials, and, if this was not in itself too serious since he had already decided he had more to say as a poet than as a painter, his freedom to write was severely restricted by the cramped and miserable conditions that he experienced as an ordinary soldier. He suffered acutely from the casual humiliations and lack of privacy of barrack-room life during his period of training, and seems to have been the victim at times of anti-semitic sentiment. Dreamy and self-absorbed, he was distressed to find that he was not a very good soldier, and was frequently given minor punishments. The worst of the bullying seems to have stopped when he was transferred to another battalion and sent to France early in 1916, but once he arrived in France he was in the line or near the line until his death nearly twenty months later, apart from one period of leave and one spell in hospital.

In many ways Owen's experience was more fortunate. As an officer he enjoyed a social standing that he had never commanded as a civilian – in France, where commissions were granted sparingly, this would have no particular significance, but in the intensely class-conscious England of this time such things were important – while his pedagogic talents and frustrated homo-eroticism were to find a certain degree of fulfilment as he devoted himself to the task of looking after his men. The period of time he spent at the Front – five months in all – was considerably less than that endured by Rosenberg, and, although his self-esteem was damaged by his being sent home suffering from shell-shock in May 1917, this meant that he spent the next fifteen months back in Britain. It was there, at

Craiglockhart War Hospital in Edinburgh, that he met Sassoon, whose polemics against the war were to have a profound effect on him, and whose influence was to be crucial in helping him to move away from the lusciousness that was always to be his main temptation towards a tighter and less self-indulgent form of expression. It was Sassoon, too, who lent Owen a copy of Barbusse's *Le Feu*, which, the latter claimed, had set him alight as no other war book had done.[5]

The meeting with Sassoon was also to have its effect on the reception of Owen's work in later years. Whereas Rosenberg's reputation was to be achieved only slowly and painfully, so that his full stature has only been fully appreciated in the last twenty-five years, that of Owen was energetically promoted by Sassoon and other friends like Osbert Sitwell from an early date, so that by the 1930s his poetry had already achieved classic status.

Quite apart from accidents of time and chance, however, it is not difficult to see why Owen's work achieved wider and more rapid recognition than that of Rosenberg in the years that followed the First World War. As soon as he experienced the reality of the fighting Owen's repudiation of the war was clear and immediate. In a letter that he wrote to his parents just before he left for the Front at the beginning of 1917 he could still say that there was 'a fine heroic feeling' about being in France and that he was in perfect spirits.[6] Less than three weeks later, after his first spell of duty at Beaumont Hamel on the Somme, his attitude had changed completely. Now the war must be brought to an end as soon as possible. 'The people of England needn't hope. They must agitate.'[7] In its definitive form, therefore, Owen's poetry avoids the aestheticism that had marred his early work and is directed to one aim – protest against the war. 'I came out in order to help these boys', he wrote in October 1918, 'directly by leading them as well as an officer can; indirectly by watching their sufferings that I may speak of them as well as any pleader can.'[8] He told Sassoon that he did not want to write anything 'to which a soldier would say No compris'.[9] And in the famous preface that he wrote for his projected volume of poems, a preface that has caused controversy ever since, the propagandist aim is openly avowed:

My subject is War, and the pity of War. The Poetry is in the pity . . . All a poet can do today is warn. That is why the true Poets must be truthful.

In sharp contrast to all this, Rosenberg's approach to the war was for the most part indirect and oblique. Once he had enlisted, it is true, he wrote a certain amount of patriotic verse, but this is so bad that it is clear that his heart was not in it. Indeed, it is because he never really believed in the war in the first place that Rosenberg did not give voice to the same bitterness and disillusionment that affected so many of the other war poets until the closing months of his life.

The reason for this detachment is not difficult to find, for it lies in the very nature of his Jewish inheritance: his parents were opposed to war on religious grounds; his father had escaped from Russia in the first place to avoid the ferocious conscription laws that operated in the Russian State; and, like many Jewish refugees from Tsarism, the Rosenberg family could hardly be expected to identify themselves with a conflict in which England was in alliance with a Russian government that had persecuted them so savagely in the recent past. There can be little doubt that Rosenberg was not unaffected by views like this. He explained to Edward Marsh:

I never joined the army for patriotic reasons. Nothing can justify war. I suppose we must all fight to get the trouble over. Anyhow I helped at home when I could and I did other things which helped to keep things going. I thought if I'd join there would be the separation allowance for my mother.[10]

Clearly the First World War was not a quarrel in which he felt personally involved, and, as 'A Worm fed on the Heart of Corinth' so vividly indicates, his basic attitude to the conflict was the immemorial Jewish one of regarding the rise and fall of mighty empires with a certain sense of déjà vu, praying only that the Jewish people would survive them all. Rosenberg was not an orthodox Jew in the religious sense: already in the poetry he had written before the war he had made clear his alienation from the patriarchal deity of Jewish tradition; and in the course of the war he was to give spectacular expression to his attraction to the idea of a female God in the dramatic poem 'Daughters of War', in which the idea is charged with a powerful eroticism to depict Amazonian figures gathering into themselves the soldiers who had died in battle. But, in his choice of subject matter and in the epic and visionary nature of his themes, Rosenberg remained intensely loyal to significant elements within the Jewish tradition.

In a number of important respects, therefore, Rosenberg can hardly be described as an 'English' poet or a 'war' poet at all, and this strangeness, this alien quality that was to disconcert so many of his early readers, was accentuated by his belief in the primacy of art. He had long held the Symbolist belief that life could only be redeemed from triviality by the transmuting power of the artist, and he was determined that in the poetry he hoped to write during the war there would be no place for mere reportage or 'penny shockers' about the slaughter. To Lawrence Binyon he wrote:

I am determined that this war, with all its power for devastation, shall not master my poetry . . . I will not leave a corner of my consciousness covered up, but saturate myself with the strange and extraordinary new conditions of this life, and it will all refine itself into poetry later on.[11]

And yet if Rosenberg, as a Jew and as an artist, approached the war with attitudes that were very different from those of the majority of his English contemporaries, both as a Jew and an artist he was immensely excited by the titanic nature of the struggle and fascinated by the possibility that, despite the suffering and the carnage, the events that were taking place in Europe might represent the birth-pangs of a new creation. In the course of the war, then, in addition to 'Daughters of War', he made other attempts to come to terms with the new situation that confronted him through the medium of poetic drama. His most ambitious idea was to depict the destructive violence and the possibly regenerative nature of the conflict in terms of the efforts made by a doomed race deprived of women to restore their vitality by carrying off the females of a neighbouring tribe. The texts entitled 'The Amulet' and 'The Unicorn' which are to be found in Rosenberg's *Complete Works* are two fragmentary drafts for this play, an enterprise that was destined to remain uncompleted.

Whether the play, even in a finished form, would have been a satisfactory piece of work and an adequate response to the issues raised by the First World War is somewhat doubtful, however. Maurice Bowra once said to Cyril Connolly, 'Whatever you hear

about the war, remember it was far, far worse: inconceivably bloody
– nobody who wasn't there can ever imagine what it was like.'[12] And
perhaps it is the case that in its scale and horror, and in its radical
discontinuity with the past, the First World War defied any attempt
at epic treatment. Romain Rolland's belief that Péguy would have
attempted an epic work on the First World War, had he survived, is
probably well-founded, but whether even a Péguy was capable of
mastering such a theme is far from certain. The most ambitious effort
to do this as far as English literature is concerned is probably David
Jones's 'In Parenthesis' which appeared in 1937, and the Catholicism
that inspired this work makes it seem at times reminiscent of Péguy's
'Mysteries'. But, despite some intensely moving passages, this is very
much an uneven masterpiece in which the suffering of the men at the
Front is diminished by the attempt to place it against a background of
Celtic myth and romance. Even so, Jones's work is rooted in the
reality of the war to a far greater degree than Rosenberg's dramatic
fragments, and it also benefitted from the fact that it was the product
of a far longer period of gestation than Rosenberg ever seemed to
have envisaged for his own work. Despite some arresting images and
an inherent vitality lacking in the poetic dramas of Lascelles
Abercrombie and Gordon Bottomley – whose work Rosenberg
deeply admired and greatly over-rated – 'The Amulet' and 'The
Unicorn' remain too distanced from contemporary events to retain
any lasting resonance.

Rosenberg's enduring reputation does not rest on these writings,
of course, but on a handful of poems where the war is faced much
more directly and in which symbol and reality are fused into one.
Amongst these must be included the much-anthologised 'Dead Man's
Dump', for, although it is somewhat diffuse and betrays a certain
clumsiness in its contruction (a result of the fact that Rosenberg
never had the opportunity for a proper revision, a common
experience for him once he got to France), it has the makings of a
profound meditation on the 'great sunk silences' of death. Even more
effective, however, are 'Returning, We Hear the Larks' and 'Break of
Day in the Trenches', in which the contrast between the plight of the
soldier and the world of nature is explored in all its many-layered
and complex ironies. In the latter poem Rosenberg contemplates the
'queer sardonic rat' with his 'cosmopolitan sympathies', who is able

to visit both sets of combatants. Meanwhile the soldier in the English trenches has to be content with sticking a poppy behind his ear. The flower, like the soldier, is 'safe' for the moment, although it has been picked and will soon die.[13]

These are poems whose full riches are only revealed after close and repeated reading. It is hardly surprising that when Rosenberg's far from complete and chaotically presented *Complete Works* appeared in 1937 their promise tended to be overlooked by a public that found itself confronted with a mass of juvenilia and the groping, tortuous verse of his dramatic fragments. In his Foreword to the work Sassoon rightly talked of the 'scriptural and sculptural'[14] nature of Rosenberg's achievement, but many readers would have agreed with the constant complaints of obscurity that Rosenberg's patron, Edward Marsh, levelled at him. Throughout his dealings with Rosenberg, in fact, Marsh was nothing if not thoroughly English in his attitudes. Although he bought some of the former's paintings, and included a speech from 'Moses' in the third volume of *Georgian Poetry*, he never really sympathised with what this eccentric Jewish artist was attempting to do. There is an unmistakable element of condescension in his reference to 'poor little Rosenberg' in the comments that he made at the opening of an exhibition of the latter's paintings in 1937.[15]

Over half a century later it is possible to take a different view. Now that the literary climate has changed so radically, Rosenberg's poetry, a body of work that cannot be fitted into the neat categories of Traditionalism and Modernism, is more likely to be accorded more sympathetic consideration. Now that the British Empire has disappeared, the prophetic nature of poems like 'A Worm fed on the Heart of Corinth' and 'The Destruction of Jerusalem by the Babylonian Hordes', can at last be recognised. Now that themes of alienation and marginalisation are the common currency of artistic debate, Rosenberg's intense, apocalyptic poetry – poetry that might have flourished more vigorously in the different setting of Central European Expressionism than amidst the English Georgians – is far more likely to be regarded with understanding.

Indeed, so much attention is now paid to Rosenberg's potential as an artist that there is a tendency today unduly to denigrate the achievement of Wilfred Owen. The charges against the latter – that his poetry is marred by sentimentality and pessimism, that, despite his development of para-rhyme, despite the influence of Barbusse's startling images and shifting angles of vision, it represents not a breakthrough to something new but a last expression of an exhausted Keatsian Romantic tradition – are, of course, familiar. Equally well known are the classic statements of this kind of criticism: Yeats's assertion in the introduction to his *Oxford Book of Modern Verse* published in 1936 that 'passive suffering is not a theme for poetry';[16] his pronouncement in a letter to Lady Dorothy Wellesley that Owen is 'all blood, dirt and sucked sugar stick';[17] Robert Graves's famous outburst, 'For God's sake cheer up and write more optimistically – the war's not ended yet but a poet should have a spirit above wars'.[18] Few would really contend today that there is not an element of truth in these comments.

And yet, having conceded all these points, the fact remains that no one conveys more poignantly or with greater authority than Owen the loss of English innocence that took place in the war. His achievement may be extremely uneven, ranging from the lachrymose in 'Greater Love' to the over-rhetorical in 'Dulce et Decorum Est'. His satirical verse may lack the pungency of Sassoon, and his use of the pastoral the subtlety and restraint of Blunden. But as an elegiac poet in 'Futility' and 'Anthem for Doomed Youth' he is unequalled by any of his contemporaries, with the exception of the much underrated poet and composer Ivor Gurney, whose work similarly articulates that nostalgia for a lost Eden that is so powerful a force within the English tradition, a force that reasserted itself in a more self-conscious way in the neo-Romanticism of the Second World War. From a European point of view it is possible to dismiss Owen as naïf and provincial, but, perhaps for that very reason, no one could depict more movingly than he the enormity of a situation in which the old were sending out the young to die on an unprecedented scale, a situation in which 'half the seed of Europe' were being slain 'one by one'. Against this kind of background many of the criticisms that have been made of him seem largely irrelevant. When Yeats, for example, compared the reactions of the poets of the First World War unfavourably with those of the heroes of Antiquity – 'In all the great tragedies, tragedy is a joy to the man who dies; in Greece the tragic chorus danced'[19] – he unwittingly revealed how little he knew about the reality of the trenches. This was a subject that did not fit into either a heroic view of the world or a scheme of things centred on Ireland, as he demonstrated on another occasion when he refused to stage O'Casey's play on the First World War, *The Silver Tassie*, at the Abbey Theatre. His attitude in these matters betrays a striking deficiency in sympathy and imagination on the part of a poet who saw so many of the wider implications of the war in his 'The Second Coming'.

But Yeats is not alone amongst Owen's critics in somehow failing to hit the target. When Graves told Owen to 'cheer up', this, perhaps, is more informative about the former's own strategy for survival than about the scale and horror of the war. Owen may be open to the charge of mawkishness and despair, but to the present-day reader, who notes his attacks on the 'Prussianism' of both alliance systems, his warnings against a vindictive peace, his anticipations of future wars and the rise of totalitarianism in 'Strange Meeting', it might seem that his forebodings concerning the future were not entirely unjustified. Indeed, to a posterity that has witnessed the way in which phrases like 'Dead Man's Dump' and 'those who die as cattle' were to take on new and even more terrible meanings in the Second World War it might seem that Owen's pessimism erred on the side of understatement.

Neither Owen nor Rosenberg were to survive to see the further disintegration of European civilisation that took place in the years after the war, however. Rosenberg was the first to be killed. The stoicism and cheerfulness with which he tried to cope with his long spells in the line are sometimes used to support the argument that his was a more positive and life-affirming view of the world than that of Owen, but comparisons of this nature are not only patronising but also very often misleading, and, if Rosenberg attempted to exclude his growing sense of despair from his poetry, his letters to Edward Marsh tell a very different story of failing health and increasing exhaustion. In a passage cancelled by the censor he wrote to Marsh on 26 January 1918:

What is happening to me now is more tragic than the 'passion play'. Christ never endured what I endure. It is breaking me completely.[20]

For a time he was sustained by the hope that he might be able to escape from the Western Front by being allowed to transfer to the Jewish battalion that was being organised by the Zionist leader Vladimir Jabotinsky to fight with the British in the Middle East. Rosenberg was obviously excited by the Balfour Declaration and by the idea that, in the midst of war and the collapse of empires, the Jews might achieve a National Home in Palestine, but when he tried to compose a battle hymn for the Jewish troops, the poem that resulted from his efforts was hardly the kind of material that would inspire any army, as Rosenberg himself ruefully admitted. A haunting and deceptively simple poem, its starkness seems to point to a dimension beyond hope and despair:

> Through these pale cold days
> What dark faces burn
> Out of three thousand years,
> And their wild eyes yearn,
>
> While underneath their brows
> Like waifs their spirits grope
> For the pools of Hebron again –
> For Lebanon's summer slope.
>
> They leave these blond still days
> In dust behind their tread
> They see with living eyes
> How long they have been dead.

Rosenberg was never to see Palestine. The British army needed to retain every man that it could to withstand the impending German spring offensive of 1918. That offensive was duly launched on 28 March. On 1 April Rosenberg was killed. The Germans rapidly swept over the area in which he was buried, and, although there is a grave bearing his name in Bailleul Road East military cemetery, it is by no means certain that the body that lies there is his.[21] An outsider and an exile throughout his life, Rosenberg may remain an outcast even in death.

Nearly five months after Rosenberg was killed, Wilfred Owen returned to France at the end of August 1918. There had been some talk of his securing a posting in England, but this was ruled out on the grounds that he had originally been sent home because of shell-shock, and Owen himself seems to have been happy that he was going back to the Front. He wrote to his mother:

I am glad. That is I am much gladder to be going out than afraid. I shall be better able to cry my outcry, playing my part.[22]

He was also determined to purge himself of the guilt that he still felt over the circumstances in which he had been returned to England in May 1917.

There were to be many opportunities for him to do so. The end of the war was in sight and the Germans were retreating, but they were putting up a series of stiff rearguard actions, and the rate of slaughter was almost as great as in the worst months of 1916 and 1917. Owen was deeply concerned about this, and, whilst he and Sassoon now maintained that Germany must be defeated, they were angry with the bellicosity of sectors of French and British public opinion that were preventing the speedy negotiation of an armistice. In 'Smile, Smile, Smile', which he wrote at this time, the divorce between the England of the press and the civilians and the England of the soldiers is now complete:

> Nation? – The half-limbed readers did not chafe
> But smiled at one another curiously
> Like secret men who know their secret safe.
> (This is the thing they know and never speak,
> That England one by one had fled to France,
> Not many elsewhere now, save under France)

And yet he also felt a strange exhilaration in being at the Front again, in sharing the camaraderie, in proving himself in battle. At the beginning of October his moment came. The 2nd Manchesters successfully assaulted the Beaurevoir-Fonsomme Line and Owen was awarded the Military Cross for capturing a German machine-gun and inflicting considerable losses on the enemy. A few days later he wrote to Sassoon:

The Batt. had a sheer time last week, I can find no better epithet; because I cannot say I suffered anything; having let my brain go dull. That is to say my nerves are in perfect order. It is a strange truth that your 'Counter-Attack' frightened me much more than the real one: though the boy by my side, shot through the head, lay on top of me, soaking my shoulder for half an hour . . . My senses are charred . . . I shall feel again as soon as I dare, but now I must not. I don't take the cigarette out of my mouth when I write Deceased over their letters. But one day I will write Deceased over many books.[23]

This was a very different Owen from the priggish young man of 1914 or the shell-shocked victim of 1917, but whether this new, harder tone would have made itself heard in his later poetry, whether he would have confounded his critics and been able to surmount the formidable problems – artistic, sexual, economic and political – that would undoubtedly have confronted him in the years after the war, are questions to which there can be no definite answer. Perhaps, like Sassoon, he would never have been able to recapture the intensity of the war years. Perhaps, again like Sassoon, he might have persisted in his hatred of war far into the 1930s, thus laying himself open even more to the charge that is often made that the influence of the war poets was one of the factors that prevented the British public from taking a resolute stand against the rise of Hitler.[24]

But this is all speculation. 'When I go from hence let this be my parting word, that what I have seen is unsurpassable.'[25] Owen quoted these words from Tagore's 'Gitanjali' on the day before his last embarkation leave came to an end, and, in communicating something of his experience to posterity, his place in history is secure. He was killed in the early hours of the morning of 4 November as he was leading an assault on the Oise-Sambre canal near Ors. One week later the guns fell silent and 'the war that will end war' was finally over.

Epilogue

Vous souvenez-vous d'un seul nom par exemple, Lola, d'un de
ces soldats tués pendant la Guerre de Cent ans? . . . Avez vous
jamais cherché à en connaître un seul de ces noms? . . . Non,
n'est-ce pas? . . . Vous n'avez jamais cherché? Ils vous sont
aussi anonymes, indifférents et plus inconnus que votre crotte
du matin . . . Voyez donc bien qu'ils sont morts pour rien,
Lola! . . . Dans dix mille ans d'ici, je vous fais le pari que cette
guerre, si remarquable qu'elle nous paraisse à présent, sera
complètement oubliée . . . A peine si une douzaine d'érudits se
chamailleront encore par-ci, par-là, à son occasion et à propos
des dates des principales hécatombes dont elle fut illustrée . . .
C'est tout ce que les hommes ont réussi jusqu'ici à trouver de
mémorable au sujets les uns des autres à quelques siècles, à
quelques années et même à quelques heures de distance . . .[1]

(Look, Lola, can you remember the name of any one of the
soldiers who were killed in the Hundred Years' War? . . . Have
you ever tried to find out one single name among them all? . . .
No, you can't; you've never tried have you? To you they're all
anonymous, unknown and less important than your morning
crap . . . You can see that they died for nothing, Lola! . . . Ten
thousand years hence I bet you that this war, all-important as it
seems to us now, will be completely forgotten . . . Possibly a
dozen or so learned men may wrangle about it occasionally, and
about the dates of the chief hecatombs for which it was
famous . . . Up to the present time that is all that humanity has
ever succeeded in finding memorable about itself, after a few
centuries have gone by, or a few years, or even a few
hours . . .)

At one level the nihilism of Céline's *Voyage au bout de la nuit* is
irrefutable. In a more mundane sense it can hardly be said that

amongst the British the memory of the First World War has yet begun to fade.

On the contrary, in Britain the fiftieth anniversary of the outbreak of the Second World War has come and gone, but the stark outlines of that earlier war remain, like those of some kind of aboriginal catastrophe, some kind of second Fall. Books, plays, television programmes and exhibitions devoted to the war appear in an endless succession. As the last surviving combatants come to the end of their lives their memories and recollections are treated with respect and veneration. Participants in a war that undermined traditional notions of the epic and the heroic, they and their comrades are now regarded as the stuff of legend.

For the French, as Jacques Darras pointed out in 'Beyond the Tunnel of History', the 1989 BBC Reith Lectures, the recollection of the massive toll in dead and wounded is so terrible, the slaughter so absurd, that they try to blot it out of their memory. Some mention of the overall losses has already been made, but a further indication of what these losses actually meant to French society can be gauged from some figures provided by Barrès in the course of his campaign to defend the cause of French higher education at the end of the conflict. Referring to the plight of the Ecole Normale Supérieure in Paris, one of the pinnacles of the French educational system, the institution which Jaurès, Péguy and Rolland had attended, Barrès pointed out that, of the 161 students of the 1911, 1912 and 1913 years of entry who had been conscripted in 1914, 81 were dead or missing and 64 were wounded by the end of the war.[2] Statistics like these reveal the qualitative as well as the quantitative nature of the losses that France sustained in the war, losses that enabled the old men to cling on to positions of power in French society far longer than they would otherwise have been able to do (one thinks of Maurras and the équipe of the Action Française, for example), losses that made it so symbolically apt that, in the hour of her defeat in 1940, the nation should have turned to an octogenarian Marshal for salvation, losses that only began to fade from the forefront of the French memory as the birth-rate began to accelerate after the Second World War and the rejuvenation of France began.

In Britain, too, the effect of the smaller but still terrible fatality figures caused by the First World War could not be ignored. There the 'lost generation' of potential leaders that Britain had lost in the conflict, and survivors like Harold Macmillan were to be intensely conscious of the fact that they were in a sense trustees for this doomed generation. But, in addition to this, it is difficult to escape the conclusion that there is in Britain a particular poignancy in the nation's memory of the war, a poignancy that derives from a deep sense of grief at the innocence that was lost in the course of the conflict.

This is an aspect of the British experience that has been emphasised at many points in this book, and it can be argued, of course, that this kind of British reaction is a form of self-indulgence and escapism, only possible in a country that did not undergo defeat and occupation during the Second World War, a symptom of the nation's continuing inability to come to terms with the demands of the late twentieth century. Comparisons with the less sentimental French, who, in any case, are far more impressed by the literary avant-garde in both the First and the Second World Wars than by the more artless sincerities of most 'war writers', immediately spring to mind. Nevertheless, English reluctance to philosophise in the face of the Absurd does not always signify ignorance and complacency, and this nostalgia for a lost innocence is an essential fact that has to be taken into account in any attempt to understand the psychology of the British. It is an aspect of the First World War that was for many years neglected by commentators from North America, such as George Dangerfield in his celebrated *The Strange Death of Liberal England*, which appeared in 1935, and Barbara Tuchman in *The Proud Tower*, which was published in 1966.

It is easy to see why both writers reacted so strongly against the idea of a mythical Golden Age that was supposed to have existed before 1914, and it is understandable that they should have pointed instead to the social tensions and Irish unrest that dominated British politics in the period before the outbreak of the conflict. It may still be felt, however, that any attempt to minimise the impact of 1914 on European society in general, or on British society in particular, runs the risk of being fundamentally misleading. After all, if none of the Frenchmen whose careers are examined in this book could foresee the scale of the catastrophe that was to overwhelm them, none of the

British writers (with the exception of Kipling) even seriously believed that a major European war would break out in which Britain would be involved. The case of Wilfred Owen may not be regarded as typical of British society as a whole, but the sequence of events that led him from his ecstatic contemplation of

> Lives
> Wakening with wonder in the Pyrenees

in his 'From My Diary, July 1914' to the anguished outburst of 'O Siegfried, make them Stop!' in one of his letters of September 1918,[3] indicates something of the dimensions of the shock that Britian experienced in the course of the war.

Perhaps it is relevant in this context to mention that, since the United States has experienced the undermining of its own idealism and its own innocence in Vietnam, there has been a marked renewal of sympathetic interest amongst American scholars in the British experience of 1914–18. This is exemplified by Robert Wohl's *The Generation of 1914*, and, above all, of course, by Paul Fussell's *The Great War and Modern Memory*, which, while illustrating the degree to which English poets were influenced by traditional images and ideas in their perception of the war, ultimately presents a vivid and intensely moving picture of a civilisation attempting to come to terms with a disaster for which, in so many ways, it was completely unprepared.

Some of Fussell's conclusions may be debatable. It may be difficult for some European observers to agree with his extremely high opinion of the pioneering qualities of Thomas Pynchon's 'Gravity's Rainbow' (a nightmarish evocation of the dehumanised universe of the Second World War by someone who was too young to participate in it) and with his assertion that, with the disappearance during the 1960s and 1970s of the concept of prohibitive obscenity, the work of Mailer, Pynchon and James Jones offers a 'new dimension' to the ritual of military memory, a dimension that is capable of revealing for the first time the full obscenity of the First World War:

The greatest irony is that it is only now, when those who remember the events are almost all dead, that the literary means for adequate remembering and interpreting are finally publicly accessible.[4]

This may be true of literature in English, but it applies far less to French writing, as the work of Barbusse and Céline testifies. In any case, before any attempt is made to pass any final verdict on the verisimilitude of the literature of the First World War, it is worth considering Bowra's comments, already quoted, on the difficulties of communicating the war experience, and Bernanos's remark, made in the context of a laudatory review of Céline's *Voyage au bout de la nuit*, that those 'realists' who followed Barbusse were far more concerned with the 'décor' of the war than with the real essence of a conflict that was for the combatants pre-eminently 'un drame intérieur'.[5] The spirit of Pynchon's work is clearly nearer to Céline (whose writings bridge both world wars) than to Barbusse, but is *Gravity's Rainbow*, remarkable though it is, very much more than a virtuoso exercise in technique?

Fussell is surely right, however, in his belief that in many ways it is only now that the full implications of the First World War can be properly appreciated, and, certainly, now is the time for historians and literary specialists of the war to work together much more closely than they have done in the past. Owen's remark to Sassoon, that he did not want to write anything 'to which a soldier would say No compris' is one that academics as well as writers can profitably consider. Immersed as he so often is in the world of political and military abstractions, the British historian may rightly be suspicious of Shelley's claim that poets are the 'unacknowledged legislators' of the world, but he must be prepared to admit far more than he has been in the past the role of writers as witnesses of their era. For his part the literary scholar must make himself far more aware of the wider social and political issues raised by the events of 1914–18 in order to avoid some of the misleading impressions that he has sometimes conveyed – the tendency to minimise German cruelties in Belgium, and an excessive optimism concerning the prospects of a compromise peace in 1916 and 1917, are examples that immediately spring to mind.

Above all, there is ample scope for both historians and literary specialists to engage themselves in comparative approaches. An attempt has been made here to illustrate some of the similarities and dissimilarities in the French and British response to the war. Much more work needs to be done comparing and contrasting the German experience with that of Germany's opponents in England, France and Russia. As far as Russia was concerned the brutalities of the war and the Bolshevik Revolution were to have enormous repercussions in the rest of Europe. In Germany there were many opponents of the war in literary circles by 1917 and 1918, and in the years of the Weimar Republic there were numerous ex-combatants – Ernst Toller, Fritz von Unruh, Ludwig Renn, Arnold Zweig and Erich Remarque, for example – who denounced the waste and futility of the conflict in terms as eloquent and as moving as those of Barbusse, Sassoon and Owen. The fact remains, however, that the Weimar intelligentsia was unable to resist the forces of aggrieved nationalism in Germany. Nor were they able to eradicate that romanticisation of violence, that contempt for easeful civilian death, the *Strohtod*, which were such powerful influences within the German tradition. The connection between the ruthlessness of the German military machine during the First World War and the methods later to be employed by the Nazis needs to be more thoroughly explored. The full implications of Elie Wiesel's contention that the road to Auschwitz began in the totally dehumanised 'battles of material resources', the *Materialschlachten*, of Verdun and after have still to be assimilated into the European consciousness.

Far from being 'completely forgotten', as Céline indicated, therefore, our understanding of the First World War has in many ways only just begun, and it is this capacity of the events of 1914–18 to remind us of later catastrophes and our own sense of vulnerability that is the last and most compelling reason why the war and human reaction to it still exercise their enduring fascination. There is Lawrence:

As for the future, that they never mentioned except one laughed at some mocking dream of the destruction of the world by a ridiculous catastrophe of man's invention: a man invented such a perfect explosive that it blew the earth in two, and the two halves set off in different directions through space, to the dismay of the inhabitants: or else the people of the world divided into two halves, and each half decided *it* was perfect and right, the other half was wrong and must be destroyed; so another end of the world. Or else, Loerke's dream of fear, the world went cold, and snow fell everywhere, and only white creatures, Polar bears, white foxes, and men like awful white snow-birds, persisted in ice cruelty.[6]

These may have been the private fantasies of Gudrun and Loerke as described by Lawrence in *Women in Love* in 1916. Today, in an era of nuclear weapons and talk of nuclear winters or other forms of environmental catastrophe, they read rather differently.

Finally, there is Péguy:

D'autres civilisations sont mortes. Cette civilisation moderne, le peu qu'il y a de culture dans le monde moderne, est elle-même essentiellement mortelle.[7]

(Other civilisations have died. This modern civilisation, the little there is of culture in the modern world, is essentially mortal.)

Péguy wrote these words in the aftermath of the First Moroccan Crisis in 1905, but as the years have passed and the true dimensions of the destructive forces unleashed during the First World War have become manifest, they have taken on a wider significance than even he could have imagined. Since 1914, it is now clear, the world as a whole has been living on borrowed time.

Notes

Unless otherwise stated the place of publication for works in French is Paris, and for works in English is London.

INTRODUCTION

1 It would require another, and much longer, book than this to record the long love–hate relationship that exists between the British and the French. Such a book would have to start with the lingering Anglo-Saxon resentment at the imposition of the 'Norman yoke' in 1066, and include an examination of the history of the two countries during the careers of Joan of Arc, Louis XIV, Napoleon and Charles de Gaulle. Suffice it to say that, during the period before the outbreak of the First World War, the mutual misunderstanding between Britain and France was symbolised by the fact that Grey, the British Foreign Secretary, spoke no French, while Paul Cambon, the long-serving French Ambassador in London, spoke no English. The latter, regarding Paris as the centre of the universe, arranged matters so that he went back there every fortnight. As a result of this, and as a result of relying too heavily on the Francophile sympathies of Nicolson at the Foreign Office, he seriously over-estimated the readiness of the English to intervene on France's behalf in 1914, and it was only the German invasion of Belgium that enabled Britain and France to unite for a common purpose. See J.F.V. Keiger, *France and the Origins of the First World War*, (1983), p. 105. See also Cambon's remarks to Barrès, in Chapter 2 above.

2 More recent works by literary specialists include Holger Klein (ed.), *The First World War in Fiction* (1976), John Cruickshank's *Variations on Catastrophe* (1982), which examines some French reactions to the war, and Peter Buitenhuis's *The Great War of Words* (1989), which deals with British writers and their involvement in propaganda during the war. All of these books indicate the possibilities that exist for interdisciplinary approaches, and underline the need for historians to participate in this

area. Two Studies in German contain interesting material: H. Cysarz, *Zur Geistesgeschichte der Weltkriege* (Berne and Frankfurt am Main, 1973); K. Vondung (ed.), *Kriegserlebnis: Der Erste Weltkrieg in der literarischen Gestaltung und symbolischen Deutung der Nationen* (Göttingen, 1980).

I JEAN JAURÈS: THE FIGHT AGAINST WAR

1 M. Auclair, *La Vie de Jean Jaurès* (1954), p. 255.
2 J. Hampden Jackson, *Jean Jaurès: His Life and Work* (1943), p. 159.
3 H. Goldberg, *Jean Jaurès* (Madison, Wisconsin, 1962; Paris, 1970), pp. 373–4.
4 Auclair, *La Vie de Jean Jaurès*, p. 536.
5 M. Bonnafous (ed.), *Œuvres de Jean Jaurès*, Vol. I, *Pour la paix; les alliances européennes* (1931), p. 43.
6 *Journal Officiel, Débats parlementaires*, 7 March 1895.
7 Bonnafous, *Œuvres de Jean Jaurès*, p. 218.
8 M. Rebérioux (ed.), *Jean Jaurès. Contre la guerre et la politique coloniale*, Vol. I (1959), p. 15.
9 M. Bonnafous (ed.), *Œuvres de Jean Jaurès*, Vol. II, *Pour la paix; la paix menacée 1903–1906* (1931), p. 247.
10 *Ibid.*, p.113.
11 G. Haupt, *Socialism and the Great War* (Oxford, 1972), p. 14.
12 C. Andler, *Vie de Lucien Herr* (1932), p. 180.
13 D. Guérin (ed.), *Rosa Luxemburg – Le Socialisme en France 1898–1912*, (1971), pp. 229–33.
14 J. Rabaut, *Jaurès* (1971), p. 220.
15 J. Joll, *The Second International* (1955), p. 111.
16 M. Lair, *Jaurès et l'Allemagne* (1935), p. 200.
17 M. Bonnafous (ed.), *Œuvres de Jean Jaurès*, Vol. VII, *Pour la paix; Europe incertaine 1908–1911* (1931), p. 428.
18 Goldberg, *Jean Jaurès*, p. 494.
19 Auclair, *La Vie de Jean Jaurès*, p. 592.
20 E. Vandervelde, *Souvenirs d'un militant socialiste* (1939), p. 171. The slowness of Jaurès's response to the crisis of 1914 and the delays that followed his insistence that the French trade unions should demonstrate their opposition to the threat of war by united and concerted action with the Socialist party have been severely criticised by A. Kriegel and J-J. Becker in their *1914. La Guerre et le mouvement ouvrier français* (1964). Whether a more rapid reaction would have made very much difference to the situation is doubtful, however. In Germany there were Socialist demonstrations against the Austrian ultimatum to Serbia, but the German Left fell into line when the news broke of the Russian

mobilisation. In France, too, the great majority of the Socialists and the trade unions rallied to the defence of their country when the Germans, in turn, threatened the Republic.

21 *Le Procès de l'assassin de Jaurès*, (n.d.), p. 179.

22 C. Péguy, *Œuvres en Prose*, Vol. II (1957), p. 1203.

23 Joll, *Second International*, p. 193.

24 M. Barrès, *Chronique de la Grande Guerre* (1920–4), Vol. XI, p. 90.

25 'He was a great man and a good one', Proust told his housekeeper, Céleste. 'The only one who would have saved us from this stupid war.' C. Albaret, *Monsieur Proust* (London, 1976), p. 204. 'My heart is breaking', was the response of Anatole France to the news of Jaurès's assassination.

26 D. Shub, *Lenin* (New York, 1950), p. 80.

27 Goldberg, *Jean Jaurès*, p. 439.

2 MAURICE BARRÈS, CHARLES MAURRAS, CHARLES PÉGUY: THE DEFENCE OF FRANCE

1 Their original findings were published in the article 'L'Esprit de la nouvelle Sorbonne', which appeared in *L'Opinion* in 1911. They were reproduced in book form as *Les Jeunes Gens d'aujourd'hui* in 1912.

2 Both Robert Soucy in his *Fascism in France: The Case of Maurice Barrès*, (Berkeley, 1972) and Zeev Sternhell in his *Maurice Barrès et le nationalisme français* (1972) underline the conservative aspects of Barrès' position, aspects that became far more pronounced as the years progressed. It may still be felt that in their efforts to demonstrate the 'Fascist' elements in Barrès's thought at the turn of the century they tend to give the impression that his thinking was more systematic than the evidence will allow. A useful corrective to the idea of Barrès as a 'thinker' is provided by the amusing portrait of him 'en pantoufles' provided by his former secretary: J. and J. Tharaud, *Mes Années chez Barrès* (1928).

3 M. Barrès, *Mes Cahiers* (1963), p. 524.

4 *Ibid.*, p. 178.

5 Maurice Barrès and Charles Maurras, *La République ou le roi. Correspondance inédite* (1970), pp. 495–6.

6 Barrès, *Mes Cahiers*, pp. 216–17.

7 *Ibid.*, Vol. V (1932), pp. 173–4.

8 *Ibid.*, Vol. XI (1938), p. 90.

9 M. Barrès, *Chronique de la Grande Guerre* (1920–4), Vol. VI, p. 38. Details of his visit to England in 1916 may be found in *ibid.*, Vol. VIII,

pp. 278–378. Despite his efforts, nursing and welfare facilities for the French troops were far worse than those of the British. This was to be a major factor in the mutinies of 1917.

10 *L'Echo de Paris*, 19 October 1914.

11 *Chronique de la Grande Guerre*, Vol. III, p. 124.

12 *Ibid.*, Vol. I, p. 226.

13 *Ibid.*, Vol. II, p. 123.

14 *Ibid.*, Vol. VI, p. 161.

15 *Ibid.*, Vol. X, p. 279.

16 *Ibid.*, Vol. XI, p. 73.

17 *Ibid.*, Vol. II, p. 90.

18 *Ibid.*, Vol. II, p. 173.

19 *Ibid.*, pp. 169–70.

20 M. Barrès, *Mes Cahiers*, Vol. XI (1938), p. 365.

21 R. Rolland, *Le Journal des années de guerre, 1914–1919* (1952), p. 131.

22 H. Massis, *Au long d'une vie*, (1967), p. 161.

23 Details of this mock trial may be found in C. Stewart Doty, *From Cultural Rebellion to Counter Revolution: The Politics of Maurice Barrès* (Ohio, 1976), p. 240.

24 *Le Table ronde*, No. 111 (May 1957), special issue: 'Maurice Barrès, L'homme et l'Œuvre', p. 20.

25 H. de Montherlant, *Essais* (1963), p. 278.

26 P. de Boisdeffre, *Maurice Barrès* (1962), p. 105.

27 M. Barrès, *Mes Cahiers* (1963), p. 251.

28 C. Maurras, *Œuvres Capitales*, Vol. IV, p. 388. A typical example of Maurras's intransigence was his refusal to be introduced to Jaurès, when they both happened to be sitting in the same café, on the grounds that he might be seduced by Jaurès's personality into moderating his attacks on the Socialist leader. Towards Jaurès's ally, Anatole France, whom he had served for a time as secretary during his early years in Paris, Maurras's attitude was more ambivalent: whilst deploring France's support of the Left he always maintained that his artistic excellence was due to his basic traditionalism, his adherence to the classical French virtues and 'la clarté française'.

29 C. Maurras, *Kiel et Tanger* (1913), p. xlv.

30 C. Maurras, *Au Signe de Flore* (1931), p. 44.

31 *Kiel et Tanger*, p. 211.

32 *Ibid.*, p. 123.

33 *Action Française*, 25 July 1914.

34 L. Dimier, *Vingt ans d'Action Française* (1926), p. 287.

35 C. Maurras, *Les Nuits d'épreuve et la mémoire de l'état. Chronique des bombardements de Paris* (1924), p. 58.

36 C. Maurras, 'Le Chemin de Paradis', in *Œuvres capitales*, Vol. I (1954), p. 29.

37 Dimier, *Vingt ans*, p. 236.

38 *Le Procès de Charles Maurras* (Lyon, 1945), p. 35. On occasions Maurras had printed the addresses of those he had denounced.

39 M. Barrès, *Chronique de la Grande Guerre*, Vol. I, p. 184.

40 P. Vandromme, *Maurras. L'Eglise de l'ordre* (1965), p. 169.

41 A Saffrey (ed.), *Péguy et Emile Moselly*, Cahiers de l'Amitié Charles Péguy (1966), p. 65.

42 C. Péguy, *Œuvres en Prose*, Vol. II, p. 1066.

43 *Ibid.*, Vol. I, p. 1275.

44 *Ibid.*, p. 519.

45 *Ibid.*, p. 852.

46 'Le Porche du mystère de la deuxième vertu', *Œuvres Poétiques Complètes* (1962), p. 615.

47 C. Péguy, *Deuxième élégie XXX* (1955), pp. 241–2.

48 M. Péguy (ed.), *Lettres et entretiens: Charles Péguy* (1954), p. 72.

49 R. Johannet, *Vie et mort de Péguy* (1950), p. 38. Péguy disliked the Tridentine Church and regarded himself as a Catholic before the Reformation.

50 B. Guyon, *Péguy* (1960; 1973), p. 264.

51 C. Péguy, *Notes Politiques et Sociales* (1957), p. 78.

52 M. Péguy, *Lettres et entretiens*, p. 148. The basic lack of understanding between Péguy and Barrès was mutual. Barrès did what he could to help Péguy, but disliked what he considered to be the shapelessness and self-indulgence of the latter's work.

53 C. Péguy, *Œuvres en Prose*, Vol. II, p. 1047.

54 C. Péguy, *Par ce demi-clair matin* (1952), pp. 24–5.

55 Péguy's optimism was widely shared in France in 1914. The French army had come to believe that the Triple Entente was more powerful than the Central Powers, while Joffre disregarded all the evidence that Germany would attack through Belgium. See D. Porch, *The March to the Marne* (Cambridge, 1981).

56 J. and J. Tharaud, *Notre cher Péguy*, Vol. II (1926), p. 188.

57 C. Péguy, *Œuvres en Prose*, Vol. II, p. 1241.

58 H. Guillemin, 'Péguy et Jaurès', *Les Temps modernes*, 18.194 (1962), p. 88.

59 C. Péguy, *Œuvres Poétiques Complètes*, p. 1028.

60 C. Péguy, *Œuvres en Prose*, Vol. II, pp. 640–1.

61 *Ibid.*, p. 1184.

62 Guyon, *Péguy*, p. 263.

63 One of the last things that Jaurès read before his death was Péguy's

defence of Bergson. Jaurès's comment was, 'C'est bien, mais pas assez technique' ('It's good, but not sufficiently technical'). Tharaud, *Notre cher Péguy*, p. 238.

3 ERNEST PSICHARI: THE CALL OF ARMS

1 C. Péguy, *Œuvres en Prose*, Vol. II, pp. 1167–8.
2 R. Girardet, *La Société militaire dans la France contemporaine 1815–1939* (1953), p. 274.
3 E. Psichari, *L'Appel des armes* (1913), p. 314.
4 H. Psichari, *Des jours et des hommes* (1962), p. 64.
5 H. Psichari, *Ernest Psichari, mon frère* (1933), p. 35.
6 Psichari, *Des jours et des hommes*, p. 10.
7 E. Psichari, 'Terres de soleil et de sommeil', in *Œuvres Complètes*, vol. I (1945), p. 278.
8 *Ibid.*, p. 280.
9 *Ibid.*, pp. 281–2.
10 *Ibid.*, p. 210.
11 *Des jours et des hommes*, p. 86.
12 C. Péguy, *Œuvres en Prose*, Vol. II, p. 831.
13 C. Maurras, *L'Action Française et la religion Catholique* (1913), p. 199, n. 1.
14 Psichari, *Ernest Psichari, mon frère*, p. 56.
15 E. Psichari, 'Les lettres du centurion', *Œuvres Complètes*, Vol. III (1948), p. 232. A number of those who replied to the 'Agathon' questionnaire looked with favour on anarcho-syndicalism as another form of 'energetic' response to the nation's ills and regarded themselves as being on the Left. The findings of 'Agathon' should not in any case be taken as typical of French youth as a whole in the years before 1914, and they should not be regarded as a blanket endorsement of Nationalism by the French people as a whole. As J.-J. Becker has stressed in his *1914, comment les Français sont entrés dans la guerre* (1983), the Nationalist revival only affected a section of the middle class, particularly in Paris. On the other hand, while it is true to say that the bulk of French youth remained detached from these developments, the spread of Nationalist and Catholic ideas amongst the élite was a phenomenon that could not be overlooked.
16 Psichari, *Ernest Psichari, mon Frère*, p. 84.
17 E. Psichari, 'Les Voix qui crient dans le désert', *Œuvres Complètes*, Vol. II (1948), p. 231.
18 E. Psichari, *Le Voyage du centurion* (1915), p. 26.

19 Psichari first mentions this incident in a letter to Barrès: see *Œuvres Complètes*, Vol. III, p. 229.

20 D. Halévy, *Péguy and Cahiers de la Quinzaine* (New York, 1947), p. 226.

21 A.M. Goichon, *Ernest Psichari* (1921), p. 242.

22 J. and J. Tharaud, *Notre cher Péguy*, Vol. II, pp. 179–80.

23 Goichon, *Ernest Psichari*, p. 350.

24 E. Psichari, 'Les lettres du centurion', *Œuvres Complètes*, Vol. III (1948), p. 330.

25 E. Psichari, *L'Appel des armes* (1913), p. 39.

26 H. Psichari, *Des jours et des hommes* (1962), p. 92.

27 A. Gide, *Journal 1899–1939* (1957), p. 522.

28 M. Barrès, *Chronique de la grande guerre* (1920–4), Vol. II, p. 123.

29 R. Maritain, *Les Grandes Amitiés* (1965), pp. 394–5.

30 J. Roy, *The Trial of Marshal Pétain* (1968), p. 83.

4 RUPERT BROOKE: THE SOLDIER

1 J. Lehmann, *Rupert Brooke* (1980), p. 38.

2 G. Keynes (ed.), *The Letters of Rupert Brooke* (1968), p. 24.

3 *Ibid.*, p. 73.

4 *Ibid.*, p. 116.

5 P. Delany, *The Neo-Pagans: Friendship and Love in the Rupert Brooke Circle* (1987), p. 49.

6 R. Harrod, *The Life of John Maynard Keynes* (1951), p. 147.

7 From the Memoir by Edward Marsh that prefaces his *The Collected Poems of Rupert Brooke* (1918), pp. xxviii–xxix.

8 Valuable discussions of Georgian Poetry may be found in C.K. Stead, *The New Poetic* (1964), and Robert H. Ross, *The Georgian Revolt: Rise and Fall of a Poetic Ideal 1910–1922* (Carbondale, Illinois, 1965).

9 T. Rogers, *Rupert Brooke, a Selection and Reappraisal* (1971), p. 189.

10 *The Letters of Rupert Brooke*, p. 603.

11 The article was reprinted in *Letters from America by Rupert Brooke* (1916), p. 174.

12 *Ibid.*, pp. 177–8.

13 *The Letters of Rupert Brooke*, p. 629.

14 *Ibid.*, p. 630.

15 *Ibid.*, p. 641.

16 *Ibid.*, p. 631.

17 J. Cohen, *Journey to the Trenches: The Life of Isaac Rosenberg* (1975), p. 153.

18 C. Sorley, *The Letters of Charles Sorley* (Cambridge, 1919), p. 263.
19 J.T. Boulton and A. Robertson (eds.), *The Letters of D.H. Lawrence*, Vol. III (Cambridge, 1984), p. 38.
20 *The Letters of Rupert Brooke*, p. 660.

5 H. G. WELLS AND BERNARD SHAW: PROPHECY AND HEARTBREAK

1 D.H. Lawrence, *Lady Chatterley's Lover* (1960), p. 47.
2 H.G. Wells, *The Way the World is Going* (New York, 1929), p. 169.
3 H.G. Wells, *Tono-Bungay* (1909), p. 490.
4 W.W. Wagar (ed.), *H.G. Wells. Journalism and Prophecy 1893–1946* (1965), p. 32.
5 I.S. Bloch's *The War of the Future in its Technical, Economic and Political Relations* appeared in six volumes in Russian in 1897. Wells presumably read the English translation of the sixth volume edited by W.T. Stead under the title *Is War Impossible?*, which appeared in 1899. Both Bloch and Stead were ardent supporters of the conferences held at The Hague in 1899 and 1907. These conferences produced conventions which attempted to strengthen the role of arbitration and apply principles of international law to the situations of war, but failed to halt the armaments race. There appears to be no definite proof that Bloch's ideas influenced *L'Armée nouvelle* of Jaurès. Nevertheless, it seems inconceivable that Jaurès and his advisers were unaware of Bloch's work.
6 H.G. Wells, *Anticipations* (1902), pp. 182–3.
7 H.G. Wells, *An Englishman Looks at the World* (1914), pp. 43–4.
8 A. West, *H.G. Wells: Aspects of a Life* (1984), p. 23.
9 H.G. Wells, *Mr Britling Sees it Through* (1916), p. 75.
10 H.G. Wells, *The War that Will End War* (1914), pp. 8–9.
11 *Ibid.*, p. 16.
12 *Ibid.*
13 G. West, *H.G. Wells* (1930), p. 207.
14 *The Daily Chronicle*, 31 December 1914.
15 H.G. Wells, *Boon* (1915), pp. 268–9.
16 *Mr Britling Sees it Through*, p. 430.
17 H.G. Wells, *What is Coming* (1916), p. 29.
18 N. and J. Mackenzie, *The Time Traveller: The Life of H.G. Wells* (1973), p. 310.
19 H.G. Wells, *War and the Future* (1917), p. 8.
20 *Ibid.*, p. 184.
21 J.P. Vernier, *H.G. Wells et son temps* (Rouen, 1972), pp. 366–7.

22 *War and the Future*, p. 12.

23 Vernier, *H.G. Wells et son temps*, p. 368.

24 H. Owen and J. Bell (eds.), *Wilfred Owen: Collected Letters* (1967), p. 483.

25 McKenzie, *The Time Traveller*, p. 326.

26 W.W. Wagar, *H.G. Wells and the World State* (New Haven, 1961), p. 24.

27 S. Orwell and I. Angus (eds.), *The Collected Essays, Journalism and Letters of George Orwell*, Vol. II (1968), p. 140.

28 H.G. Wells, *The Bulpington of Blup* (1932), p. 315.

29 G.P. Wells, *The Last Books of H.G. Wells* (1968).

30 McKenzie, *The Time Traveller*, p. 446.

31 This proposal first appeared in *The Daily Chronicle*, 18 March 1913. It is reprinted in G.B. Shaw, *What I Really Wrote About the War* (1931), p. 11.

32 Dan H. Laurence (ed.), *Bernard Shaw: Collected Letters 1911–1925* (1985), p. 220.

33 'Commonsense About the War' is reprinted in *What I Really Wrote About the War*, pp. 22–110.

34 For details of this affair, see Dan. H. Laurence (ed.), *Bernard Shaw: Collected Letters 1898–1910*, (1972), pp. 722–3.

35 S. Weintraub, *Bernard Shaw 1914–18: Journey to Heartbreak* (1973), p. 61.

36 From a press interview given by Shaw that appeared in *The New York American*, 26 June 1915; quoted by Weintraub, *Bernard Shaw*, p. 93.

37 A. Ransome, *Six Weeks in Russia in 1919* (1919), p. 78. When someone laughed at this remark, Lenin added: 'He may be a clown for the bourgeoisie in a bourgeois state, but they would not think him a clown in a revolution.'

38 *Bernard Shaw: Collected Letters 1911–1925*, p. 474.

39 *Ibid.*, p. 460.

40 Shaw's account of his trip to the Front in 1917 may be found in his articles entitled 'Joy Riding at the Front' which appeared in *The Daily Chronicle* of 5, 7 and 8 March 1917. They are reprinted in *What I Really Wrote About the War*, pp. 248–79.

41 *Ibid.*, p. 98.

42 *Bernard Shaw: Collected Letters 1911–1925*, p. 442.

43 D. MacCarthy, *Shaw* (1951), p. 144.

44 G.N. Bergquist, *The Pen and the Sword: War and Peace in the Prose and Plays of Bernard Shaw* (Salzburg, 1977), p. 199.

45 Dan H. Laurence (ed.), *Platform and Pulpit* (1962), pp. 286–92.

46 R. Brustein, *The Theatre of Revolt* (1965), p. 205.

6 RUDYARD KIPLING: STOICISM AND EMPIRE

1 R. Kipling, *The Fringes of the Fleet* (1915), p. 205.
2 E. Wilson, 'The Kipling that Nobody Read', in *The Wound and the Bow* (1952 edition), pp. 94–161.
3 K. Amis, *Rudyard Kipling and his World* (1975), p. 81.
4 C. Carrington, *Rudyard Kipling* (1978 edition), p. 402.
5 R. Kipling, *Stalky and Co.* (1917 edition), p. 271.
6 H. Orel (ed.), *Kipling: Interviews and Recollections*, Vol II (1983), pp. 256–7.
7 T.S. Eliot, *A Choice of Kipling's Verse* (1941), p. 19.
8 M. Cohen (ed.), *Rudyard Kipling to Rider Haggard: The Record of a Friendship* (1965), pp. 33–4.
9 Carrington, *Rudyard Kipling*, pp. 420–1.
10 *Ibid.*, p. 168.
11 Lord Birkenhead, *Rudyard Kipling* (1978), p. 252.
12 R. Kipling, *Souvenirs of France* (1933), pp. 21–2.
13 Orel, *Kipling*, p. 363.
14 *Ibid.*, pp. 323–4.
15 R. Kipling, *France at War* (1915), p. 12. Relations between the ranks in the French army deteriorated sharply in the course of the war as losses within the officer corps were made up with professional NCOs. Far more of the war writers in France served in the ranks than in Britain.
16 *Ibid.*, pp. 19–20.
17 R. Kipling, *The New Army* (1915), p. 15.
18 A. Wilson, *The Strange Ride of Rudyard Kipling* (1977), pp. 299–300. In 'The Morning Post' of 22 June 1915 Kipling was reported as having said at his recruiting speech in Southport that 'there are only two divisions in the world today, human beings and Germans'.
19 E.C. Gilbert (ed.), *O Beloved Kids* (1983), pp. 212–13.
20 *Ibid.*, p. 220.
21 Cohen, *Rudyard Kipling to Rider Haggard*, p. 87.
22 A. Wilson, *The Strange Ride of Rudyard Kipling*, p. 304.
23 Cohen, *Rudyard Kipling to Rider Haggard*, p. 97.
24 J. Gross (ed.), *Rudyard Kipling* (1972), p. 147.
25 Cohen, *Rudyard Kipling to Rider Haggard*, p. 110.
26 C.M. Bowra, *Memories* (1966), p. 189.
27 Birkenhead, *Rudyard Kipling*, p. 284.
28 *Souvenirs of France*, p. 4.
29 Birkenhead, *Rudyard Kipling*, p. 351.
30 A. Wilson, *The Strange Ride of Rudyard Kipling*, p. 300.

31 S. Orwell and I Angus (eds.), *The Collected Essays, Journalism and Letters of George Orwell*, Vol. II (1968), p. 215.
32 See, for example, B. Dobrée, *The Lamp and the Lute* (1964), and Elliot Gilbert, *The Good Kipling* (1972).
33 W.W. Robson, *Modern English Literature* (1970), pp. 15–16.

7 ROMAIN ROLLAND: ABOVE THE BATTLE

1 R. Rolland, *Mémoires* (1956), p. 197.
2 Quoted in W.T. Starr, *Romain Rolland: One Against All* (The Hague, 1971), p. 84.
3 R. Rolland, *Vie de Beethoven* (1908), p.v. This, a very short work, was first published in the *Cahiers de la quinzaine* in 1903, and should not be confused with Rolland's massive biography, *Beethoven. Les Grandes Epoques créatrices*, which was published in seven volumes between 1928 and 1945.
4 R. Rolland, *Jean-Christophe* (1966 edition), p. 1027.
5 *Ibid.*, p. 1559.
6 *Ibid.*
7 C. Hassall, *Edward Marsh: A Biography* (1959), p. 144.
8 E.M. Forster, *Two Cheers for Democracy* (1973), pp. 226–7.
9 A. Gide, *Journal 1889–1939* (1951), pp. 543, 551, 661.
10 M. Proust, *Contre Sainte-Beuve* (1971 edition), p. 308.
11 R. Cheval, *Romain Rolland, l'Allemagne et la guerre* (1963), p. 205.
12 *Ibid.* In terms of musical history, of course, Alban Berg's *Lulu* seems the most obvious 'daughter' of *Salomé*.
13 *Ibid.*, pp. 205–6.
14 *Jean-Christophe*, pp. 1434–5.
15 *Ibid.*, p. 392.
16 Richard Strauss and Romain Rolland, *Correspondance, fragments de Journal* (1951), p. 118. The second opening phrase of this tone-poem has become known throughout the world as the musical leitmotif of space exploration. It is interesting to speculate on Rolland's likely response to this conjunction of Nietzsche, German music and German-inspired technology in the late twentieth century.
17 Rolland, *Le Cloître de la rue d'Ulm* (1952), p. 174.
18 R. Rolland, *Péguy*, Vol. II (1944), p. 118.
19 R. Rolland, *Chère Sofia. Choix de lettres de Romain Rolland à Sofia Bertolini Guerrieri-Gonzaga*, Vol. II (1960), p. 120.
20 Cheval, *Romain Rolland*, p. 191.
21 *Ibid.*
22 J. Robichez, *Romain Rolland* (1961), p. 65.

23 R. Rolland, *Le Voyage intérieur* (1959), p. 146.

24 *Ibid.*, p. 267.

25 R. Rolland, *Le Journal des années de guerre 1914–1919* (1952), pp. 32–3.

26 Quoted in F.J. Harris, *André Gide and Romain Rolland: Two Men Divided*, (New York, 1973), p. 17.

27 R. Rolland, 'Au-dessus de la mêlée (1915), p. 16.

28 *Ibid.*, pp. 36–7.

29 *Ibid.*, pp. 60–1.

30 *Die Fackel*, Nos. 484–98 (October 1918), p. 127. For further details of Kraus's hostility towards Rolland, see my *The Last Days of Mankind: Karl Kraus and His Vienna* (1967), pp. 129–30 and 207.

31 N. and J. McKenzie, *The Time Traveller*, p. 301.

32 D.J. Fisher, *Romain Rolland and the Politics of Intellectual Engagement* (Berkeley and Los Angeles, 1988), p. 69.

33 M. Barrès, *Mes Cahiers*, Vol. XI (1938), p. 365.

34 Massis had published a pamphlet, 'M. Romain Rolland, ou le dilettantisme de la foi', in 1913. This was incorporated with other material in another pamphlet, 'Romain Rolland contre la France', which was published in 1915.

35 Cheval, *Romain Rolland*, p. 490.

36 *Le Journal des années de guerre*, p. 271.

37 *Ibid.*, p. 940.

38 R. Tagore, *Nationalism* (Westport, Connecticut, 1973), pp. 76–8.

39 *Le Journal des années de guerre*, p. 1063.

40 *Ibid.*, p. 1832.

41 R. Rolland, *Inde* (1951), p. 252. The encounter between Rolland and Gandhi was not without its moments of comedy. For the first twenty-four hours of the visit the latter observed one of his periodic days of silence. When he did speak he was noticeably more sympathetic to Britain and more critical of the Soviet Union than Rolland. Later Indian visitors to Rolland's home included Nehru, together with his daughter Indira.

42 Barbusse's contribution to the debate may be found in *Clarté* (3 December 1921, 1 February 1922, 1 April 1922). Rolland's views may most conveniently be studied in his *Quinze ans de combat* (1935), pp. 38–58. See also my *Three French Writers and the Great War* (Cambridge, 1975), pp. 55–60.

43 Shaw only gave his support to this initiative reluctantly, however. He wrote to Augustin Hamon, 'People now take no more notice of a Barbusse–Romain Rolland manifesto than of the clock of Notre Dame

striking twelve.' See Dan H. Laurence (ed.), *Bernard Shaw: Collected Letters 1926–1950* (1988), p. 295.

44 *Quinze ans de combat*, p. xxvii.

45 J. Pérus, *Romain Rolland et Maxime Gorki* (1968), p. 249.

46 M. Nadeau, 'Romain Rolland', *Journal of Contemporary History*, 2 (1967), p. 217.

47 Pérus, *Romain Rolland et Maxime Gorki*, p. 332.

48 D.D. Nedelkovič, *Romain Rolland et Stefan Zweig* (1970), p. 195.

49 Rolland denounced Gide's book in a letter to the steel-workers of Magnitogorsk. It was published in *L'Humanité* on 5 January 1937.

50 Pérus, *Romain Rolland et Maxime Gorki*, p. 328.

51 R. Johannet, *Vie et mort de Péguy*, p. 377.

52 R. Rolland, *Péguy*, Vol. 1 (1944), p. 8.

53 N. Mandelstam, *Hope against Hope* (1971), p. 381.

54 D. Shostakovitch, *Testimony* (1979), pp. 153–4.

55 There was indeed a proposal that Rolland's remains should be buried in the Panthéon, but, after counter-suggestions that Péguy and Bergson should be interred there at the same time, the idea was dropped. Rolland's final resting place was, as he wished, at Clamécy, where he was born. For details of this, see Fisher, *Romain Rolland and the Politics of Intellectual Engagement*, p. 297. Rolland's Russian stepson was killed on the Eastern Front during the war, but this information did not reach France until after Rolland's death.

8 D.H. LAWRENCE: NIGHTMARE AND ESCAPE

1 D.H. Lawrence, *The White Peacock*, ed. Andrew Robertson (Cambridge, 1983), p. 146.

2 J.T. Boulton (ed.), *The Letters of D.H. Lawrence*, Vol. 1 (Cambridge, 1979), p. 503.

3 *Ibid.*, p. 544.

4 D.H. Lawrence, *Phoenix*, Vol. 1 (1955 edition), pp. 304–6.

5 *Correspondance André Gide – Arnold Bennett*, ed. L.F. Brugmans (1964), p. 199.

6 G.J. Zytaruk and J.T. Boulton (eds.), *The Letters of D.H. Lawrence*, Vol. II (Cambridge, 1981), p. 218.

7 D.H. Lawrence, 'With the Guns', *Encounter*, 33 (1969), p. 6.

8 *The Letters of D.H. Lawrence*, Vol. II, p. 268.

9 *Ibid.*, pp. 407–8.

10 K. Sagar, *The Life of D.H. Lawrence* (1980), p. 83.

11 *The Letters of D.H. Lawrence*, Vol. II, p. 365.

12 *Ibid.*, p. 392.

13 *Ibid.*, p. 547.

14 *Ibid.*, pp. 330–1.

15 *Ibid.*, p. 414.

16 *Ibid.*, pp. 424–5.

17 D.H. Lawrence, *Kangaroo* (1950 edition), p. 240.

18 *The Letters of D.H. Lawrence*, Vol. II, pp. 611–12.

19 *Ibid.*, Vol. III (Cambridge, 1984), p. 48.

20 *Ibid.*, Vol. II, p. 608. Like Wells, and unlike Rolland and Shaw (*The Adventures of the Black Girl in Her Search for God* (1932)), Lawrence never thought that the West could learn anything from Africa or Asia. After his visit to Ceylon, en route for Australia, in 1922, he would often say in later years of the representations of the seated Buddha there, 'Oh I wish he would stand up!' See E. Nehls, *D.H. Lawrence: A Composite Biography*, Vol. II (Madison, 1958), p. 119.

21 *Ibid.*, Vol. I, (1957), p. 479.

22 *Kangaroo*, p. 286.

23 *The Letters of D.H. Lawrence*, Vol. III, p. 143.

24 F. Kermode, *Lawrence* (1973), p. 154.

25 E.D. McDonald (ed.), *Phoenix: The Posthumous Papers of D.H. Lawrence*, Vol. II (1936), p. 110.

26 *The Letters of D.H. Lawrence*, Vol. II, p. 181.

27 H.T. Moore (ed.), *The Collected Letters of D.H. Lawrence* (1962), p. 1045.

28 *Ibid.*, p. 933.

29 D.H. Lawrence, *Lady Chatterley's Lover* (1960 edition), p. 362.

30 *Ibid.*, p. 204.

31 D.H. Lawrence, *Aaron's Rod*, ed. Mara Kalnins (Cambridge, 1988), p. 118. In an essay on 'Boy', the small volume of eighteen poems that Lawrence published in 1919, Keith Cushman has pointed out that it is hardly a model of military verisimilitude: 'There is not a trench in sight in "Boy", though about half the poems are set on the Western front. Poems like "Bombardment" and "Ruination" even suggest that Lawrence believed that the war in France and Belgium was mainly fought in towns – (similarly in "England, My England" he seems confused about what exactly a machine gun is).' See G. Salgādo and G.K. Das (eds.), *The Spirit of D.H. Lawrence* (1988), p. 187. In 1915 Lawrence had talked wildly of getting away from the Home Front by going out to France, 'not to shoot', but 'to be a bus-conductor at the front'. Moore, *Collected Letters*, p. 338.

32 *Lady Chatterley's Lover*, p. 362.

33 'Apropos of Lady Chatterley's Lover', *ibid.*, p. 34.

34 Kermode, *Lawrence*, pp. 138–9.

35 The ideals of the young in any generation may be extravagant, and the judgements of historians cannot be anything other than subjective, but could the following passage have been written about any periods of the twentieth century in England other than the 1960s or the overheated years before 1914?

At Eric Gill's instigation, Jacob Epstein, Ambrose McEvoy and I used to gather at my studio in the King's Road, Chelsea, to discuss the question of a New Religion. Gill's idea took the form of a Neo-Nietzschean cult of super-humanity under the sign of Ithyphallus. Epstein, more simply, would be realised by the apotheosis of himself on a colossal scale, alone, and blowing his own trumpet. I was in favour of the rehabilitation of the Earth – Mother and Child, whose image installed in a covered waggon would be drawn by oxen and attended by dancing corybantes.

Augustus John, *Chiaruscoro* (1952), pp. 75–6.

9 ISAAC ROSENBERG AND WILFRED OWEN: ANTHEMS FOR DOOMED YOUTH

1 D. Hibberd, *Owen the Poet* (1986), p. 34.

2 H. Owen and J. Bell (eds.), *Wilfred Owen: Collected Letters* (1967), p. 282.

3 *Ibid.*, pp. 283–6.

4 J. Liddiard, *Isaac Rosenberg: The Half-used Life* (1975), p. 158.

5 B. Bergonzi, *Heroes' Twilight: A Study of the Literature of the Great War* (1965), p. 104.

6 *Wilfred Owen: Collected Letters*, p. 421.

7 *Ibid.*, p. 429.

8 *Ibid.*, p. 580.

9 D.S.R. Welland, *Wilfred Owen: A Critical Study* (1960), p. 68.

10 G. Bottomley and D.W. Harding (eds.), *The Complete Works of Isaac Rosenberg* (1937), p. 300.

11 *Ibid.*, p. 373.

12 C. Connolly, *The Evening Colonnade* (1973), p. 39.

13 An excellent examination of 'Break of Day in the Trenches' is to be found in P. Fussell, *The Great War and Modern Memory* (1975), pp. 250–3.

14 *The Complete Works of Isaac Rosenberg*, p. ix. One of the many curious features of this edition of Rosenberg's works is that it is described as *The Complete Works of Isaac Rosenberg* on the spine, and *The Collected Works of Isaac Rosenberg* on the title page.

15 J. Cohen, *Journey to the Trenches: The Life of Isaac Rosenberg 1890–1918* (1975), p. 183.

16 W.B. Yeats, *The Oxford Book of Modern Verse* (1936), p. xxxiv.

17 *Letters on Poetry from W.B. Yeats to Dorothy Wellesley* (Oxford, 1940), p. 113.

18 *Wilfred Owen: Collected Letters*, p. 596.

19 Yeats, *The Oxford Book of Modern Verse*, p. xxxiv.

20 Cohen, *Journey to the Trenches*, p. 3.

21 *Ibid.*, pp. 5–6.

22 *Wilfred Owen: Collected Letters*, p. 568.

23 *Ibid.*, p. 581.

24 Criticism of the unrepresentative nature of the responses of Graves, Sassoon and Owen to the war and the way in which this kind of literature paved the way for the appeasement of the 1930s may be found in John Terraine's introduction to Graham Greenwell's *An Infant in Arms* (1972), p. xiii, Terraine's *The Smoke and the Fire: Myths and Anti-Myths of War 1861–1945* (1980), Correlli Barnett's article 'A Military Historian's View of the Great War', *Essays by Divers Hands*, 36 (1970), pp. 1–18, and his *The Collapse of British Power* (1972), pp. 424–35. It may be felt that, like some of the criticisms of Owen made by Yeats and Graves, these objections are well-founded but do little to affect the validity of Owen's reactions to the war. Barnett's claim that working-class soldiers were less sensitive to the horror than middle-class war poets may be true, but how can one really tell? In any case, it seems that the industrial working classes with whom Owen came into contact were themselves not unaffected by English sentimentality and the appeal of the pastoral. Almost immediately after joining the 2nd Manchesters at the end of 1916 Owen reported that the favourite song of the soldiers, that they sang 'everlastingly', was:

> The roses round the door
> Make me love mother more.
>
> Wilfred Owen, *Collected Letters*, p. 423

25 *Wilfred Owen: Collected Letters*, p. 430, n. 1.

EPILOGUE

1 L.F. Céline, *Voyage au bout de la Nuit* (1932), pp. 73–4. For the English translation I have used the version by John H.P. Marks, *Journey to the End of the Night* (1966 edition), p. 57.

2 M. Barrès, *Pour la haute intelligence française* (1925), p. 80.

3 *Wilfred Owen: Collected Letters*, p. 578.
4 P. Fussell, *The Great War and Modern Memory* (1975), p. 334.
5 G. Bernanos, *Le Crépuscule des vieux* (1956), p. 194.
6 *Women in Love*, ed. David Farmer, Lindeth Vasey and John Worthen (Cambridge, 1987), p. 453.
7 *Par ce demi-clair matin*, p. 37.

Bibliography

The following list is only a short selection from the available secondary sources, but it consists of those books that I have found particularly useful in writing this study. Primary published sources that have been used are detailed in the Notes. Unless otherwise stated the place of publication for works in French is Paris, and for works in English is London.

General
France

R. Arbour, *Henri Bergson et les lettres françaises* (1955).

J.-J. Becker, *The Great War and the French People* (1985)

P Bernard and H. Dubief, *The Decline of the Third Republic 1914–38* (Cambridge, 1985)

V. Cronin, *Paris on the Eve, 1900–1914* (1989)

J. Cruickshank, *Variations on Catastrophe: Some French Responses to the Great War* (Oxford, 1982)

J. Darras, *Beyond the Tunnel of History* (1990)

C. Digeon, *La Crise allemande de la pensée Française* (1959)

J.B. Duroselle, *La France et les français 1900–1914* (1972)

R. Girardet, *La Société militaire dans la France contemporaine 1815–1939* (1953)

R. Griffiths, *The Reactionary Revolution: The Catholic Revival in French Literature 1870–1914* (1966)

J. Guéhenno, *La Mort des autres* (1968)

A. Horne, *The Price of Glory: Verdun 1916* (1962)

J.F.V. Keiger, *France and the Origins of the First World War* (1983)

J.M. Mayeur and M. Rebérioux, *The Third Republic from its Origins to the Great War 1871–1914* (Cambridge, 1984)

M. Rebérioux, *Le Socialisme français* (1974)

R. Shattuck, *The Banquet Years: The Arts in France 1885–1918* (1969)

M. Tison-Braun, *La Crise de l'humanisme*, 2 vols. (1958 and 1967)

B. Tuchman, *The Proud Tower* (1966)

R. Wohl, *The Generation of 1914* (Cambridge, Massachusetts, 1979)

T. Zeldin, *France 1848–1945*, 2 vols. (1973 and 1977)

Britain

C. Barnett, *The Collapse of British Power* (1972)

J. Batchelor, *The Edwardian Novelists* (1982)

B. Bergonzi, *Heroes' Twilight: A Study of the Literature of the Great War* (1965)

P. Buitenhuis, *The Great War of Words: Literature as Propaganda 1914–1918 and After* (1989)

G. Dangerfield, *The Strange Death of Liberal England* (1961 edition)

J. Darras, *Beyond the Tunnel of History*, (1990)

P. Fussell, *The Great War and Modern Memory* (1975)

D Halévy, *The Rule of Democracy 1905–1915*, 2 vols. (1953)

J.H. Johnston, *English Poetry of the First World War* (1964)

C.E. Montague, *Disenchantment* (1922)

W.W. Robson, *Modern English Literature* (1970)

R.H. Ross, *The Georgian Revolt* (1966)

M. Roucoux (ed.), *English Literature of the Great War Revisited* (Amiens, 1989)

A. Rutherford, *The Literature of War* (1978)

J. Silkin. *Out of Battle: The Poetry of the Great War* (1972)

C.H. Sisson, *English Poetry 1900–1950, An Assessment* (1971)

A.J.P. Taylor, *English History 1914–45* (1965)

J. Terraine, *The Great War 1914–18* (1965)

    The Smoke and the Fire: Myths and Anti-Myths of War 1861–1945 (1980)

M. Wiener, *English Culture and the Decline of the Industrial Spirit* (Cambridge, 1981)

R. Williams, *The English Novel from Dickens to Lawrence* (1970)

J.M. Winter, *The Great War and the British People* (1986)

Individual Personalities
Jaurès

C. Andler, *Vie de Lucien Herr* (1932)

M. Auclair, *La Vie de Jean Jaurès* (1954)

M. Drachkovitch, *Les Socialismes français et allemand et le problème de la guerre* (Geneva, 1953)

H. Goldberg, *The Life of Jean Jaurès* (Madison, 1962; Paris, 1970)

G. Haupt, *Socialism and the Great War* (Oxford, 1972)

J.H. Jackson, *Jean Jaurès: His Life and Work* (1943)

J. Joll, *The Second International* (1955)

A. Kriegel and J.-J. Becker, *1914. La Guerre et le mouvement ouvrier français* (1964)

M. Lair, *Jaurès et l'Allemagne* (1935)

G. Lefranc, *Le Mouvement socialiste sous la IIIᵉ République* (1963)

J. Rabaut, *Jaurès et son assassin* (1967)
Jaurès (1971)

C. Rappoport, *Jean Jaurès, l'homme, le penseur, le socialiste* (1915)

E. Vandervelde, *Souvenirs d'un militant socialiste* (1939)

C. Willard, *Les Guesdistes* (1965)

Barrès

P. de Boisdeffre, *Maurice Barrès* (1962)
Barrès parmi nous (1969)

M. Curtis, *Three Against the Third Republic: Sorel, Barrès and Maurras* (Princeton, 1959)

J.M. Domenach, *Barrès par lui-même* (1954)

J.S. Doty, *From Cultural Rebellion to Counterrevolution: The Politics of Maurice Barrès* (Ohio, 1976)

R. Lalou, *Maurice Barrès* (1950)

H. Massis, *Barrès et nous* (1962)
Au long d'une vie (1967)

C. Maurras, *Maîtres et témoins de ma vie d'esprit* (1954)

R.J. Soucy, *Fascism in France: The Case of Maurice Barrès* (Berkeley, 1972)

Z. Sternhell, *Maurice Barrès et le nationalisme français* (1972)

J. and J. Tharaud, *Mes Années chez Barrès* (1928)

A. Thibaudet, *La Vie de Maurice Barrès* (1921)

E. Weber, *The Nationalist Revival in France 1905–1914* (Berkeley, 1959)

Maurras

R. Benjamin, *Charles Maurras, ce fils de la mer* (1932)

G. Bernanos, *Nous autres français* (1938)
Scandale de la vérité (1939)

L. Dimier, *Vingt ans d'Action Française* (1926)

J. de Fabrègues, *Charles Maurras et son Action Française* (1966)

H. Massis, *Maurras et Notre Temps*, 2 vols. (1961)

M. Mourre, *Charles Maurras* (1958)

C.C. Peter, *Charles Maurras et l'idéologie d'Action Française* (1972)

L.S. Roudiez, *Maurras jusqu'à l'Action Française* (1957)

P. Vandomme, *Maurras. L'Eglise de l'ordre* (1965)
E. Weber, *Action Française* (Stanford, 1962)

Péguy

E. Cahm, *Péguy et le nationalisme français* (1972)
P. Duployé, *La Religion de Péguy* (1965)
H. Guillemin, *Charles Péguy* (1981)
B. Guyon, *Péguy* (1960; 1973)
D. Halévy, *Péguy and the Cahiers de la Quinzaine* (New York, 1947)
R. Johannet, *Vie et mort de Péguy* (1950)
J. Onimus, *Incarnation. Essai sur la pensée de Péguy* (1952)
A. Robinet, *Péguy entre Jaurès, Bergson et l'église* (1968)
R. Rolland, *Péguy*, 2 vols. (1944)
A. Rousseaux, *Le Prophète Péguy*, 2 vols. (1946)
J. and J. Tharaud, *Notre cher Péguy* (1926)

Psichari

A.M. Goichon, *Ernest Psichari* (1921)
A.G. Hargreaves, *The Colonial Experience in French Fiction* (1981)
M.A. Loutfi, *Littérature et Colonialisme* (1971)
R. Maritain, *Les Grandes Amitiés* (1965)
H. Massis, *Notre Ami Psichari* (1936)
H. Psichari, *Ernest Psichari, mon frère* (1933)
 Des jours et des hommes (1962)

Brooke

P. Delany, *The Neo-Pagans: Friendship and Love in the Rupert Brooke Circle*
 (1987)
C. Hassall, *Edward Marsh: A Biography* (1959)
 Rupert Brooke (1963)
J. Lehmann, *Rupert Brooke* (1980)
T. Rogers, *Rupert Brooke, a Selection and a Reappraisal* (1971)
C.K. Stead, *The New Poetic: Yeats to Eliot* (1964)

Wells

J. Batchelor, *H.G. Wells* (Cambridge, 1985)
B. Bergonzi, *The Early H.G. Wells* (1961)

R.D. Haynes, *H.G. Wells: Discoverer of the Future* (1981)

M.K. Hillegras, *The Future as Nightmare: H.G. Wells and the Anti-Utopians* (1967)

P. Kemp, *H.G. Wells and the Culminating Ape* (1983)

N. and J. Mackenzie, *The Time Traveller: The Life of H.G. Wells* (1973)

J.R. Reed, *The Natural History of H.G. Wells* (1982)

J.P. Vernier, *H.G. Wells et son temps* (Rouen, 1972)

W.W. Wagar, *H.G. Wells and the World State* (New Haven, 1961)

G.P. Wells, *The Last Books of H.G. Wells* (1968)

A. West, *H.G. Wells: Aspects of a Life* (1984)

G. West, *H.G. Wells* (1930)

Shaw

G.N. Bergquist, *The Pen and the Sword: War and Peace in the Prose and Plays of Bernard Shaw* (Salzburg, 1977)

R. Brustein, *The Theatre of Revolt* (1965)

N. Grene, *Bernard Shaw: A Critical View* (1984)

M. Holroyd, *Bernard Shaw: The Search for Love* (1988); *Bernard Shaw: The Pursuit of Power* (1989)

(ed.), *The Genius of Shaw* (1979)

D. MacCarthy, *Shaw* (1951)

M. Moore, *Bernard Shaw et la France* (1933)

S. Weintraub, *Bernard Shaw 1914–18: Journey to Heartbreak* (1973)

A. West, '*A Good Man Fallen amongst Fabians*' (1950)

E. Wilson, *The Triple Thinkers* (1952)

Kipling

K. Amis, *Rudyard Kipling and his World* (1975)

Lord Birkenhead, *Rudyard Kipling* (1978)

C. Carrington, *Rudyard Kipling* (1978)

E. Gilbert, *The Good Kipling* (1972)

J. Gross (ed.), *Rudyard Kipling* (1972)

H. Orel (ed.), *Kipling: Interviews and Recollections*, 2 vols. (1983)

A Rutherford (ed.), *Kipling's Mind and Art: Selected Critical Essays*, (Stanford, 1964)

A. Sandison, *The Wheel of Empire* (1967)

J.M.S. Tompkins, *The Art of Rudyard Kipling* (1977)

E. Wilson, *The Wound and the Bow* (1952)

Rolland

J.-B. Barrère, *Romain Rolland par lui-même* (1955)
  Romain Rolland, l'âme et l'art (1966)

R. Cheval, *Romain Rolland, l'Allemagne et la guerre* (1963)

D.J. Fisher, *Romain Rolland and the Politics of Intellectual Engagement* (Berkeley and Los Angeles, 1988)

M. Kempf, *Romain Rolland et l'Allemagne* (1962)

H. March, *Romain Rolland*, (New York, 1971)

D.D. Nedelkovič, *Romain Rolland et Stefan Zweig* (1970)

J. Pérus, *Romain Rolland et Maxime Gorki* (1968)

J. Robichez, *Romain Rolland* (1961)

W.T. Starr, *Romain Rolland: One Against All*, (The Hague, 1971)

S. Zweig, *Romain Rolland. Der Mann und das Werk* (Frankfurt am Main, 1921)

Lawrence

P. Delany, *D.H. Lawrence's Nightmare* (1979)

E. Delavenay, *D.H. Lawrence: The Man and His Work* (1972)

C. Heywood (ed.), *D.H. Lawrence: New Studies* (1987)

G. Hough, *The Dark Sun* (1956)

F. Kermode, *Lawrence* (1973)

F.R. Leavis, *D.H. Lawrence, Novelist* (1955)

J. Meyers (ed.), *D.H. Lawrence and Tradition* (1985)

E. Nehls, *D.H. Lawrence: A Composite Biography*, 3 vols. (1957–9)

K. Sagar, *The Art of D.H. Lawrence* (Cambridge, 1966)
  The Life of D.H. Lawrence (1980)

G. Salgado and G.K. Das (eds.), *The Spirit of D.H. Lawrence* (1988)

S. Sanders, *D.H. Lawrence: The World of the Major Novels* (1973)

Rosenberg

J. Cohen, *Journey to the Trenches: The Life of Isaac Rosenberg* (1975)

D.W. Harding, *Experience into Words* (1963)

J. Liddiard, *Isaac Rosenberg: The Half-used Life* (1975)

J.M. Wilson, *Isaac Rosenberg: Poet and Painter* (1975)

Owen

D. Hibberd, *Owen the Poet* (1986)

H. Owen, *Journey from Obscurity: Wilfred Owen 1893–1918*, 3 vols. (1963–5) *Aftermath* (1970)

J. Stallworthy, *Wilfred Owen* (1974)

D.S.R. Welland, *Wilfred Owen: A Critical Study* (1960; 1978)

Index

Printed in the United Kingdom
by Lightning Source UK Ltd.
119226UK00001B/32